Your Life User Manual

Practical Insights
for Living a
Meaningful Life

Evan L Wride

Your Life User Manual

Practical Insights for Living a Meaningful Life

© 2018 By Evan L Wride

All rights reserved. No portion of this book may be reproduced, stored in a retrieval system, or transmitted in any form or by any means – electronic, mechanical, photocopy, recording, scanning or other – except for brief quotations in critical reviews or articles, without the prior written permission of the copyright owner.

Scripture quotations are taken from the Holy Bible, New Living Translation, copyright © 1996, 2004. Used by permission of Tyndale House Publishers, Inc., Wheaton Illinois 60189. All rights reserved.

ISBN 13: 978-09998540-0-6

Editor: Patrick Hurley

Dedication

To God's Undeniable Glory!

To those who want to live a better, more meaningful and fulfilling life;

To those who live a biblical lifestyle every day;

To my mother, who loved and taught me more than anyone;

To my brother, who is always there for me;

To my wonderful children;

To my beautiful Soul Mate.

This book is not about me. It is all about God and His instruction manual, the Bible, written with love to and for all of us. This book is simply my humble thoughts, perspectives and observations on living a meaningful life according to the Bible.

All profits from this book will be donated to charity.

yourlifeusermanual.com

Contents

Introduction	1

Everyday Life

Your Choices Matters	8
Life is Short	21
Life Priorities and Plans	28
Adapting to an Ever-Changing World	42
Your Personal Finances	51
Your Physical Health	85
Your Mental Health	97
Addiction	125

Relationships

Marriage and Family	132
Friends and Mentors	147
Relationships at Work	165
Sex	174
The Power of Love	187

Your Life Purpose

You are Unique	200
Why are You Here?	206
Partnering with God	215
How to Live Forever	229
Why I Believe the Bible	253
Next Steps	261
Epilogue	266
Acknowledgements	269

Introduction

"The Bible is one of the greatest blessings bestowed by God on the children of men. It has God for its author; salvation for its end and truth without any mixture for its matter. It is all pure." John Locke, English philosopher, physician and enlightened thinker.

Congratulations! You are someone who cares about yourself, is curious about the Bible and desires to know how it provides practical direction to successfully manage your life in personally dynamic ways. When you decide to read and use the Bible, it will positively impact every area of your life.

My overriding goal is to demystify the Bible and make it understandable for everyone. Writing this book has taken me deeper into the Bible and resulted in new perspectives and relevant ways to live. If you give the Bible a chance, it will do the same for you.

It truly is **"Your Life User Manual"** – that God provided to each of us to help us find our way in this chaotic, often troubled world. The Bible is about hope, encouragement, love and change, no matter your past or current situation.

No life is ever so far gone that diligently reading and applying the Bible cannot help.

Please understand, I am not on a mission to convert you to a particular religion, preach my beliefs or show the world how smart I am. This book is part personal memoir, consisting of my own search for a useful and relevant faith and part how I practically use and rely on the Bible to run my daily life. My objective is to clearly demonstrate how truthful, insightful and pertinent the Bible's advice is for living a magnificent life.

My perception is that there are millions of ordinary individuals searching for a new way to live and achieve a grand life. If you are one of them and reading these pages helps you in any way, my effort has been worth it.

Let's begin with a great metaphor on the power of the Bible,

There was a famous zoo that featured a powerful lion. He was housed in a structure with a tin roof next to the adjoining monkey cage surrounded by large trees. Unfortunately, the zoo officials failed to take into account the smart and playful monkeys. It wasn't long before they discovered that tossing coconuts on the tin roof was insufferable torture on the trapped lion, driving him to roar in misery every day.

The officials called in an animal expert who quickly sized up the situation and wisely offered a solution, "You don't have to protect a lion; he is the King of the Jungle. If you want to put the monkeys in their place, simply *open* the lion's cage and natural order will be quickly restored!"

End of problem.

Like the powerful lion, the Bible doesn't need to be defended, apologized for or constantly questioned. Just release the Bible in your life to restore the order, peace, love and hope planned for you!

My sole purpose in this book is to unlock the Bible, so it can roam freely in your mind, heart and everyday life. If you have an open mind and apply it daily, it will transform you, just like it remade me.

The Bible is God's Blueprint for living an excellent life.

If you are willing to believe that, then read on. If it sounds a little too religious for you, then at least take the time to read and study the Bible for your own intellectual edification and knowledge. Your preconceived theories and notions of God and the Bible may be altered. The Bible makes complete sense in today's disturbing world and no other literary set of life truths and rules can accomplish what the Bible succeeds in doing.

"The truth is like a lion; you don't have to defend it. Let it loose; it will defend itself." Saint Augustine.

Just don't ignore the Bible or merely accept what you have heard from parents, friends, culture or traditions. Most people have *never* actually read the Bible. Discovering how the Bible's message directly relates to you and your unique life is a surprising epiphany that will positively and, at times, miraculously lead you to your destiny.

It did for me.

The Bible will meet you right where you are. It is a guide that can be used by everyone, of any race, belief, language, education, geography, age or position in society.

If this is the first time you are reading about the Bible, God or religion, this book may initially be intimidating and difficult to understand. But, persist, the results will be well worth your time.

My hope is that you will see how exciting and brilliantly beneficial it is to use the Bible as your authority for creating a significantly better and wholly meaningful life. Most search everywhere, except the Bible, for practical solutions to today's problems. Are you open to discovering God's wonderful plan for you?

Your life is not a practice session; there are no second tries.

Life is always going to be a struggle. Left to our own ways we often make a complete mess of our lives. A wise man once said,

"We spend the first half of our lives digging ourselves into a hole and the second half climbing out of it." Unknown.

Youth is foolish and irresponsible. Maturity and meaning only comes from taking responsibility for your life, gaining a little wisdom and, hopefully, self-control. The Bible is filled with succinct guidance, ageless wisdom and practical life rules.

Following God can be difficult, He expects a lot from us. For me, trusting the Bible came later in life and it has been a long, gradual, evolutionary process, not always in a straight line. There is no right or wrong way to discover the Bible. We all decide, intentionally or unknowingly, who or what authority to trust to manage and direct our daily lives. We all need help; no one successfully goes it alone.

"When you discover something that nourishes your soul and brings joy, care enough about yourself to make room for it in your life." Jean Shinoda Bolenc, psychiatrist and author.

If you are traveling from New York to California there are several highways that will get you there, depending on your preference for large or small roads, climate, topography, town size, natural wonders and how much time you have. You can use a written or on-line map, travel guide, as well as, Google attractions, restaurants and hotels along the way. If you become lost you can ask locals for directions and recommendations.

Similarly, our terrestrial journey is always going to be a struggle with numerous routes we can choose to travel! It may surprise and hopefully please you to discover a *"user manual"* for specifically what path to take. It is called the Bible! Living according to the Bible helps you overcome roadblocks, find detours and discover points of importance along the way to reach your pre-planned destinations for a complete, joyful and meaningful life.

The Bible will guide you to truth for the precise route that is *personally* best for you. Understanding and applying the Bible will be a lifelong journey that maps the way to your best life and ultimate destiny.

I am an ordinary man. I do not have a theology, psychiatry or philosophy degree. I am not a motivational speaker, nor claim to have any special understanding, knowledge or superior intelligence. What the Bible has done for my life is nothing short of a miracle – encompassing the most meaningful and impactful changes I have ever made. The Bible takes me to unanticipated, incredible destinations that I have never encountered, while simultaneously, comforting and guiding me to my destiny.

If there was a picture of me in the dictionary or Wikipedia, the defining words next to it would be, "an ordinary guy."

It is the Bible that makes me special, confident, content and assured about my future - it makes my life *come alive.*

If you pay attention just a smidgeon, you occasionally sense that there must be more to life. Like many of you, I knew there was something missing in my existence. Life couldn't be that shallow and purposeless. You and I have a soul that persistently encourages us to search for more. Your soul never ages, lasts forever and is the "Blue Print" for who you are and your destiny. Thus, it wants us to make the right choices so after death your soul (you) will arrive at the destination where it was designed to live permanently - eternity.

In addition, the Bible is filled with mystery, drama, betrayal, deception, adventure, murder, sex, inequality, discrimination, miracles, wisdom, joy, sadness, empathy, greatness, human nature, corrupt government officials, unwanted consequences, relationships, faith, tragedy, challenges, personal growth, humor and the greatest and most unimaginable examples of love ever experienced.

Does the above all sound exactly like life today? Yes! Biblical times were just as corrupt, chaotic, unfair and dangerous as we see and experience now.

That is because, while our modern-day society has advanced technically, is filled with modern conveniences and instantaneous communication, the real, heart-filled needs of our "humanness" and psyche have not changed. We are just as emotionally, mentally, spiritually and physically needy now as in ancient times.

So, I have attempted to show how the Bible is directly relevant to your world and life today.

This book is organized as follows.

The **Introduction** is a synopsis of the book to set the stage and expectations for what you will read, learn and experience.

The **Everyday Life** and **Relationships** sections take on some of life's most common, pertinent and important opportunities and challenges for living a meaningful life.

The **Your Life Purpose** section describes what the Bible says about your specialness, why you are here, how to partner with God, how to relate to God, why I believe the Bible and a few next steps.

Each chapter contains applicable and relevant Bible verses for the topic being discussed, with my interpretation of the Bible's guidance and how I personally apply the Bible in my life.

The **Take Away** in each chapter is the main point and lesson from that chapter.

In the **Epilogue** I attempt to "bottom line" the rationale for why to use the Bible to manage your special life.

My hope is to challenge your current beliefs and paradigms, as well as, inspire your heart, mind and soul. Once you read the Bible and consistently apply it in your life, you will discover it is literally indispensable for creating the life you have always hoped for.

"Study this Book of Instruction (the Bible) continually. Meditate on it day and night, so you will be sure to obey everything written in it. Only then, will you prosper and succeed in all you do." Joshua 1:8.

Would you like to prosper and succeed? Read on so you can decide for yourself what is true and real, meaningful and pointless, as well as, where the secular and spiritual worlds collide.

If someone doesn't tell you about the Bible and the future it has for you, you may never give it a second thought and miss out on God's best for you.

It's time to get started.

EVERYDAY LIFE

Your Choices Matter

"It's in the moment of a decision that your destiny is being shaped." Tony Robbins, author and entrepreneur.

Decision: the action or process of resolving a question.
Choice: an act of selecting or making a decision when faced with two or more possibilities.

A *wise* decision can dramatically change your life. A *foolish* one can doom you for years to come. A self-centered, spur of the moment misguided choice can be disastrous; *making irrational investments, holding a hateful grudge, carrying on an adulterous affair, losing your temper, offending a friend/loved or marrying the wrong person.* Each choice has the power to set you back years, even decades or miraculously spring you forward.

A decision is a fork in the road; one path will allow you to reap rewards, the other will lead to regrets, pain and possibly ruin for a long, long time. Or, as the Bible succinctly puts it,

"A wise person chooses the right road; a fool takes the wrong one." Ecclesiastes 10:2.

Making good decisions is a non-negotiable imperative for success. It is a skill *not* grasped by millions. Just read the paper, search the internet or watch the evening news and you will see endless tragedies and bad outcomes because of countless individual's poor choices, some big, some small – at times, life altering.

According to the National Endowment for Financial Education, 70% of lottery winners or those who get a big windfall end up broke. What kind of choices do you think they made?

Your key decisions, as well as, everyday choices determine your life outcomes and your status in life. The better your decisions the better your life. Your decisions matter!

It is no wonder there are so many mediocre marriages, numerous divorces, parentless children, unsuccessful careers, corrupt politicians, crime, alcohol and drug abuse, homelessness and hundreds of other social ills plaguing our nation. People have always made bad choices and continue to do so every day.

"Nothing is more difficult, and therefore more precious, than to be able to *decide*." Napoleon Bonaparte, French military and political leader.

Why is it so difficult for us to make good decisions? Some are afraid to make *any* decisions, thus choosing to randomly float through life, apathetically accepting the choices of others. Other reasons include, fear of failure, peer pressure, cowardice, selfishness, laziness, lack of personal responsibility, ignorance, lack of truthful information or just being too stubborn to ask for help and a hundred other rationales and excuses. We are endlessly creative when it comes inventing excuses and blaming others.

"In any moment of decision, the best thing you can do is the right thing, the next best thing is the wrong thing, and the worst thing you can do is nothing." Theodore Roosevelt, American President.

So, where do you begin to ensure healthy decision-making? You don't start with choices made in the 'heat of the moment'; that is worst time to make big decisions. It is difficult to instantly know what to do when you are under pressure, angry or emotional. Wisdom needs to be planned and nurtured in advance. To be prepared for tough, confusing situations you must read the Bible everyday so the accumulated wisdom will already be ingrained in your thinking, behaviors and habits. What are your criteria and values for making decisions and controlling your behavior? You have to go back to the *source* of truth – the Bible.

"It's not hard to make decisions when you know what your values are." Roy Disney, businessman and older brother of Walt Disney.

If your values are pleasure, fame, power or other short-term human desires; your motives for decisions will be based upon your desires at the *moment*. Great decision-making must be based on sound information, a long-term perspective, as well as, moral, ethical and spiritual foundations.

To have the right foundation and values, we must go to the most ethical, trusted guide in human history: The Bible. It has never been easier to access and understand the unchanging truths in the Bible. The internet has provided direct access to many different presentations of the Bible. There are many books, blogs, devotionals and sermons to help you interpret the Bible. I often do a Google search, "What does the Bible say about _____?"

We enjoy the freedom and power to make our own choices, it's called "free will". However, there are always strings attached. We are accountable for the resulting outcomes of our choices. Ah, regrets. We are the, "woulda, shouda, coulda capital of humanity. We are all experts - *after* the fact.

 So many bad decisions, so few do overs.

The other side of the "freedom coin" is that while we are entitled to choose, we are not free from the inevitable consequences of every choice we make. Consequences and outcomes are what validate the wisdom or foolishness of our latest choice. Everyone wants and likes independence, but few consider the long-term consequences of their decisions. I have learned that the pain and inconvenience of a disciplined life is always less than the pain of regret.

"You say, "I am allowed to do anything" – but not everything is beneficial." 1 Corinthians 10:23.

Today, as in Bible times, it is the ability to consciously choose how to conduct our lives that determines our outcomes and ultimate destiny. This *distinguishes us from all other life forms that primarily function on instinct* rather than complex reasoning and judgment.

"The difficulty we have is accepting responsibility for our behavior which lies in the desire to avoid the pain of the consequences of that behavior." M. Scott Peck, psychiatrist and author.

Regardless of your station in life, you have the freedom to choose. This puts you in the powerful, but precarious position of determining your destinations in life. Most of us do not fully comprehend the implications of our earthly decisions. And, we do not get to dictate or negotiate the consequences of our choices. As the Bible says,

"Look, today I am giving you the choice between a blessing and a curse! You will be blessed if you obey the commands of the Lord your God (Bible) that I am giving you today. But you will be cursed if you reject the commands of the Lord your God and turn away from him and worship gods (money, power, fame, possessions) you have not known before." Deuteronomy 11:26-28.

I believe, the most interesting twist to God's plan is graciously giving us complex minds to succeed or fail by making purposeful choices throughout our lives. This is a powerful gift and it demonstrates God's unlimited omnipotence. He fully knows that we may not follow His desires and commandments.

But, that will always be *our* loss, not His. He will never stop loving or pursuing you. His overriding goal is to love you and develop a personal relationship with you. That is why we were created.

We each get to choose the extent of our exposure to society, media, other influencers, as well as, the Bible. When these differing worlds collide, we have to be wise in deciding what and who to follow. Who or what authorities, motivators and influencers do you trust?

"The fear (respect, revere) of the LORD is the beginning of knowledge, but fools despise wisdom and instruction." Proverbs 1:7.

In the above verse, "fear" can be interpreted to mean dread of God's judgment or reverence and respect for His omnipotence. There is no reason to be frightened of Him, as He only wants the best for you. In my case, it appears God has more faith and confidence in me then I do in myself.

The following verse tells us that while we can choose to "do this", meaning obey the Bible, that "God will bless you", but if you "refuse to listen" and *go your own way*, the consequences could be devastating.

"If you <u>do this</u>, you will live and multiply and the Lord your God will bless you …. But, if your heart turns away and you <u>refuse to listen</u> and if you are drawn away to serve other gods, then I warn you now that <u>you will certainly be destroyed</u>." Deuteronomy 30:15-18.

The desire and ability to make decisions based upon the Bible's guidance is one of the most important forms of wisdom. However, it is almost impossible for most, even Christians, to pull that off for one good reason: **They don't know enough about the Bible to use it as the foundation for their decisions.** As a result, they make critical choices based solely on their *own* understanding, selfish motives and ever-present friends and social media influencers.

"For God has not given us a spirit of fearfulness, but one of power, love, and sound judgment." 2 Timothy 2:7.

Our choices tell the world who we are and what we value. Admittedly the Bible doesn't specifically address every issue we face, making it difficult, at times, to determine its guidance. However, there are hundreds of verses that we can apply to our individual situations and predicaments to get an accurate indication of what would simultaneously make God smile and improve our life.

I have found that as I accumulate more wisdom and knowledge from continuously reading the Bible, I can usually find a specific verse regarding my issue or apply similar principles and behaviors in the Bible. Additionally, a good Bible will have an index to find verses and topics related to my specific question.

Here is a major clue for you; **if your choice doesn't align with the Bible, it's not a good choice.**

The men and women of the Bible were far from perfect and struggled with decisions just as we do. They were called "saints" "disciples" and "apostles" not because they were spiritually flawless, but because of their consistent passion to live according to the teachings in the Bible. A few examples of bad choices by key biblical figures include:

Adam and Eve ignored God's directions; Abraham lied about his marriage to his wife, Sarah; Noah passed out drunk following the flood; Lot's wife looked back to see God's destruction of Sodom and

Gomorrah; Moses tapped the rock against God's order not to do so; David committed adultery with Bathsheba and tried to cover it up by murdering her husband; Peter denied knowing Jesus and Paul demeaned and killed Christians.

God blessed all these people in spite of their major flaws in character and errant decisions because they asked for forgiveness. As in biblical times, pride and sin (going against the teachings in the Bible) play a significant role in the majority of our poor decisions today.

Now, it is time to talk *solutions*.

In the Garden of Eden, Adam and Eve had time to walk away from the Devil. David could have fled from the roof before he went after Bathsheba. Moses could have put down his rod and obeyed God and Peter could have proclaimed his devotion to Christ. You usually have a choice to leave, avoid or respond appropriately to tempting situations.

"...run from all these evil things (temptations). Pursue righteousness and a godly life, along with faith, love and perseverance, and gentleness." 1 Timothy 6:11.

If you want a different and better reality, you must think, speak and behave *differently*, which will lead you to better decisions.

"Insanity is doing the same thing over and over again and expecting different results." Albert Einstein, theoretical physicist.

Are you going to repeat your bad decisions or *learn* from them?

Here is a template on how to make wise decisions based on the Bible. Follow this approach to figure out which, "fork in the road," to take the next time you have to choose. Remember, it is always easier to get into a relationship, business transaction or commitment than to get out of it.

1. Begin with prayer. Seek His will from the Bible.

"Give me a helping hand, for I have chosen to follow your commandments." Psalm 119:173.

2. Gather information for and understand all aspects of the decision, so you can make an informed one. Don't rush into any important choice, take all the time you need. Information is power!

3. Be honest and objective about the pros and cons of your decision. Don't make up your mind until you have seriously thought through every facet of the pending decision and the potential short and long-term consequences.

4. Consult with a trusted mentor, pastor, reliable friend, spouse, sibling or parent who knows the most about you and the circumstances.

   "Plans go wrong for lack of advice; many advisers bring success." Proverbs 15:22.

5. Whatever the time of day, it is usually best to postpone your decision and don't sign anything, until the following morning. Your head will be clearer and your perspective will be sharper.

   "No good decisions were ever made after 1:00 in the morning." Unknown.

6. Don't confuse making a decision with knowing all the answers and solving all the potential problems. Diligent decisions and planning come first, then problem solving and solutions are discovered as you make progress.

   "The most difficult thing is the decision to act, the rest is merely tenacity. The fears are paper tigers. You can do anything you decide to do. You can act to change and control your life; and the procedure, the process is its own reward." Amelia Earhart, American aviation pioneer and author.

7. Be willing to revise or change your mind if you don't have inner peace or you receive new information. The majority of breakthroughs are a result of incremental improvement, a change in direction or minor adjustment.

Jesus was amazingly flexible, often changing His plans to help others. He was always willing to be inconvenienced to help others.

"No eye has seen, no ear has heard, no mind has conceived what God has prepared for those who love him." 1 Corinthians 2:9.

Here is a powerful thought:

Your decision to trust the Bible to manage your life is one of the most consequential turning points you will ever make in your life.

But that is only the beginning. The hard part is to actually apply the Bible in *all* aspects of your life. Will you apply the Bible to your finances, marriage, relationships, work, leisure time, lifestyle and all the rest? This is where you see if you are a secular or a Bible-driven person.

A lot of people mock believers by saying, "Christianity is a crutch." But we all base our lives and choices on a particular **authority**. It's just a matter of which influencer, motivator, educator, ethics, values, standards or laws you choose to follow.

Don't turn to God or the Bible only in times of crisis or when you have run out of options. In the past, I only deferred to the Bible or God when it was consistent with what I wanted to do or I was at the end my rope. I seldom let the Bible guide me regarding money, relationships and my behaviors at work. I wanted to be in charge.

I now do my best to depend on the teachings in the Bible for all my decisions, in every area of my life. My financial choices are now consistent with the Bible. I engage in relationships that benefit others, not just me. I now choose to volunteer to help others. I have surprisingly discovered that it is virtually impossible to live according to the Bible, put others first and not be blessed and benefitted to the maximum. James, the half-brother of Jesus wrote:

"Whatever is good and perfect is a gift coming down to us from God our Father, who created all the lights in the heavens." James 1:17.

Most will not believe what I write next, but it is absolutely true - *The Bible does not restrict or limit you, it frees you!*

I have found that living by the rules and guidance of the Bible actually results in *more* freedom, *less* worry, *abundant* joy and a life that can only be described as super naturally inspired. *The purpose of the Bible is not to limit you, but to transform your life.* I can't take credit for the unbelievable life I now enjoy.

Most people have chosen to deny or simply overlook the Bible and God because they are afraid of turning their life over to someone or something else. In the end, it comes down to who or what you are going to trust to manage and control your life. Trust God to lead you, the Bible is **"Your Life User Manual"** for every part of your life.

"Jesus said to the people who believed in him, 'You are truly my disciples if you remain faithful to my teachings. And, you will know the truth and the truth will set you free.'" John 8:31-32.

My history contains times of searching for God and times of ignoring Him; times my ego and pride have ruled my thoughts and behaviors; stretches when I followed the trends of society and also times that I have lived according to the Bible. **Thus, I am simply an ordinary, struggling human, like everyone else**, searching for how to live a meaningful life.

There are some things we cannot choose, like parents, siblings, race and the neighborhood we grew up in. On the other hand, we each have the power to make the most important life choices: friends, partners, positions, faith and where to find wisdom, love and who to trust. The daunting aspect of that power is that we must live with the consequences of *our* choices - whether good, mediocre or bad.

Your past doesn't have to determine your future, that is your responsibility.

Replicating this cycle of decisions and the resulting consequences, repeatedly, throughout life is *how we learn.* You get to choose the lessons from the outcomes of the decisions you make. You can learn from each choice and gradually make better choices or ignore the whole process and continue to make poor choices. For better or worse, we *inevitably end up exactly where we decide to be*.

I and a good friend worked with the homeless at our church for three years. One day I asked him, "Why several of the same individuals remain homeless year after year?" He simply said, "They have made poor choices in the past and continue to make poor decisions now." Apparently, we are not very good at seeing that our future is connected to our present-day choices.

"I have chosen to be faithful, I have determined to live by your (Bibles) regulations." Psalm 119:30.

By "regulations", the Psalmist is referring to the rules and guidance in the Bible, not some city zoning code. This is about a meaningful life, a spiritual life and death; not a bureaucratic fiat. It is about your life! Where do you ultimately want to end up? Who or what are you going to trust and believe in with your one and only life?

Yet, just like the shallow Israelites moaning and groaning across the desert for 40 years because they ignored God, the Bible's direction seems to elude our thinking today. We occupy ourselves with technology, money and fame as if they are the essence of life itself. This attitude is self-serving and short-term. We cope with our pathetic shallowness by obsessing on social media, buying things and staying busy, while remaining illiterate of the Bible that will be recited at our funerals.

God must be shaking His head at His wondrous creations relying on electronic games and social media.

Let me put it this way. Apps are fun and enjoyable for entertainment purposes and, at times, educational as well. But, there is no comparison between *Snapchat, Pokémon Go and Facebook Messenger* when compared to the Bible. To paraphrase Jesus from Mark 12:17:

Render to Apps the things that are App's, and to God the things that are God's.

Apps may be entertaining and make you productive, but the Bible can *transform* your life. Spending hours and hours on social media are the smart phone's plan for your life, which may replace the Bible's plan for you. To be frank, on judgment day, the first thing that will be noticeably absent will be a smart phone. Everyone will be looking up, not down at their screen.

What if we used our smart phones to read and understand the Bible as much as we do for our recreational and social activities?

So, why not start giving the Bible app *equal* time. It is not only your play toy; it could also be your ticket to the Bible's truth about your life. Since we love The Social Network why not create an *alternative* one that has eternal benefits; The **Spiritual Network,** which comes with all the moral, ethical and wisdom we need today and forever.

Maybe we can coin it, *"Faithbook Messenger."* The app that allows you to **network** with a Loving God. **"Add"** God as a friend, **"Share"** His verses and **"Like"** His abundant life posts for you and your friends. You can even text with God; it's called *"Prayer."*

Many people use their smart phones for only trivial, non-consequential activities. Often, we use it as a distraction from reality or to appear busy and important. But, busyness is no guarantee of spending our time on activities that make a difference in our lives. And, "augmented or virtual reality", the newest technological trend is interesting, but don't believe it is real, it is entertainment.

I use the **YouVersion** Bible app every day. There are many faith and Bible apps to choose from. A few are **gotquestions.com, idailybread.org, bible.com, biblehub.net** and **biblegateway.com.** Discover the one that works best for you. You can simply ask a question on any search site about what the Bible says on any topic, there are many to choose from.

Here is the bottom line for all of you who claim to want the best for your lives. It is impossible to make biblical based decisions until you *know* the Bible. You don't guess at wisdom; you absorb it on a day to day basis just like your all-consuming apps. You can't spiritually survive on one hour at church, 40 hours at work and 40 hours online every week.

If you truly want to manage your life according to the Bible, you must be proactive in the time you allocate to the Bible. It must become a daily habit.

I use my cell phone to get several daily devotionals, research Biblical questions, listen to meaningful sermons and look up verses from the Bible to help me in specific life situations and my overall life objectives, priorities and plans.

The knowledge and wisdom I have accumulated over the last few years has resulted in some amazing breakthroughs and allowed me to live according to the Bible more than ever before. My smart phone is one of my most important knowledge resource. It is my *"Divine Device."*

Of course, I use my cell phone for many activities, but *balancing* worldly activities with Biblical understanding is critical to living a meaningful life.

And, a funny thing happened to me along the way; I started making decisions based on the Bibles direction. My life became more meaningful, interesting, relevant, pleasurable and spiritually healthier. There are numerous distractions in life, don't let your cell phone be *another* one.

Take Away: The power of wise decision-making, resulting consequences, learning and adapting, is how we persistently move through our lives one day at a time. Decision making is what determines where you will be tomorrow, next year and where you will spend eternity.

No judgment is more important than making sound choices. The standards, values and truths you trust with your life are the most critical decisions you will ever make.

Choose the Bible as **"Your Life User Manual"** for living your one and only, personally meaningful and successful life.

"For we are each responsible for our own conduct." Galatians 6:5.

In other words, take on a spiritual perspective by understanding the Bible, thinking long-term, even eternally. Remembering our lives are short and life, on the other side of death, is forever.

"If you need wisdom, ask our generous God, and he will give it to you. He will not rebuke you for asking. But when you ask him, be sure that your faith is in God alone. Do not waver, for a person with divided loyalty is as unsettled as a wave of the sea that is blown and tossed by the wind. Such people should not expect to receive anything from the Lord. Their loyalty is divided between God and the world and they are unstable in everything they do." James 1:5-8.

Scripture is a non-negotiable daily opportunity to help you cope with the day-to-day struggles, dangers and pitfalls of life, as well as, learning how to live purposefully. The Bible is nutritious food for your life and soul.

"Trust in the Lord with all of your heart; do not lean on your own understanding. Seek his will in all you do, and he will show you which path to take." Proverbs 3:5-6.

Life is Short

"How frail is humanity! How short is life, how full of trouble! We blossom like a flower and then wither. Like a passing shadow, we quickly disappear." Job 14:1-2.

After my mom passed away in 2014, I clearly internalized how temporary everything is in this world. She had been with me my entire life; she was 95. I painfully asked myself how she could be gone? But, when I thought realistically about it, nothing lasts forever. Structures deteriorate, forests regenerate, the earth weathers from wind, water and geological movements. Meteors and suns burn out – nothing is permanent, particularly human beings. Even my loving, strong mom was temporary. God and eternity are all that remain.

"Seventy years are given to us! Some even live to eighty. But even the best years are filled with pain and trouble; soon they disappear and we fly away. Who can comprehend the power of your anger? Your wrath is as awesome as the fear you deserve. Teach us to realize the brevity of life, so that we may grow in wisdom." Psalm 90:10-12.

A blink of an eye vividly describes how long we actually live on earth. When measured against the life cycles of nature's milestones, a human life is a *nit*. Our time on earth is nothing compared to eternity as described in the Bible.

"Lord, remind me how brief my time on earth will be. Remind me that my days are numbered – how fleeting my life is. You have made my life no longer than the width of my hand. My entire lifetime is just a moment to you; at best, each of us is but a breath. We are merely moving shadows. And all our busy rushing ends in nothing." Psalm 39:4-6.

I recall my mom, in her 90's, telling me how fast her life had passed. She didn't know if time actually moved faster as she aged or if she was just more anxious to get on with life. I can now relate to her comments.

When I was a kid, I had lots of time. As a child, time painfully oozed along very slowly. In my child-like wonderment craving to enjoy summer and winter vacations, May was the longest month and Christmas Eve was the longest day. As a teenager, I can remember watching the clock in school as it shuffled by at an agonizingly slow pace. Weekends, holidays and summers zoomed by in a blur. But, as the years passed, the velocity of life increased like a cheetah tracking an antelope in the Serengeti!

I look back and realize my years have raced by too quickly.

Time is the most precious, perishable and valuable resource we possess. We may have abundant wealth, love, hope, health, meaning, excellent children and a soulmate. However, none of us will ever have enough time and there is nothing we can do about it.

Time only moves relentlessly forward. I appreciate and value time more. I am willing to spend money to "save time," and say no to unnecessary or meaningless activities. I can't really "save time," but I can choose to allocate my time in ways that are most important, meaningful and useful, thus increasing the value of what it produces. Turns out time is unstoppable.

Why do years seem to pass more quickly? It's as if I measure time by different scales as I age. Now I sense, based on my own horizons, that life is *accelerating* toward the end. I don't take life for granted as I did in my youth. I value life more than ever because my time is finite. I, like you, never know how limited *our* time is, (and truthfully, that is fine with me) but, it is always less *today* than it was yesterday.

How do we slow life down, appreciate it more, do more good, love more and ensure meaning before the end of our story? From where I am, in my 60's, I can already see my earthly finish line. I intend to finish strong, not letting age or the world distract or slow me down. I read the Bible every day to gain a deeper understanding of why I am here and what I should be doing.

If you only had 12 months to live, what would you value, who would you want to be with and what would you spend your time doing during that final year?

We each answer that question differently, but I am sure your activities would include telling those you care about how much you love them, perhaps reconcile with alienated family members and update your will. You would most likely spend your valuable time on activities that really *matter*. I often struggle to put my all-important "to do list" aside so I can be with those I love, be more patient with everyday frustrations and take time to help those who may need a little help, encouragement or just a smile.

From an eternal perspective, if you are a believer you would also make sure your soul has been secured. You would deepen your relationship with God, tell others about Jesus, pray and read the Bible in a more passionate and personal way.

Occasionally, I catch myself lost in a moment staring at a sunset, an ocean, a majestic mountain or a grand view, with absolutely nothing on my mind. It is awesome! I am completely content, nothing is missing – maybe that is actually the way life was meant to be lived, spontaneous, unmeasured and unplanned. With a nod to the music group, The Eagles, it is, *"a peaceful easy feeling."* The Apostle Paul, stated this concept personally and eloquently,

"I know how to live on almost nothing or with everything. I have learned the secret of living in every situation, whether it is with a full stomach or empty, with plenty or little. For I can do everything through Christ who gives me strength." Philippians 4:12-13.

Consider those few times when you met someone for the first time and ended up having a spontaneously fantastic time together, each of you just accepting the other, not judging or wanting something or to be somewhere else. That kind of acceptance, relatable connection and mutual empathy is a rare gift.

Meditation and worry are similar. Both take over your mind but the outcomes are opposite. Meditation is all about letting go of everything, calming, stopping your mind and just being alive and content in the moment. Worry is the inverse causing stress, nervousness and insecurity. Serenity is mostly defined as, "experiencing reality without analyzing, evaluating or trying to make life better."

"Focus on your priorities, but take things in stride. Make decisions, not excuses. Live one moment at a time. Count your blessings, not your troubles. Let the wrong things go. Look for lessons in unforeseen obstacles. Ask for help. Give as much as you take. Make time for those who matter. Laugh when you can. Cry when you need to. And always stay true to your values." Melchor Lim, author.

I try to consciously put myself in the *moment*, but it is much harder than I expected. Thinking about nothing is a real challenge. With practice, I have been able to enter the *"right now"* reality for short periods of time, with no judgement or analysis - just love and gratefulness. Maybe that is why Xanax, Valium, marijuana and alcohol are so popular. They facilitate escaping time and reality. But, the goal is to be deeply into the moment, not escape it.

So, how do you appreciate the time you have so you can use it wisely?

"Until you value yourself, you won't value your time. Until you value your time, you will not do anything with it." M. Scott Peck, psychiatrist and author.

It is not so much time management as it is *self*-management. Time is simply one tool we use to measure life. As a result, you have to believe that your life and time are important or you will never truly appreciate the life you have been given.

Time is life; use it wisely. Consider "life-time" as the most precious resource you have. You can earn more money, but you can never make more time. Humans have created astounding technology and wonderful techniques to manufacture endless items. But, no one has ever created more time!

We have all heard the phrase, "Time is money." It is actually more important, finite and valuable than money. View each day as the most treasured gift of your life - treat it like gold.

"One of the greatest labor-saving inventions of today is tomorrow." Vincent T. Foss.

Here is King Solomon's bottom line on our use of time.

"So be careful how you live. Don't live like fools, but like those who are wise. Make the most of every opportunity in these evil days. Don't act thoughtlessly, but understand what the Lord wants you to do." Ephesians 5:15-17.

None of us want to come to the end of a week, month or year and regret how we spent our precious time. Certainly, no one wants to come to the end of life and wish they had accomplished and loved more. But some do! There is no regret more devastating than looking back at your life and seeing how you wasted so much time on meaningless activities and marginal relationships.

Generally, weekdays have three, 8-hours segments: Personal time, work time and sleep. Work and sleep are usually determined for you. So, that only leaves your personal time to manage and prioritize your options. This might include entertainment, education, playing with your kids, dating, time with your spouse, sports and the mundane activities of shopping, cooking, cleaning and yard work that are all required to simply survive. Saturday and Sunday are "bonus days" for you to control and allocate your time to only that which is important to you.

How do you intentionally spend your free time?

For me now, spending my precious time on meaningful, life enriching activities, with those I *love* is the only way to live. Maybe it's *time* for you to prioritize your life before it is gone forever?

"The bad news is time flies. The good news is you're the pilot." Michael Altshuler, author.

Through all your life choices, you must decide how to use your limited time, which determines your life outcomes and where you go when you pass through death to the other side.

Someday is not a day of the week or specific time frame, it is a fantasy.

Your *time* is the best gift you can give anyone – only you can give it. You can call, email, text or tweet them; all are effective ways of staying in touch. However, language is so imperfect and, at times, ineffective at communicating love, sorrow and emotions. Nothing is as powerful as your personal *presence*. Simply being together, face to face, smiling, sharing a meal with that special person is the most powerful human experience. It is the best way to say I care, you are valuable and I love you.

The best use of your time is to love God, family and others. Love is the only way to make your "life-time" useful, meaningful and aligned with the ways of the Bible.

We have all been helped, cared for and encouraged by numerous people along life's long path. Conspicuously, take time for all those you love, those who helped you and those who are important to you. And, don't forget those you don't know, who are in need, lost or down on their luck – we all need help, compassion and love.

How we treat others is our life's legacy and we don't have much time to establish it on earth. Strive to be as amazing, while you are alive, as mourners will express at your funeral.

"How do you know what your life will be like tomorrow. You are just like the morning fog - it's here a little while then it is gone." James 4:14.

There is no going back, only regret for time you didn't spend or gratitude for the time you did spend with those who count. Time passes, excuses are easy and competing priorities will always be there, but you and those you love will be gone, maybe sooner than you think.

Now is the only time you have to actually live and invest your time on what matters.

While we can live a healthier life and, maybe a little longer, there is no bargaining with God for more time. There is no way to specifically know when our "life time" will run out, the stopwatch will be pressed or the game clock will buzz. And, there won't be another "life game or season." Well lived, one life time is enough.

"Life is uncertain. Eat dessert first." Ernestine Ulmer, author.

Life is short and uncertain, don't believe you won't be touched by time. Looking back, I realize that I spent enormous time on temporary earthly pursuits and inadequate time on family, relationships, loving people and locking in my eternal goals. I'm trying to change this.

In investment terms, the potential payback on eternity is enormous compared to our puny earthly lives. Unfortunately, because we are mere humans, it is impossible for us to fully comprehend God's perspective and plan for eternity. You see, everyone's soul lives forever, it is just a matter of where you will reside next.

Take Away: Every living creature is transient. Time is limited, use it wisely. You can't make more time.

"But you must not forget this one thing, dear friends: A day is like a thousand years to the Lord, and a thousand years is like a day. The Lord isn't really being slow about his promise, as some people think. No, he is being patient for your sake. He does not want anyone to be destroyed, but wants everyone to repent." 2 Peter 3:8-9.

In the end, only human relationships and your relationship with God will matter.

Life Priorities and Plans

"Time is a great teacher, but unfortunately it kills all its pupils." Hector Berlioz, French composer.

We have **86,400 seconds in each 24-hour day**. One of the most important powers we have is to decide how to allocate or "spend" our precious time. Unlike cell phone plans, you do not get to carry time forward to the next month. We are on the *"use-it-or-lose-it"* plan.

Everyone seems to want our time – family, work, friends, church, school, thus, you quickly run out of time and energy. We get busy, someone calls or drops in to say hi, a crisis pops-up, all of which can deflect our attention away from what is actually important.

Do you write down your most important priorities and develop plans to achieve them?

"The prudent understand where they are going, but fools deceive themselves." Proverbs 14:8.

In this verse King Solomon is bluntly saying if you create priorities and develop life plans you are *wise* and if you do not you are *foolish*. Additionally, the following verses plainly say that our plans and motives must align with God's purpose because that is the only way our daily life will succeed.

"For I know the plans I have for you, "says the Lord." They are plans for good and not for disaster to give you a future and hope." Jeremiah 29:11.

"We can make our own plans, but the Lord gives the right answer. People may be pure in their own eyes, but the Lord examines their motives. Commit your actions to the Lord, and your plans will succeed." Proverbs 16:1-3.

None of us set out to look foolish, so, why do most of us *not* plan our lives? Most couples spend more time and energy planning their wedding or family vacation than they do arranging their lives. I read that fewer than 10% of Americans actually have *written* plans of any type. That is sad. My guess is that the wise 10% also earn more money and possibly, have more successful lives.

All successful companies develop objectives, priorities, strategies and plans to achieve sales, profit and other important goals. **Your life is infinitely more important than any company and deserves your serious attention to guide you along life's long arc.** No sophisticated company, smart explorer, builder or intelligent inventor would start a project without a plan.

Neither should you.

Benjamin Franklin's insightful slogan rings true here: *"If you fail to plan you're planning to fail."*

We all need to determine our priorities and develop plans for our life. Otherwise, we are just aimlessly bumping along each day encountering life on the spur of the moment, seldom with direction or purpose. If you want a rewarding life you must develop priorities, objectives and plans.

Life Priorities

Some of us have misplaced priorities.

Four golf buddies are on the course for their weekly game. As one of the players was about to putt, a funeral procession and hearse drove by. The golfer backed away from his putt and removed his cap. He bowed his head and showed his respect, as did his partners.

After the cars moved on, one of the golfers turned to his putting partner and remarked, "That was a lovely gesture of respect you showed as that hearse passed by." The golfer looked at him and nodded, "It's the least I could do, I was married to her for 40 years!"

Priorities: The things that someone cares about and thinks are important. The condition of something being more important than something or someone else and, therefore, being dealt with first.

📖 "You got to do what you *HAVE* to do before you can do what you WANT to do. It's called Priorities." Anonymous.

Most of us simply wander through our hectic lives letting life happen to us; accepting life outcomes as inevitable. But, we must proactively set priorities and develop plans for what is essential to a life worth living. If you don't have a list of priorities or you make *everything* a priority, you effectively have *no* priorities. Your life will quickly become overwhelmed with the trivial, non-essential or the individuals who yell the loudest.

Stated another way, hopes and dreams make for fun conversation, but without plans they are useless; only a fantasy. Without detailed priorities, coupled with plans, you are living by the seat of your pants. There is a vast difference between hopeful *dreams* and hopeful *plans*.

"For a ship without direction, any port or destination will do." Anonymous.

Your life is too important to drift on an open sea. Setting priorities for your passions, dreams and goals requires reaching the right ports at the right time. Otherwise, others and society will gladly drag you in their direction, on their schedule, for their needs and benefit.

"Do not go where the path may lead, go instead where there is no path and leave a trail." Ralph Waldo Emerson, essayist and poet.

You are responsible! You must be the designer of your life and destiny. When you focus and prepare, you will become historic and memorable.

What is important to you? What do you value most?

The answer is easily revealed; simply look at your *calendar* to see where you spend your time and your *checkbook and credit/debit card statements* to see where you spend your money. Where you allocate your time and money will tell you precisely *what* is important to you. This is what captures your heart in life. What you talk or brag about is also a good indicator of what is central to your self-esteem.

 **We do what we really want to do.**

We each get to decide what really matters in our lives and whether to focus on them or not. Deciding what is essential and following through on those objectives will lead you to your pre-planned destinations. You didn't arrive where you are by accident, but by your personal, "smart" design.

Are you pleased with your life outcomes and destinations?

Individuals in the Bible, are excellent examples of misplaced, often selfish, priorities:

-Adam wanted to be as powerful as God so he ignored God's command and ate fruit from the middle of the Garden in Eden.

-David wanted to seduce Bathsheba so he ignored God and joined her for an ill-fated rooftop tryst leading to the murder of her husband and disfavor with God.

-James and John got a little heady with power and arrogantly asked for permission to bring down fire from heaven to destroy an inhospitable Samaritan village. Jesus firmly rebuked them.

-Simon Peter thought his human life was more important than his eternal allegiance to Jesus when he denied Christ on the night of Jesus's arrest.

We are all capable of gross behaviors and ego-driven desires, given the right opportunity, means and the perfect time. It makes no difference if you were alive in biblical times or today.

"For everyone has sinned; we all fall short of God's glorious standard." Romans 3:23.

Let's face it, there is a lot of drama in everyday life. However, not much of what we do each day will matter tomorrow and certainly not in a year. We each get to decide what truly matters to us short and long-term. Deciding what is important and focusing on those priorities is essential for a meaningful life. Additionally, you need to set goals that are much larger than you can possibly achieve by yourself. Expect the "supernatural" to show up in order for your biggest and most outrageous dreams to come true.

This book is an example of an impossible goal I could never have achieved by myself. I had a dream and knew generally what I wanted to do but not *how*. As I started simply putting words on paper, God inspired me to keep going and filled my mind with ideas. My editor, a godly man, refined what I had randomly compiled. My wife encouraged me and helped with proofreading. Friends chipped in with suggestions and encouragement throughout the endeavor. Like all great achievements in life, it was a collaboration that was much bigger than just me.

And, here is the book! This is a powerful WOW, far beyond my capabilities.

Unless you develop a biblical value system, you are perfectly capable of following the wrong priorities and desires right off a cliff. When it comes to right and wrong you absolutely cannot trust yourself to consistently do what's right. It is not in our nature to be holy. How do your priorities align with God's values?

So, what should you do? While I will dispense some advice and hopes here, please know that I am neither wise nor superior. I am just as bewildered as most with the growing complexities of modern society, declining morals, lack of worldwide peace and the deepening mysteries of life. I also realize there is no one recipe for life that applies to everyone, but your life is too special not to plan.

Some time ago, I read the statement, **"Health is the greatest gift, contentment the greatest wealth and faithfulness the best relationship."** I had not even considered these *three* attributes crucial to my success. As a result, I was further inspired to develop my own list of **"Major Life Priorities"**.

Over the years, I have added to and deleted from my priority list, changing them as I learned more about who I was, who I needed to be, what I wanted to achieve and how God worked in my life. Gradually, I assembled a biblical set of life priorities. I have settled on the following objectives beginning with the foundation for everything else in life.

1. My relationship with God

Every life priority must begin and end with God and the Bible. When I have flaws in the rest of my priorities I can always go back and start over with this one. If you believe this is negotiable, you will be lost forever.

In the past, I claimed God was my top priority, but I often relegated Him to a lower priority. There is no room for compromise here. Your best reasoning, money, fame, power and human relationships can never replace a meaningful relationship with God.

There are no other good options.

Much of what we call loneliness or boredom is actually the void of not having a relationship with God. Sure, you should develop trusting relationships with family and others, but if you miss the most important relationship of all, nothing can fill that hole in your heart; the God void.

"What else does this craving and this helplessness, proclaim but that there was once in man a true happiness, of which all that now remains is the empty print and trace? This he tries in vain to fill with everything around him, seeking in things that are not there the help he cannot find in those that are, though none can help, since this infinite abyss can be filled only with an infinite and immutable object; in other words, by God himself" Blaise Pascal, French mathematician.

As long as I honor God, the rest of my life priorities will be easier to identify and will fall into their proper place. But, if I lose my faith or don't trust in Him, I am vulnerable to following the least consistent influence in the world, me.

"Seek the Kingdom of God above all else and live righteously and he will give you everything you need." Matthew 6:33.

The primary threats to my top priority are pride, selfishness, a desire for immediate pleasure, as well as, apathy.

"...all the people did whatever seemed right in their own eyes." Judges 21:25.

Adam sinned against God because of pride, the first sin in the Bible and we live with his selfish choice to this day. If you become rich, famous or accomplished, it will be tempting for you to replace God with yourself. If you lose a loved one or suffer in a major way, it is possible for you to become disillusioned or angry with God and be tempted to turn your back on Him. Although these are understandable and powerful rationalizations for rebellion, don't give in to them. God is completely enamored with you, loves you unconditionally and always wants the best for you. Nothing can replace Him.

We all trust in someone, thing and/or a system of beliefs to manage our lives day to day. Atheists believe in themselves, that they are all powerful and this world is all there is. Thus, they manage prideful lives to their sole advantage. There are many who prioritize money, materialism and other earthly idols. There are some who believe appearance is all important so they prioritize fashion and physical preening. Even family is second to God. Granted there are the Christian hypocrites who proclaim to believe in God, but do not live or base their lives on the Bible. They are just as lost as non-believers.

You have the freedom to decide what to believe and follow to manage your special life. You could believe in a person, thing, theology or lifestyle as your standard, moral or principle to manage the outcomes of your life.

Core principles like forgiveness, "Love your neighbor as yourself," the Ten Commandments and the other teachings from scripture are essential for living a full and meaningful life. For me, it has become the very best way to live life. The Bible is brilliant; it is the handbook for a good life. You can't get this kind of advice, wisdom and inspiration anywhere else.

"Whoever pursues righteousness and unfailing love will find life, righteousness, and honor." Proverbs 21:21.

If there is no God, then you just live your life and die; it's over. Granted, it does make life simpler. There really is very little to live for except to have a good time, do what is best for you and get all you can, in any way you can, for as long as you can. Life would be very short-term focused, you live 70-100 years and then die. However, if God and eternal life are real, you have a very important decision to make.

I have discovered, God is the missing piece in life's complex jigsaw puzzle. Without a deep relationship with Him, I will always be looking for more and having less. With the Bible, life is more meaningful and life's lesser priorities simply fall into their proper place and perspective. Every major choice in my life must pass through the "Bible filter".

"Sensible people keep their eyes glued on wisdom, but a fool's eyes wander to the ends of the earth." Proverbs 17:24.

2. **Physical and Mental Health**

"Physical training is good, but training for godliness is much better, promising benefits in this life and in the life to come." 1 Timothy 5:8.

According to a growing body of scientific evidence, people of faith, who attend church, believe in God and pray regularly, tend to be healthier than those who eschew faith. I believe it is impossible to be completely healthy, mentally or physically without God. Of course, I do my part by exercising, eating nourishing foods, getting plenty of rest and having a positive attitude.

"Don't you realize that your body is the temple of the Holy Spirit, who lives in you and was given to you by God?" 1 Corinthians 6:19.

If you respect and take care of your body, your body will take care of you. Living a long life is the goal of most people, but life is only enjoyable if you are healthy, energetic and thriving.

Mental health is just as important as physical health. You are and become what you think about most. Your thoughts can make you sick or empower you.

It is possible to mentally talk yourself into or out of your destiny in life.

3. **Relationships and Family**

Meaningful relationships with family, friends and work associates are essential to a good life. Without them, your life will be unfulfilling. Unfortunately, relationships have never been my strong point, but I have been working on this weakness. I have learned to value all relationships and to cultivate them easily and deeply for my benefit, as well as, others. If you don't have meaningful relationships you will miss much of what life is all about.

I tend to be somewhat of an introvert. However, through feedback from my wife and close friends and the Bible, I have experienced improvement in my relationship building skills. I have found that relationships can be "messy" and especially challenging for males. However, I am dedicated to improving my relationships to fully enjoy others and follow the commandment in the Bible to love God and love others.

4. Financial Objectives

Money will not bring you long-term happiness or contentedness, but it can make life a little easier. I now believe this, but for a long time, I was a believer that wealth should be my primary objective. I always wanted more and more, believing it would bring happiness.

It didn't and doesn't!

In today's modern world, it is very important to plan your finances so you can take care of your and your family's needs. Life is more complex than it was in the past and adequate wealth is required to provide for just the basics today. To do this you need a budget, a decent paying job, a savings and investment plan and appropriate health and life insurance. All of this takes time, effort and knowledge, but you don't have to be a genius and it is well worth the time spent.

The key is to treat your financial life as just one of the many requirements you must manage to be successful. If you do not spend adequate time on your finances throughout your younger years, you will likely be very disappointed, maybe even angry, when you are old, out of time and have significantly fewer options to earn money.

5. Career and Job

Your job is important because you will spend a lot of time earning a living to finance your life. Much of your identity, friends and status in society will come from your chosen profession. What is one of the first questions most strangers ask you, "So, what kind of work do you do or want to do?" Choose your career carefully.

Consider not only how much you will earn, but more importantly, is it meaningful labor, does it have a future and are you passionate about your work? If you are naturally nurturing and caring, be a nurse, teacher or mom. If you love analysis be a scientist, computer expert or financial advisor. If you like physical activities be in construction. Doing what you enjoy and enlarges your life!

"Never get so busy making a *living* that you forget to make a *Life*." Dolly Parton, singer, actress.

Whenever making life critical choices, search the Bible for insight, get advice from your spouse, friends and mentors. It was a caring professor in junior college who told me to major in data processing, which changed my career, financial standing and the trajectory of my life.

What are your life priorities?

There are many other major life priorities: wealth, fame, happiness, success, friends, nice car, big house, world travel, a good education, etc. And, there is nothing wrong with any of them. However, in my case, I have settled on the five above. You must find the major priorities that are right for you.

Additionally, be aware that change is the only constant, so set long-term goals and adapt as required. Don't be apathetic or indifferent about your life and certainly do not let society make these choices for you. It's really quite easy to just "go along with the rules and ways of the world". Don't, intentionally decide what your priorities are for your future.

A poem I recently read sums it up nicely: **"Aim with your heart, adjust with your mind and always love."**

Your Life Plans

Now that you have prioritized your major life priorities, the minimum you should do is write down the short-term objectives you want to accomplish at the beginning of each year. Review them a few times during the year to see how you are doing, revise them as needed and, at the end of the year, evaluate how you actually did.

Ask yourself at the end of each year: What have I accomplished? What have I learned? How can I do better in the future and what needs to change? Additionally, if you miss a few dates or fail to reach an objective, don't stress, just adapt, learn and set new or revised objectives and move on.

Your life plan is simply writing down specifically what you want to happen and the steps to get there. A few simple objectives may include: Taking a class in college, spending time with your children, losing 20 pounds, getting a promotion, going on a vacation, saving to purchase a home or car, anything that is important to you.

For more complex, longer-term goals, you may need to develop a **detailed plan with specific/relevant objectives, action steps, measurable outcomes and a completion date** for each step to keep you on track. You can have objectives for each area of your life: family, career, relationships, education, financial, health, volunteering, spiritual.

This is not a complicated process, these are the basic nuts and bolts of any meaningful Life Plan.

I was surprised how often objectives and plans that I took the time to write down and track actually got accomplished, often surpassing my initial expectations.

There is something magical about *specifically* writing down what you want to happen, the steps to get there and paying attention to achieve your important life goals. Detailed planning allows you to accomplish more than you thought possible, be more in control of your life and actually live the life you want to live.

Additionally, you will be better equipped to anticipate and adapt to problems or bumps in life's long road. Likewise, as new opportunities arise you can evaluate them against your existing life plans. This provides a point of comparison for evaluating life's spontaneous alternatives and outcomes and making adjustments.

There are numerous books and internet sites if you need help getting started. Simply Google "life plan" and numerous "how to" plan suggestions will appear. Objectives and plans can be as simple or complex as you need them to be.

This process is for you and no one else, so you can keep it confidential if you wish. However, I have found it very helpful to include others in order to provide new ideas, illuminate blind spots and potential pitfalls. Plus, ask your spouse and friends to hold you accountable for doing what you say you want to get done.

Plans are simply a tool to help you manage your life and achieve your most important life goals.

I have found that as I go through life there are many life stages, each requiring different preparation, skills and attention. In every life, the timing and purpose for your plans varies depending on what you want to accomplish, as the Bible says:

"For everything there is a season, a time for every activity under heaven. A time to be born and a time to die. A time to kill and a time to heal. A time to tear down and time to build up. A time to cry and a time to laugh. A time to grieve and a time to dance. A time to scatter stones and a time to gather stones. A time to embrace and a time to run way. A time to search and a time to quit searching. A time to keep and a time to throw away. A time to tear and a time to mend. A time to be quiet and a time to speak. A time to love and a time to hate. A time for war and a time for peace." Ecclesiastes 3:1-8.

You have only so much time, energy, talents and money, so it is critical for you to plan how to invest and develop each of these limited resources. I read a story that had an interesting take on these vital resources of life as we grow and age.

"During your child/pre-teen and teenage years you have time and energy, but no money. During your working age years, you have money and energy, but no time. In old age, you have time and money, but limited energy and health." Unknown.

There are tradeoffs which require critical thinking, priorities and planning in every stage of life. The objectives and plans you set during your working years, (usually the longest life stage), are critical for your lifestyle, happiness and long-term financial security. It also determines the resources you have when you retire and grow older.

"The older I get the more I understand that it's okay to live a life, others don't understand." Jenna Woginrich, author.

Clearly, priorities, objectives and plans aligned with the Bible's bigger plans will succeed enormously. Whereas, selfish plans are likely to have mediocre outcomes. We often pray for God to bless our plans and activities *after* we make them and are frantically trying to accomplish them. Doesn't it make more sense to ask God to help you create your plans and align them with His strategies when you are *planning*, rather than after you have unilaterally made your plans?

"The mind of man plans his way, but the Lord directs his steps." Proverbs 16:9.

Following God is always a partnership. It is a delicate balance between trusting God and knowing everything is dependent on Him, while simultaneously planning and doing your part, as if everything depends on *you*.

"Now all glory to God, who is able, through his mighty power at work within us, to accomplish infinitely more than we might ask or think." Ephesians 3:20.

Remember, God is omniscient, He knows the past, present and future and there is no better counselor and partner to lead you.

Take Away: Setting priorities and planning your life is the best way to live successfully. Your past doesn't have to define you, nor determine your future. Rather, it often prepares you to take on the rest of your life. As you learn and grow from life's experiences, you are better equipped to plan your future.

Develop priorities, objectives and plans for your life and diligently work to achieve them. Determine your own destiny and lifestyle. Don't ignore the spiritual possibilities of life just because you don't understand them; there is more than you can see.

"Don't copy the behavior and customs of this world, but let God transform you into a new person by changing the way you think. Then you will learn to know God's will for you, which is good and pleasing and perfect." Romans 12:2.

Create meaningful life plans consistent with biblical principles, so you clearly determine and reach your destiny.

"We can make our own plans, but the Lord gives the right answer. People may be pure in their own eyes, but the Lord examines their motives. Commit your actions to the Lord, and your plans will succeed." Proverbs 16:1-3.

That's priority One.

Adapting to an Ever-Changing World

"There are three reasons that we fear change. The first, and in my opinion, most important, is that humans fear the unknown. The second is that, at our very cores, we're creatures of habit. And third, we fear failure and loss. What if, by making a change, we're starting down on the long road towards failure?" Helena Bala, writer.

America and the world have dramatically changed in the last 50 years and we must change with it. The problem is that most of us don't like change; we are creatures of habit. We like things we are familiar with; the way things have always been. We don't want to risk what we have. So, we dig in our heels and do all we can to avoid what we don't know. We love our comfort foods and our comfort zones unless we are *forced* to adapt or die.

"Some people will change when they see the light. Others change only when they feel the heat." Caroline Schoeder, author.

At first glance, voluntary and forced change appear to be the same, but there is a distinction between the two. Proactively taking risks as we venture into a new area we are unfamiliar with is your choice. But, much of the change in life is not your choice. Change is what happens *to* us. And, it can be overwhelmingly challenging, if not downright painful, mentally, psychologically and physically.

Change: "To become different; to become something else."

Change is the only constant in our world. The perpetual, relentless evolution of everything, living or not, is inevitable and persistent. You might as well accept and understand this fact and lead your life in ways that allow you to *continually adapt.*

"If you don't like something change it; if you can't change it, change the way you think about it." Mary Engelbreit, artist.

Think about it, nothing stays the same or lasts forever. Everything is *temporary*. Nations thrive and then disappear – think the Roman Empire. Even the redwoods, which live for hundreds of years, eventually die, decompose and return to the earth. The earth's surface, geology, atmosphere and every aspect of the planet is constantly moving through earthquakes, volcanoes, wind and water.

Learning, growing and changing is the only choice to stay relevant throughout our lives. We must keep learning at a rate that is greater than the rate of change. And, don't count on age and experience to make change easier. As we age, change becomes more difficult and more important. Once you stop learning and adapting, in any area of your life, you start regressing, gradually knowing and understanding less; irrevocably migrating toward irrelevance. While physical aging can only be slowed, mental capabilities and perspectives can keep growing for your entire life.

"Intelligence is the ability to adapt to change." Stephen Hawking, physicist.

Playing it safe is not a long-term strategy. The more you take rational risks the more likely it is the impossible will occur. Most want to experience a miracle without doing anything. However, it is not possible to experience a miracle unless you are working hard to do the impossible. The more often you step out in faith, the more likely it is the supernatural will show up and take you to the incredible.

"But, whenever someone turns to the Lord, the veil is taken away. For the Lord is the Spirit and wherever the Spirit of the Lord is, there is freedom. So all of us who have had that veil removed can see and reflect the glory of the Lord. And the Lord – who is the Spirit – makes us more and more like him as we are changed into his glorious image." 2 Corinthians 3:16-18.

The dynamic changes in American society experienced from the mid 1960's forward launched us into a dramatically different world. This tidal wave of change was initiated by an explosion in technology, protests and a revolution of equal rights for women and minorities. Also, sexual freedoms and an overwhelming attack on the four pillars of our society - church, state, family and education were unleashed. All hell was breaking loose…

And, then there was Vietnam.

America was fending off turmoil as much as it was advancing technology. We were simultaneously a nation of modern brilliance and moral bankruptcy. There were shouts of, "God is dead!" politicians trumpeted, "The Great Society" and, "The Silent Majority." We were a schizophrenic blend of lawlessness and "Law and Order" according to Richard Nixon, who was leading the way to government corruption.

Change had arrived in America whether we liked it or not. The old days of peace and prosperity were gone and the new days were filled with assassinations, violence, racism, anger, drugs, free sex and a conflict in Southeast Asia that tore our nation apart. On one side were hippies; on the other were hard hats. We saw killings at Kent State, riots in Watts and soldiers dying in a foreign land every night. Forget about the status quo, the roller coaster was close to jumping the tracks. We had never seen an America like this one.

Technology has given us tremendous opportunities and a more informed life. Our progress and new lifestyles also bring anonymity that isolates us from social face-to-face contact that has connected us together as humans.

Mobility led to the disintegration of multi-generational families and fractured a normal, consistent home life.

Instant worldwide communication has led to both equalizing information availability, as well as, an emerging media that use their pulpit for "specific agendas" that blurred the line between truth and lies.

All of our new, ever increasing freedoms, birth control, the sexual revolution and easy credit have led us to unanticipated moral consequences. Additionally, economic prosperity has resulted in a wider division between the rich and poor than ever before.

The unfortunate flipside of "unlimited freedoms for everyone," is the never-ending, exaggerated wants and demands of every selfish individual, extremist and social deviate. This was all done under the ethical guise of inclusiveness and equality with no counterbalance of taking responsibility, accountability or consequences.

Common sense morals, values and standards for positive social interaction evaporated. Even today, no one understands or has a clue really, where all these freedoms and contemporary developments will lead us. The world is a misguided route to freedom.

We are realizing that without universally accepted truths and morals, consensus and democracy will be replaced by power and money, which leaves fairness, reason and justice abandoned. American politics is already experiencing corruption as lobbyists and big money, has, for the most part, replaced a politician's constituency. Corruption has entered the American political arena. The Bible warns about bribes:

"The wicked take secret bribes to pervert the course of justice." Proverbs 17:23.

"Take no bribes, for a bribe makes you ignore something that you clearly see. A bribe makes even a righteous person twist the truth." Exodus 23:8.

You get to individually decide what authority, values and morals to base your life choices on. The Bible determines how I view, interpret and manage my life in modern society and the world's ever-changing landscape of vanishing mutual respect, inconsistent justice, malleable truths and destructive, anti-biblical agendas.

I am accountable for my behavior and respecting others opinions. I am diligent in finding the balance between charity that helps the less fortunate versus enabling an irresponsible and unaccountable lifestyle. I vote in every election and respect the outcome. However, our insular, self-serving, always growing governments are too big and powerful to be successfully managed. The Bible, family and close friends sustain me, not government or society.

"The grass withers and the flowers fall, but the word of our God endures forever." Isaiah 40:8.

No one is perfect; we are all fallible, imperfect and, at times hypocritical, yet want and need to keep growing. Most of us would like to change some aspect of our life.

However, *lasting* change is very difficult, most of us fail at it and many don't even try. Countless numbers of us only change when we are forced to because of a life altering experience like a serious illness, job loss, crippling addiction, natural disaster, near death encounter or some other dramatic incident. Fortunately, this does not happen to many of us. Our proximity to death and tragedy definitely gets our attention and provides the most impetus for change. The threat of death makes "life" real and can be the ultimate motivator for getting things done.

Thus, we are often left to our own inner strength and motivation when trying to change.

"Change is painful. Few people have the courage to seek out change. Most people won't change until the pain of where they are exceeds the pain of change." Dave Ramsey, author, radio host.

Adapt your life to the truths of the Bible, which interestingly, never changes. Unlike the world's trends and schemes that periodically change, the Bible is an everlasting rock to anchor your life to.

"I am the Lord, and I do not change." Malachi 3:6.

Thus, the Bible is the perfect **Life User Manual** and can be relied on for honest, unbiased direction for both everyday living, as well as, changing our lives. If you take a first step by simply following the Ten Commandments, your life will be measurably improved.

The Bible is written in a way and with uncompromising truth so it remains as relevant today as when it was written. It is a mystery to me how the Bible has remained successfully immutable over centuries.

Like all difficult, complex questions in life, don't let what you don't understand stop you from using what you do know about how to live an exquisite life. I don't understand the details of how jets fly or comprehend how huge ships float, but that doesn't stop me from using them for my benefit.

"The Lord our God has secrets known to no one. We are not accountable for them, but we and our children are accountable forever for all that he has revealed to us, so that we may obey all the terms of these instructions (in the Bible)." Deuteronomy 29:29.

Throughout my life, I have always believed that I was open to change and had the ability to adapt to most situations. But, much of the change I experienced had to do with success at work. Since I retired and work was eliminated from the equation, I have been persistently striving to change and improve the personal and spiritual expanses of my life. This has been quite different from my career and, thus, I needed to find reliable approaches to accomplish these more significant changes.

It hasn't been easy.

I have struggled to change in the "softer" areas like interpersonal and relationship skills, expressing love and humility. Thus, I have thought a lot about change and have tried many techniques in my quest to stay relevant. As I have thrown myself into these critical life changes, I have read many books, testimonials, talked to friends and even used Google for ways to change. Here is what I came up in my search to be a better human being.

The first step is to clearly describe on paper, specifically *what* and *how* I want to change, the exact outcome I expect and a target date. I have found that if I don't make an *intentional* choice to change and be willing to let go of my old ways, very little happens. Writing always helps me think through, clarify and understand the specific change I want to make. I do the following to hold myself accountable.

-place my **change objectives** where I see them periodically.
-put **reminders** on my phone calendar to review my plans.
-**read** everything I can about the behavior I want to change.
-**pray** about the changes daily and be **grateful** for any progress.

The **second step** is identifying **strategies for staying motivated.** Practicing willpower, feeling guilty or being pressured to change, have never been durable motivators for me. A few strategies that have worked include: fear of God and knowing that one day I will have to explain myself to Him. In addition, my family and close friends help and hold me accountable. Relationships are power tools for change.

"But even though a person sins a hundred times (doesn't follow the Bible) and still lives a long time, I know that those who fear (revere) God will be better off. The wicked will not prosper, for they

do not fear God. Their days will never grow long like the evening shadows." Ecclesiastes 8:12-13.

The **third step** is to **be very aware of what I say to myself, as well as, to others** about the change. Positive, encouraging "self-talk" is very effective for changing your mind. Also, by forcing myself to say kind comments to others and not make grumpy, condescending barbs; I am *retraining* my brain to believe that this is my new way of behaving. It takes a load of discipline and it is a long, slow process, but it works.

The **final step** is to believe **that deep change is the work of the Holy Spirit and not me**. Significant change is *not possible* with only human willpower. I pray, asking God to give me an attitude of faith and expectancy so that my desired change will become reality.

"Don't copy the behavior and customs of this world, but let God transform you into a new person by changing the way you think. Then you will learn to know God's will for you, which is good and pleasing and perfect." Romans 12:2.

Change of any kind is tough, not a single point in time, but an evolutionary process. Fortunately, changing to live according to the Bible is always worth the time and energy.

"Throw off your old sinful (irrational) nature and your former way of life, which is corrupted by lust and deception (not aligned with reality). Instead, let the Spirit (Bible) renew your thoughts and attitudes. Put on your new nature (reasoning), created to be like God—truly righteous and holy." Ephesians 4:22-24.

This verse defines how you can purposefully decide to behave differently, to live an *entirely* different lifestyle and be transformed into the person you were intended be.

I have also found that, at times, it is better for me to simply change my *behaviors and habits* and my mind will follow. For example,

> **If you are greedy, start giving money away.**
> **If you struggle with jealousy, start complimenting others.**
> **If you fear something, learn about it and start doing it.**
> **If you are judgmental, forgive the individual and be kind.**

A few years ago, I caught myself frowning in the mirror and decided I looked mean. So, from that moment on I tried to start smiling at everyone. The payback has been that I look better and the reactions I get from others are wonderful.

So, if you're having a bad day, smile at others and your day will turn around!

"Do everything without complaining and arguing, so that no one can criticize you. Live clean, innocent lives as children of God, shining like bright lights in a world full of crooked and perverse people. Hold firmly to the word of life (Bible)..." Philippians 2:14-16.

The Bible is all about change and restoration. It provides everything we need to live productive, joyful and fulfilling lives. The Bible makes it clear that, while it is tough, we are not to fear change; but to embrace it for our own long-term good.

"That is why we never give up. Though our bodies are dying, our spirits are being renewed every day. For our present troubles are small and won't last very long. Yet they produce for us a glory that vastly outweighs them and will last forever! So we don't look at the troubles (of the world) we can see now; rather, we fix our gaze on things that cannot be seen (spiritual). For the things we see now will soon be gone, but the things we cannot see will last forever." 2 Corinthians 4:16-18.

Change is not a suggestion, it is a *mandate*. We are not on this earth to sit idly by, selfishly ignoring others and lazily overlooking the devastating outcomes in the world. We are called to demonstrate, through our lifestyle and what we say, that we are driven by the Bible, not the world.

"You are the light (encouragement) of the world – like a city on a hilltop that cannot be hidden. No one lights a lamp and then puts it under a basket. Instead a lamp is placed on a stand where it gives light to everyone in the house. In the same way, let your good deeds shine out for all to see, so that everyone will praise your heavenly Father." Matthew 5:14-16.

Become the "light", the encouragement and hope we all crave. So, don't chafe at God's urging to move you out of your comfort zone, into greatness through your courage and His power. We are only on this earth for a short time compared to eternity. We don't have the luxury of meandering at a selfish and leisurely pace; doing all we can to avoid change.

"For God is working in you, giving you the desire and the power to do what pleases him." Philippians 2:13. **"And I am certain that God, who began the good work within you, will continue his work until it is finally finished…"** Philippians 1:6.

Take Away: Change is the only constant. Be open to criticism, challenge assumptions, try new activities, meet new people, avoid stereotypes and continually learn in order to remain relevant and useful. To do otherwise is to regress and fall behind.

Before you criticize others or attempt to correct their behaviors or beliefs, it is best to assess and have your own house in order. The Bible is insightful and direct about critiquing or demeaning other's before you work on yourself.

"Hypocrite! First get rid of the log in your own eye; then you will see well enough to deal with the speck in your friend's eye." Matthew 7:5.

Whatever your season of life, you have a choice to follow the teachings in the Bible or the ways of the world. Critical thinking is mandatory to determine when you are right, wrong or uninformed and change is required.

The serenity prayer is useful for all of us:

"God grant me the serenity to accept the things I cannot change, courage to change the things I can and the wisdom to know the difference." Reinhold Niebuhar, theologian.

Your Personal Finances

Wealth

"I don't find it hard to meet expenses. They're everywhere." Anonymous.

The most mentioned words and concepts in the Bible are money and materialism. Jesus was constantly addressing it. Of course, He used different words, like flock, sheep, grain, fields, wine and olive oil. He knew the power of wealth on individual's souls and the danger it posed to worshipping God. That is why this is one of the longest chapters in the book.

"Those who love money will never have enough. How meaningless to think that wealth brings true happiness? The more you have, the more people come to help you spend it. So, what good is wealth, except perhaps to watch it slip through your fingers." Ecclesiastes 5:10-11.

While money, by itself, can't bring happiness or eternity, it does directly impact every area of your life. Wealth can determine the quantity and quality of your food, housing, children's education, health care, security, peace of mind and your ability to help others. If you do not get your finances right it will cause arguments, stress, sleeplessness, turmoil and other grief.

"Wherever your treasure is, there the desires of your heart will also be. No one can serve two masters. For you will hate one and love the other; you will be devoted to one and despise the other. You cannot serve both God and be enslaved to money." Matthew 6:21 & 24.

Being wealthy is nice, but it is not a primary requirement in God's economy. He is much more interested in your heart, character, love and obedience. Your priorities and balance are key here.

"Better to have little, with godliness, then to be rich and dishonest." Proverbs 16:8.

People who long to be rich fall into temptation and can be trapped by many foolish and harmful desires that often plunge them into debt, lies and, occasionally, crime. Some people crave money so much that they bring heartache and regret on themselves.

"Yet true godliness with contentment is itself great wealth. After all, we brought nothing with us when we came into the world and we can't take anything with us when we leave it. So, if we have enough food and clothing, let us be content. But, people who long to be rich fall into temptation and are trapped by many foolish and harmful desires that plunge them into ruin and destruction. For the love of money is the root of all kinds of evil. And, some people, craving money, have wandered from the true faith and pierced themselves with many sorrows." 1 Timothy 6:6-10.

Paul's direction to Timothy is spot on here. One can never depend on money. Look at celebrities, professional athletes, business owners and lottery winners who wind up in bankruptcy with increased sorrow in their lives!

The goal of wealth should not be to amass it, rather to use it to care for yourself, family, helping the less fortunate and further God's plan on earth.

"Teach those who are rich in this world not to be proud and not to trust in their money, which is so unreliable. Their trust should be in God, who richly gives us all we need for our enjoyment. Tell them to use their money to do good. They should be rich in good works and generous to those in need, always being ready to share with others. By doing this they will be storing up their treasure as a good foundation for the future so that they may experience true life." 1 Timothy 6:17-19.

Based on the numerous times the Bible discusses money and wealth, it is obviously a significant issue. Only recently have I put God *first* and money further down my life's priority list and the results have been profound.

"Don't love money; be satisfied with what you have. For God has said, "I will never fail you. I will never abandon you." Hebrews 13:5.

I continually remind myself to be content with what I have and to love God and people more than money. I generously share what I have, realizing that when I die money will be meaningless. This attitude and related behaviors are the foundation for a healthy financial life.

📕 The only way I have found that wealth can possibly provide long-term meaning or happiness, is to give it away.

"Then Jesus said to His disciples, 'I tell you the truth, it is very hard for a rich man to enter the kingdom of heaven. I'll say it again - it is easier for a camel to go through the eye of a needle, than for a rich man to enter the Kingdom of God." Matthew 19:23-24.

This verse reinforces that salvation only comes from God and has nothing to do with us *earning or buying* our way into heaven. Additionally, Jesus then quickly said following verse to make it clear that with God anything is possible, including the rich entering eternity.

"Jesus looked at them intently and said, 'Humanly speaking it is impossible. But with God everything is possible.'" Matthew 19:26.

Making money and being wealthy is not a sin or even a bad goal; **the worship and love of money, more than God and others, is the overwhelming problem.** Having money is not the issue; it is how you think of money and your relationship with wealth that is the key to a balanced and blessed life. A biblical mindset regarding wealth is imperative to a successful financial lifestyle and a balanced life.

 **Money is a tool and resource, not an end in itself.**

Many wealthy individuals don't care about the latest fads or fashion; they are frugal and disciplined about everything. They take full responsibility for conservatively managing their wealth. They work extremely hard to earn, save, invest and are often very generous. They plan and consciously make both financial and life decisions based on both short and long-term facts and goals, not spur-of-the-moment emotions.

Look at Bill and Melinda Gates, he made *billions*. Now he and his wife work full time to give it away! They realize that helping others is the only way money can make your life meaningful. They live by a *different set of rules and values* then those who do not succeed financially.

The average American doesn't budget or plan. They listen to marketing ads, make impulsive purchases and don't have a saving or investment strategy. This is a recipe for financial disaster. We see it played out in our world and on the news every day.

When it comes to money what motivates and inspires you?

If your idea of success is the accumulation of more stuff and money, then you are probably addicted to money and possessions. I was addicted for many years. Everyone was doing it; how could it be wrong? I lived in Orange County, California, where materialism is loved, worshiped and flaunted. I eventually realized that most things I purchased ultimately ended up in a garage sale, donated to charity or in a storage shed that cost even more money every month.

It was a life changing wakeup call!

Possessions are all just short-term highs. The 'buzz' quickly wears off and our stuff ends up costing a lot to acquire, store and maintain. If you purchase stuff on credit the 'buzz' ends long before the payments.

"We buy things we don't need with money we don't have to impress people we don't like." Dave Ramsey, author and radio host.

What are your priorities? Do you have a budget and plan for earning, spending and investing your money? What are your motives for earning more money? These are key questions you need to honestly answer as a responsible and accountable human.

It is said that a person's true priorities can be easily determined by looking at their checkbook and credit card statements. Take a look at your financial records, you may be surprised by what you discover.

"Choose a good reputation over great riches; being held in high esteem is better than silver or gold. The rich and poor have this in common: The Lord made them both." Proverbs 22:1-2.

Take Away: Money is not good or evil, it is currency. Your perspective on and relationship with wealth is key. The Bible has a lot to say about it and will keep your life in balance. It is fine to be wealthy, just make sure God is your #1 priority, not money or power and invest your wealth to help others and fulfill God's plan on earth.

Earning a Living

The joy of working for a living…

In bed, it's 6:00 a.m. You close your eyes for five minutes and its 7:45. At work, it's 1:30 p.m. You close your eyes for five minutes and its 1:31.

What is your work ethic? More importantly, do you *have* a work ethic?

A good life is effortful. Hard work is mandatory to succeed. How do you work and what's your motivation for the labor you do? Work, career, job, profession, whatever you choose to call it, is a responsibility we each face in today's demanding, expensive world.

"A hard worker has plenty of food, but a person who chases fantasies ends up in poverty. The trustworthy person will get a rich reward, but a person who wants quick riches will get into trouble." Proverbs 28:19-20.

Most people, must work just to provide shelter, feed and clothe themselves and their families. The Bible addresses all those who work diligently; this verse was written by Solomon, the wealthiest man who ever lived.

"Lazy people want much but get little, but those who work hard will prosper." Proverbs 13:4.

How hard and long you work are also choices that say a lot about what you value. I chose to work enormous hours rather than be at home with my family. Thus, I missed other activities in life; like once in a lifetime experiences with my children. Balancing all of life's alternatives is essential to living a complete life. I should have read and used the Bible's advice much earlier in my life.

"Don't wear yourself out trying to get rich. Be wise enough to know when to quit. In the blink of an eye wealth disappears, for it will sprout wings and fly away like an eagle." Proverbs 23:4-5.

The other implication is that you will excel at what you work on and invest in the most. The analogy with agriculture is that you can only "harvest what you plant,", which is completely applicable to life.

Remember, you decide how hard to work, whether to do what you love or a job that pays well, to get a college degree or start a business; these choices determine how much you earn and thus, how much you have to give away. Listen to the Apostle Paul,

"Remember this – a farmer who plants only a few seeds (works little) will get a small crop. But the one who plants generously (works hard) will get a generous crop." 2 Corinthians 9:6.

If you invest well financially you will harvest additional money. If you raise your children well, you will likely see them succeed. If you invest time in people, you will have stronger family relationships and many close friends.

Of course, the inverse is also true. If you are corrupt, you will harvest jail time. If you don't work hard, you will probably not succeed financially or at your job. If you don't help others, they likely will not help you when you are in need and alone.

Or, as the Bible succinctly states it:

"Those unwilling to work, will not get to eat." 2 Thessalonians 3:10.

There are too many Christians in the work force who erroneously believe their boss is the person supervising them. Your ultimate authority is not called boss; He is referred to as God. Yes, respect your supervisor, but remember you are in the end working for God.

"Work willingly at whatever you do, as though you were working for the Lord rather than people. Remember that the Lord will give you an inheritance as your reward (eternity) and that the Master you are serving is Christ." Colossians 3:23-24.

Put God first, rather than pride, ego, fame and fortune. Always do what is right in all areas of your life, never compromise, cheat or lie. Never sacrifice your beliefs, values or character for your career or investments.

If you are ever in doubt about a decision of any kind ask yourself, *"What Would Jesus Do?"*

Unfortunately, I seldom contemplated the long-term consequences of the career choices I was making. I primarily focused *on my immediate personal success.* I couldn't stop incessantly striving and achieving; I was helplessly addicted to my career and money - nothing else mattered.

I thrived on crisis management and undertook many activities at once, believing I was invincible and could conquer anything. However, never mistake a busy life for a *meaningful* life. Often our hectic schedules, like any addiction, drown out everything else important in life. My career took up most of my energetic 20's, 30's and 40's and was central to my dysfunctional life and purpose. I was driven, even ruthless at times. My motives were ego and achievement centered rather than spiritual and relationship oriented.

Looking back on my career, while providing a very good living financially, is a regretful phase in my life. What was useful was the income that allowed me to provide for my family, retire early and help a few special individuals. All of the titles, achievements, big offices, and business travel are trivial now. I write this only to say we need to balance all aspects of life. I didn't then, but I do now.

"For wherever there is jealousy and selfish ambition, there you will find disorder and evil of every kind." James 3:16.

It is remarkable to me, as I write this, how insightful and applicable the verse above and many others are to my past life and the one I live now. Because in the end, I have come to understand that loving God and others and living according to the Bible is what matters most.

King Solomon asked an interesting question:

"What do people really get for all their hard work? I have seen the burden God has placed on us all. God has planted eternity in the human heart, but even so, people cannot see the whole scope of God's work from beginning to end. So, I concluded there is nothing better than to be happy and enjoy ourselves as long as we can. And, people should eat and drink and enjoy the fruits of their labor, for these are gifts from God." Ecclesiastes 3:9-13.

I was a hard-headed, stubborn learner. As a Christian, if what I say and how I behave is not based on the Bible, it doesn't mean much in this life nor in the *eternal* scheme of things.

Take Away: Do your best to select a career or job that has meaning for you, not simply a job that pays the most or is available. And, whatever job you do, work at it honestly and diligently, like you are working directly for God. Never forget to balance your job with all the other, often more important, aspects of a meaningful life, like family. And, don't forget to enjoy life, use your vacation time. Have fun!

Professional Sales Persons and Banks

This is the area where most of us get off on the wrong financial foot: We are emotional buyers, not prudent planners and fact-based purchasers.

Take for example, buying a car. We go to an auto dealership just to, "look around." In most cases, we wind up buying a new car! What happened?

The salesperson is charming and seemingly helpful in understanding my personal needs. They ask key questions like,

"How much can you afford a month?"

"You really like this car, right?"
"If I could arrange a special deal, so it fits into your budget, would you buy it?"

Then, he springs the trap...

The salesperson will even waive your first monthly payment to give you time to prepare for your six-year loan at a huge interest rate. This is all designed to make you feel good at the outset about signing your financial life away. You have little to no understanding of the financial storm about to descend upon you.

Of course, in most cases *we don't have a budget*! And, because of our pride, we hate to admit we cannot afford the car. We haven't researched how much our trade-in or the new vehicle is actually worth, nor our credit score and a fair interest rate for an automobile loan. We are unprepared and thus, *vulnerable*. This is all, pre-planned, sales gibberish to manipulate our egos and emotions. Their motive is to get you to trust the sales person, convince you that you "deserve" this beautiful vehicle and that you can park it in your garage tonight.

You give the dealership a check for $1,000 and drive away feeling like you made a great deal and wow, it feels good driving a new, shiny car! And, did I mention the new car smell? Of, course, the monthly payments will start soon, you have no idea if you can afford them or what the total cost of your vehicle will be at the end of six years. Trust me, the number is much higher than you imagined. You will be significantly "underwater" with the vehicle long before your last payment.

Welcome to professional sales people and the insidious world of credit.

Take Away: You cannot, I repeat, CANNOT ever beat banks, credit card companies and professional sales people. Never, never, never!

But you can be prepared to minimize the cost. My philosophy on purchasing vehicles is to always drive yours as long as you can, update your budget, do your research before you start looking at vehicles, always buy a used car, save and pay cash and try to purchase the vehicle from a private party.

Budgeting

"**We might come closer to balancing the budget if all of us lived closer to the Commandments and the Golden Rule.**" Ronald Reagan, 40th President of the United States.

Most of us are not **rational** when it comes to our finances. Like the above scenario, we show up at the car lot without a budget or plan for purchasing a car, so our **emotions** guide us, rather than our fiscally responsible brain. We fall victim to an emotional, "spur of the moment" impulse buy.

"**He who is impulsive exalts folly.**" Proverbs 14:29.

Car salespeople are the greatest psychologists in the world. They see us coming, have been methodically trained to sell by making us "feel good" and practice their profession every day, for a living. To have a chance at a fair deal, you must thoroughly prepare or you will be taken advantage of. This is not rocket-science, it is smart, but takes knowledge, planning and self-control.

No wonder most of us lack savings, are always short on cash and in debt. It is not hard to understand how money and materialism has us in its grip. When you lack a budget, you are vulnerable to many bad decisions.

"**Good planning and hard work lead to prosperity; but hasty shortcuts lead to poverty.**" Proverbs 21:5.

Financial budgeting is not optional; it is mandatory! It will make the difference between economic success and disaster, as well as, peace of mind and stress. A lack of budgeting will lead to debt and, can even lead to divorce, poverty, bankruptcy and thoughts of suicide.

Be smart. Do your homework, be prepared.

"**But, don't begin until you *count the cost*. For who would begin construction of a building without first calculating the cost to see if there is enough money to finish it? Otherwise, you might** complete only the foundation before running out of money and then everyone would laugh at you. They would say, there's the person who started that building and couldn't afford to finish it." Luke 14:28-30.

Don't be that person. Or as the Bible instructs:

📖 "The prudent understand where they are going, but fools deceive themselves." Proverbs 14:8.

Don't be deceived. There is no way to manage your financial life if you don't know how much you make and where you spend your money. That is the power of a personal budget.

The Bible is clear on this basic financial premise:

"Know the state of your flocks (resources, money) and put your heart in to caring for (manage) to your herds (assets), for riches don't last forever and the crown (inheritance) might not be passed to the next generation." Proverbs 27:23-24.

A budget is the *foundation* for all your financial responsibilities and decisions. Because *money influences every other area of your life*, you will effectively be measuring and managing every critical part of your life. Quotes from two premier business thinkers:

"You can't manage what you can't measure." Peter Drucker, author, management consultant.

"In God we trust, all others must bring data." W. Edwards Deming, author, engineer.

Every company, charity and business, of any size, has a budget. Every month they measure and analyze the difference between money coming in and money going out. The difference is either a profit or a loss. Then they make decisions and adjustments on what to do the following month and the rest of the year. If you follow the stock market you know that every quarter each company reports their actual financial performance versus budget. The consequences of the company's financial choices are obvious and is quickly reflected in their stock price. This feedback causes immediate changes in their decisions, cash flow and investments. You need to do the same.

You and your family are infinitely more important than any company. You must emulate what companies do so you have the information to make better financial choices. If you do not intelligently and diligently manage your money and finances you are ignoring reality and ignorant about how the world works.

A company's stock price is like your net worth. Your net worth is the difference between your assets (cash, savings, retirement accounts, home and car value) minus your debt (car, student and other loans, home mortgage, credit card debt). Your finances directly impact you and your family's self-esteem, lifestyle, outlook and opportunities. If you care about yourself, love your family, you will create and live by your budget.

"A budget is telling your money where to go instead of wondering where it went." Dave Ramsey, author and radio host.

If you don't have a plan and budget for your life you have no idea where you are, where you are going, nor where you will end up. Most importantly, you will never have enough money.

"Budget: a mathematical confirmation of your suspicions." A.A. Latimer, author.

📖 **You either tell your money what to do or the lack of money will control you.**

It is mandatory to know where your money is being spent, so you can take control of it. This does involve a little work. You will have to spend time *tracking* receipts to determine how much you spend eating out, entertainment, phone, cable, internet, clothing, food, gas, insurance, healthcare, mortgage or rent and all other expenses.

This tedious work will eventually become second nature and the extra money you save will definitely be worth it, as well as, immensely rewarding. By spending a little time each month comparing your *actual expenses and income* to your *budget* you will have knowledge. You are now equipped to begin to adjust your lifestyle and make decisions based on *facts,* not desires, dreams and emotions.

As a result, you will be in control, experience less stress and increased confidence. I guarantee that you will spend far **less** time budgeting than you will resolving the resulting financial problems and excessive debt of not budgeting. And, don't forget the brutal, helpless and humiliating consequences from a lack of retirement income.

📖 **There is absolutely no other way to get control of your income and expenses without a detailed budget.**

The sooner you realize that fact and apply it, the quicker you will right your financial ship and the stronger your financial life will become. There is nothing wrong with buying stuff once in a while if the financial facts warrant it. Let your budget dictate your spending not your desires, emotions or marketing ads.

📖 *It is your choice*, **budget your finances or live with the consequences.**

Most people *do not have a practical, working budget*, so they do not save for retirement, donate generously, prepare for emergencies or take advantage of investment opportunities. Wealthy individuals *do have budgets* and train themselves to know where their money is coming from and where it is going. They know it is a choice to intelligently manage their finances and not be lackadaisical about personal finances. That's how they became wealthy!

There are many tools and much advice on the internet to help you create and maintain a budget. It is not "rocket science" and only requires basic math skills.

"Winning at money is 80 percent behavior and 20 percent head knowledge. What to do isn't the problem; doing it is. Most of us know what to do, but we just don't do it. If I can control the guy in the mirror, I can be skinny and rich." Dave Ramsey, author and radio host.

Take Away: If you don't learn or do anything else from this chapter, at least create and maintain a personal budget. Do it because you are smart, want the best for yourself, family, help others and because the Bible instructs you to be diligent in financial matters. It will keep you out of debt, avoid financial arguments and stress. Plus, you will experience financial peace, send your children to college, take a vacation, donate to charity and, possibly retire early!

Saving and Investing Money

"The wise have wealth and luxury, but fools spend whatever they get." Proverbs 21:20.

Rick Warren, the dynamic pastor of Saddleback Church in Southern California, teaches the **10-10-80 rule** in allocating your income: the first 10% to God (the church you regularly attend) and 10% to your savings/retirement, which leaves 80% to live on. (If possible, I suggest increasing your savings to 15%). This is a very wise plan and more importantly, a financially biblical one.

Here is a great question for you,

Are you responsible with what God has given you to manage on earth?

Don't answer quickly. Think about it first.

Most Americans do not save enough. We save on average about 2-4% of our income, while numerous European and Scandinavian countries average savings of over 10%. Saving is simply planning and preparing for the future. Your future may include unanticipated expenses, buying a house or car, vacation, Christmas, birthdays, education, retirement and other priorities important to you.

It amazes me how many people seem to be *surprised* when Christmas arrives in December every year. As well as by the overall cost of Christmas that *forces* them to purchase gifts on their credit cards.

Prior to credit cards and easy to get loans, most people saved to make major purchases. Now we borrow and accumulate debt to make most acquisitions, instead of saving. This has led to many families being in debt with no savings. Credit cards are addictive. You don't actually see and touch your physical money leaving your wallet.

Guess what? It DOES.

"You have spent your years on earth in luxury, satisfying your every desire. You have fattened yourselves for the day of slaughter (judgement)." James 5:5.

The previous verse speaks to those who only live for today, thus are vulnerable to the future. Proactive, smart investing is an essential part of preserving and growing the money, you have already earned. It is serious business, because sound investments will significantly grow your wealth, while uninformed investments can lose your money.

Bonds, savings accounts, government CD's and money market accounts are safe, insured and fine for the funds you may need to access quickly. But, your return will be *minimal*, often less than the inflation rate. **To meaningfully grow and achieve your long-term investments goals, you must invest in stocks, low cost mutual funds and ETF's.**

The best recommendation is to take the time to learn how investing actually works, regardless if you are making the investments yourself or getting help from a professional. Do not just unilaterally trust anyone with your money. Do your diligence to know all about your broker and the company they work for. Never invest in anything you do not understand completely, because all investments come with risk.

If you just don't feel comfortable or competent in your financial investment capabilities, carefully select a financial advisor to help you. Consider recommendations from trusted friends and interview several advisors before you make a choice. They all charge fees for their services so always negotiate lower fees, evaluate their investment philosophy and make sure they are governed by the **fiduciary rules for financial advisors**. Never blindly trust any advisor; remember Bernie Madoff?

Consider testing them with a portion of your savings before giving them additional funds to invest. There is no replacement for you developing at least a basic understanding of financial markets, the risks of different types of investments and how your proposed investments work. Ask questions, even second-guessing your advisor, it is how you learn, screen and eventually trust someone with your money.

In the beginning, be very conservative and avoid taking any large investment risks.

There are risks with everything, thus the goal is to intelligently and rationally increase the probability of your success. Generally, the younger you are the more *risk* you can take to potentially earn more, because if the investment does not work out, you have time to earn additional money and let your investment recover. As you near retirement, be more *conservative*. This is because you will no longer be earning additional money and you do not have the time to let your investment recover from the down turn. As the Bible warns us:

"A prudent person foresees danger and takes precautions. The simpleton goes blindly on and suffers the consequences." Proverbs 27:12.

A key investing rule is to be **diversified:** invested in different types of stock, bonds, real estate and other asset types. Not surprisingly, the Bible stated this truism 3,000 years ago.

"Divide your investments among many places, for you do not know what risks might lie ahead." Ecclesiastes 11:2.

God is the ultimate financial advisor!

This is yet another example of the Bible's enduring and accurate advice on how to live your life, in this case, your *saving and investing* life. And, haven't we all heard that pearl of investment wisdom, "Don't put all your eggs in one basket"?

To paraphrase Proverbs 22:7: **Remember, those with the wealth make the rules, they have the power.**

You can get no better investment advice than from 87-year-old Jack Bogle, founder of the Vanguard Group. He recommends: **"Regular investing, diversified investing and above all, low-cost investing."**

To me, paraphrasing him, this means:

1. **Invest in the stock market**; there are few alternatives
2. Invest in several **diversified** broad market indexes
3. Invest for the **long-term**, don't try to time the market and don't panic when the market goes up or down.

4. Invest in the **lowest cost** mutual funds, ETF's, seldom individual stocks. The total of all fees should be less than 1%.
5. Start now, the younger you are the better; **compounding** of interest takes a lot of time.
6. No investment is a sure thing, there are **no guarantees.**

Bogle says: **"We live in an uncertain world and face not only the risks of the known unknowns, but also the unknown unknowns – the ones that we don't know we don't know. Despite these risks, if we are to have any chance for meeting our long-term financial goals, invest we must."**

If your employer offers a pension, you are blessed. Don't underestimate the value of a pension long term. If you have a 401K at work, at least invest enough to get all the company match and, preferably, the maximum contribution allowed. If there is no retirement plan available, start your own IRA or Roth IRA.

I do not suggest trading individual stocks. If you decide to, make certain you have a thorough understanding and training on how to invest and are willing to spend full-time managing your investments. A word of warning here: Do not be a "day trader," they are professionals and understand the instant profit and loss that can sink an amateur.

Real estate is just another form of investing. Like the stock market it almost always goes up in value over decades. There will of course, be periods of growth and downturns for all investments, at times, lasting years. Here is a tip, always attempt to purchase the *least* expensive house in the neighborhood or a "fixer" you can add value to.

I sold my prized Corvette when I was 26 years-old to make my first real estate purchase. At the time, it was a difficult decision, but looking back now it was brilliant. The lesson I learned was, it is always right to purchase assets appreciating in value, think **house**, and sell assets that go down in value, think **vehicle.**

Always defer immediate gratification for future gain.

Remember, all investments come with risk; there are NO sure or guaranteed investments. So, before investing in anything, you

must understand completely what you are investing in. Consider potential upside opportunities, downside risks, tax implications, costs and why you are investing. Get help from trusted, knowledgeable mentors.

While historical performance is not an indicator of future performance, it can be a good place to learn how the investment performed in both up and down markets.

"Do your planning and prepare your fields before building your house." Proverbs 24:27.

The verse means to do your planning, research and work in the right order before proceeding with your investment, project, starting a business or other important effort. It is excellent advice no matter what your project or investment. The Bible is the wisest advisor in the investment business!

Over the past 100 years the stock market has gone up an average of **5 to 6%** per year. Remember, the average includes multiple years in a row that *the stock market was down double digits and multiple years the market was way up.* Do not try to time the market; invest for the long-term. Real estate follows a similar pattern.

"Wealth from get-rich quick schemes quickly disappears; wealth from hard work grows over time. Proverbs 13:11.

Take Away: Think of money as a resource for not only today's needs, but also for future necessities when you are no longer able to earn more money. Diligently save and intelligently invest money. Save, Save, Save - then SAVE some more.

There is no substitute for *knowledge* when it comes to investments. Don't invest in anything you do not understand.

Debt

"Debt: A trap which a man sets and baits himself, and then deliberately gets into." Anonymous.

Of course, God has a rational way of looking at it,

"The wicked borrow and never repay; but the godly are generous givers." Psalms 37:21.

No one just *wanders* into debt. With few exceptions, debt is the result of many, consistently poor and often selfish choices. If you spend more than you make; you will be in debt! This is not high-finance, it's 5th grade math and common sense. Learn to live within your means or you will no longer have any means!

📖 **Save to purchase an item and do not acquire anything you cannot afford. Live within your means.**

"So be careful how you live. Don't live like fools, but like those who are wise. Make the most of every opportunity in these evil days. Don't act thoughtlessly, but understand what the Lord wants you to do." Ephesians 5:15-17.

Debt is not God's will for you

"Debt means you had more fun than you were supposed to." Greg Fitzsimmons, comedian and radio host.

Approximately 70% of Americans have debt. That is beyond sad! While the goal is to have no debt, in the short-term you *may* need debt to resolve an emergency or obtain a long-term objective. Debt to acquire an appreciating asset (anything that goes up in value over time), like a mortgage on a house or loan to earn a college degree may make sense. But, debt to acquire depreciating assets (anything that goes down in value over time) like a car, boat, golf clubs, clothing, furniture or vacation, are not smart transactions and should not be done.

A loan you can handle can be enabling; a loan you cannot handle is enslaving.

Whatever debt you have must be paid off as soon as possible. Making all payments on time and make extra payments. Otherwise, you will often spend more on interest than the original cost of the item.

"Give to everyone what you owe them: Pay your taxes and government fees to those who collect them and give respect and honor to those who are in authority. Owe nothing to anyone – except for your obligation to love one another." Romans 13:7-8.

Smart, rational individuals save for items they want to purchase. Emotional purchasers borrow money or foolishly use credit cards to purchase items.

"Just as the rich rule the poor, so the borrower is servant to the lender." Proverbs 22:7.

Never loan money to a stranger, friend or relative. It will always put a strain on the relationship, could potentially ruin it and at a minimum, make the relationship more difficult.

"Don't agree to guarantee another person's debt or put up security for someone else. If you can't pay it, even your bed will be snatched from under you." Proverbs 22:26-27.

If you must help another person out financially, I suggest you give them the money with no *expectation* that they will ever pay you back. This will not lead to hard feelings, will preserve your relationship and you will feel good.

Take Away: Intentionally save and invest your money carefully and wisely. Make it a goal to never owe money to anyone. If you are in debt, work hard to quickly pay off your debt as soon as possible. Always spend less then you make, don't use credit cards if you can't pay them off entirely every month.

Generosity

"It is more blessed to give than to receive." Acts 20:35.

How much should you give? The Bible has specific direction for you.

"Give in proportion to what you have. Whatever you give is acceptable if you give it eagerly. And give according to what you have, not what you don't have. Of course, I don't mean your giving should make life easy for others and hard for yourselves. I only mean that there should be some equality. Right now you have plenty and can help those who are in need. Later, they will have plenty and can share with you when you need it. In this way, things will be equal." 2 Corinthians 8:11-14.

"Give and you will receive. Your gift will return to you in full – pressed down, shaken together to make room for more, running over and poured into your lap. The amount you give will determine the amount you get back." Luke 6:38.

"Give freely and become more wealthy; be stingy and lose everything. The generous will prosper; those who refresh others will themselves be refreshed. People curse those who hoard their grain. But, they bless the one who sells in time of need. If you search for good, you will find favor; but if you search for evil, it will find you! Trust in your money and down you go! But, the godly flourish like leaves in spring." Proverbs 11:24-28.

You see a pattern here? There are numerous ways to give: money, time, food, expertise, hospitality, clothing, joy, encouragement, blood, gifts, used household items…

Give generously!

I was shocked how many verses in the Bible discuss giving. Obviously, it is important to God! Many verses say God loves a generous giver. My understanding is that you should give what God leads you to give; what you honestly believe is appropriate.

You should never go into debt or deprive your family in order to give to others. Use your heart, logical mind and budget to reach the correct level of generosity for you.

I have tested what the Bible says about giving and my experience confirms what it proclaims, every time. The more I give, the more I get, the better life is and the closer I am to God. Remember, when I say "get" it may not be just wealth, but rather joy, inner peace, understanding, friendship and fulfillment. Don't expect to always experience the fruits of your giving right away. Often, you will see the results from your generosity later in life, not immediately.

"Wait patiently for the Lord. Be brave and courageous. Yes, wait patiently for the Lord." Psalms 27:14.

God often uses money to test our faith, to see if you will follow through and really trust Him. It isn't just about giving, many give, but their motives for being "generous" are often selfish, using it only for a tax write off, to receive accolades from others or driven by ulterior motives.

"If someone has enough money to live well and sees a brother or sister in need, but shows no compassion – how can God's love be in that person?" 1 John 3:17.

In 2008, like many, my wife and I lost a significant amount during the stock market crash. While visiting the kids we attended our previous church, where we were married and baptized. The sermon that Sunday happened to be on a financial crisis the church was experiencing. A few of the church's bond holders were demanding payment of several hundred thousand dollars due in a few weeks.

In spite of the fact that we had lost lots in the stock market we decided to donate a meaningful sum to the church we had not attended for seven years. The church ended up raising more than they needed in a matter of weeks to pay off the few disgruntled bond holders. A few years later we not only regained what we had lost in the stock market, but significantly *more.* And, we felt joy and gratitude because of giving to help the church that taught, married and baptized us.

Coincidence? Not based on my understanding of the Bible and how God's financial world works.

I recount this story because it demonstrates that God is always at work in everything. The church is now thriving, helping many in the community and God's plans for us and the church are powerfully moving forward. We benefited greatly, financially, peace of mind and spiritually, by living according to the Bible's instructions.

"You must each decide in your heart how much to give. And don't give reluctantly or in response to pressure. 'For God loves a person who gives cheerfully.' And God will generously provide all you need. Then you will always have everything you need and plenty left over to share with others. As the Scriptures say, 'They share freely and give generously to the poor. Their good deeds will be remembered forever.'" 2 Corinthians 9:7-9.

Keep your eyes, attitude and faith *open* to God showing up at exactly the right time and place to benefit you and others, as well as, to further His plan on earth. It is about trusting God with your life and resources. I have tested this and learned:

 You cannot out give God! Believe it.

Take Away: Remember God does not bless and prosper you so you can have a comfortable life. He blesses you so you can bless others. You get what you give. Give generously!

Tithing

"Give God what's right -- not what's left." Anonymous.

So, what is *tithing?*

Giving 10% of your income to the church you regularly attend is called tithing. God says to give the *first* 10% of your total income to His church. To me this means give the first 10% of your *gross* income, from all your income sources, to your church. God created the church and it is of utmost importance to Him! It is His plan to save the world, one believer at a time. There is no plan B. Here is what Jesus said to Peter about building the church,

"Now I say to you that you are Peter (which means 'Rock'), and upon this rock I will build *my* church, and all the powers of hell will not conquer it." Matthew 16:18.

Most believe that giving is a good and noble thing to do. However, many prioritize giving *last*, after spending and saving.

The Bible teaches us to:
Give first,
Save second
Spend third.

"One tenth of the produce of the land, whether grain from the fields or fruit from the trees, (all sources of your income) belongs to the Lord must be set apart to him as holy." Leviticus 27:30.

The reason to tithe is because the Bible says to, because it reminds you that God must be *first* in your life. God uses money to test you, to see if He can trust you with what He has already given you before He gives you more.

"Well done my good and faithful servant. You have been faithful in handling this small amount, so now I will give you many more responsibilities. Let's celebrate together." Matthew 25:23.

So, do you believe the Bible and what Jesus promised or do you trust your own understanding of how the monetary world works?

"You must set aside a tithe (10%) of your crops (*income*) – one-tenth of all the crops you harvest each year. Bring this tithe to the designated place of worship, *(the church you regularly attend)* – the place the Lord your God chooses for his name to be honored and eat it there in his presence. This applies to your tithes of grain, new wine, olive oil and the firstborn males of your flocks and herds. *(your total income, from all sources)*. Doing this will teach (remind) you always to fear (respect or revere) the Lord your God." Deuteronomy 14:22-23.

Re-read that last line, "teach you always to fear the Lord your God." The purpose of tithing is to remind us to put God first.

I seldom see God move first, rather He waits for me to take the first step and then He shows up at exactly the right time to provide blessings. This makes my faith *real*, rather than me simply hoping for a miracle.

Faith in God and eternity is what we are talking about. You must believe before you can experience it, because faith unlocks the power of God in you. Everyone has faith – we place faith in airline pilots, parent's, friends and our cars every day. Every human invention started as a dream that became a vision and someone who took appropriate action to make that vision a reality because of their faith if their initial idea. Faith in God gives you the strength, confidence and knowledge to persevere and the resilience to move forward.

"Faith shows the reality of what we hope for; it is the evidence of things we cannot see." Hebrews 11:1.

The best quote I have ever heard about tithing, giving and volunteering is; **"There is no better feeling or deed, then to give to someone who can never repay you."**

I admit there have been times when things didn't work out like I had hoped. Perhaps a church did something I disagreed with or someone I helped let me down or didn't behave as I had expected. But, then I remembered all those who have helped me over decades. They didn't see any immediate results in me either.

Take Away: Tithing is a practical and simple discipline to demonstrate who is First in your life. Also, it reminds us that everything we have comes from God and develops an appropriate perspective on other aspects of our lives. We are directed to support God's church, its leaders, spreading understanding of the Bible and doing good for everyone, especially the "least of these" in our community.

Consumerism

Has all your consumption left you empty, in debt, wanting and needing more?

This was a real eye opener for me since my answer was a resounding yes! This may be an opportunity to sincerely think about the life you have been living and decide if it is providing the results, inspiration, contentment and hope that you expected.

I think we have all been sold lies through the marketing of large corporations. Companies and web-browsers know us better than we know ourselves. They relentlessly study us as consumers. The manipulative inventions of Black Friday, Internet Monday, amped up Halloween and demand to give flowers on Valentine's Day effectively separate us from our hard-earned money. They even hijacked Christmas, turning it into a buying pandemonium beginning in October. Easter, the most sacred of holidays, is now a chocolate bunny fest, praising little yellow chickees and Peter Cottontail.

Marketing organizations use the term "mindshare" to describe the awareness, in consumers' minds, of their product or service. What is your "mindshare" of the Bible?

You may have also noticed that working ridiculous hours, spending every cent you make, accumulating credit card debt and taking out loans to purchase more stuff has not resulted in the fulfilling, happy life the conniving ad men promised us. Rather, it has produced more profits for companies and more debt for customers.

Time and experience has taught me that what I once thought brought me happiness and purpose no longer satisfy me, it was all a tragic illusion. Money, acquisitions and entertainment were distractions or artificial fulfillment that quickly ended. All the earthly options left me feeling empty or not feeling anything at all. It is time to flip our thinking around and realize that life is *not* about more money and stuff.

A meaningful life is not about things. It is about loving God, our precious family and friends and helping those in need.

When I freely give my time, talent or money to someone directly or to a charitable organization, I rarely know where or how it will be spent. The gift could go on and impact many generations into the future for decades. If I give money to a family for a child's education, that child may then raise a child and send them to college and so on. Possibly one of them will create an important invention or become an influential leader, positively impacting the lives of millions.

I choose to volunteer, make donations and let life take its fascinating, random course. There are endless simple ways to give: sincerely empathize with and listen to someone; let the other person win an argument or game; reconcile with someone; bless someone anonymously; secretly buy someone's meal; volunteer wherever you feel most passionate; smile; be kind; compliment someone or just have a meaningful conversation. It doesn't take much to make someone's day!

"Joy can only be real if people look upon their life as a service and have a definite object in life outside themselves and their personal happiness." Leo Tolstoy, Russian Author.

As long as I trust the individual or charitable organization, it is not necessary for me to know my contributions final outcome. A gift or service, of any kind, freely given to the needy, elderly, sick or helpless is the best, most personally satisfying thing I have ever done.

"It is one of the most beautiful compensations of life that no man can sincerely try to help another without helping himself." Ralph Waldo Emerson, essayist and poet.

The insight from the Bible is that generosity is the way to live a fun, enriching and rewarding life. I now understand that joyfully giving of my time, talents and treasures always helps others, makes me feel great and simultaneously, honors God.

"Blessed are those who are generous, because they feed the poor." Proverbs 22:9.

"Whoever gives to the poor will lack nothing, but those who close their eyes to poverty will be cursed." Proverbs 28:27.

My wife and I volunteer at our church, the Salvation Army and other organizations throughout the year, as well as supporting food pantries and serving meals. We help build houses with Habitat for Humanity, deliver lunches for Meals on Wheels and donate blood. We have helped homeless families get off the street and spent a week at MDA camp. We are currently helping several foster kids with college. The opportunities to give and feel great and useful are endless.

After each of those experiences, we feel uplifted and grateful. We knew we had done something meaningful for others, as well as, ourselves. We never get that same kind of feeling earning more money or acquiring more stuff. I never experienced this kind of deep enrichment with my career accomplishments.

"Give generously to the poor, not grudgingly, for the Lord your God will bless you in everything you do. There will always be some in the land who are poor. That is why I am commanding you to share

freely with the poor and with other Israelites in need."** Deuteronomy 15:10-11.

Take Away: Joy, contentment and peace are only found in a relationship with God and other people, not possessions. The more grateful you are for what you do have, the happier you will be. Give generously and you will be blessed!

Legacy

Who do I want to be? What do I want to happen in my life? What do I want to be remembered for?

If you have those thoughts, then work hard toward those purposes and **intentionally create your legacy**. This is a significant, never-ending challenge for me. I have seen incremental *improvements* in my financial behavior, generosity and relationship goals. Each small change encourages and reminds me that it is possible to keep maturing and creating my hoped-for legacy.

We each become known for something; for who we really are. This comes about through what we say, our behaviors and choices. Everyone has a unique image, reputation and personality. Intentionally decide who you want to become, then work toward living that life. The key is to take the focus off of you and put it on God and others. That perspective will secure the legacy we all hope for.

A key principle of the Bible is that whatever you do, good or bad, it will come back to you. Here is an amazing paradox: **If you want or need more of something, start giving it away!** Want to become richer, be more generous. If you need more time, volunteer. If you need to develop a skill, work with someone who has that skill for free. It is seemingly counter intuitive, but it works.

Just like an agricultural harvest, a single seed planted (given away to the soil), produces a harvest several times the number of seeds planted. Thus, investing your money, time or talents to help other individuals will return to you many times over.

"Do not judge others and you will not be judged. Do not condemn others or it will all come back against you. Forgive others and you will be forgiven." Luke 6:37.

Alternatively, causing harm or grief to others will also return to you many times over. By not donating, giving or helping others may result in you having less money, friends and happiness.

"Bring all the tithes into the storehouse so there will be enough food in my Temple. If you do "says the Lord of Heaven's Armies," I will open the windows of heaven for you. I will pour out blessings so great you won't have enough room to take it in! <u>Try it! Put me to the test!</u> Your crops will be abundant, for I will guard them from insects and disease. Your grapes will not fall from the vine before they are ripe, "says the Lord of Heaven's Armies." Malachi 3:10-11.

This may be the only verse in the Bible where God says to test Him! When He says "open the windows of heaven" and, "blessings so great you won't have enough room to take it in," you can believe your blessings will surprise and overwhelm you. You can count on God, He always keeps His promises.

Be a blessing to other people.

Take Away: There is a place or "knowing" deep down inside each of us where we simply recognize, that in spite of us being a mere speck in the entire universe, it is not only right, but imperative that we do good and be kind to others. Generosity and love are how we honor God, bless others and create the legacy we desire. Choose to live the incredible life that will create the reputation you want others to remember and think about at your funeral.

Greed

"Greed is a bottomless pit which exhausts the person in an endless effort to satisfy the need without ever reaching satisfaction." Erich Fromm, German social psychologist.

Wanting more and more can be an idol.

📖 **"They were always greedy and never satisfied. Nothing remains of all the things they dreamed about."** Job 20:20.

Greed is the intense and selfish desire for more, especially wealth, possessions, power and fame. Our persistent drive to acquire more is constantly fueled and reinforced by tempting marketing ads. If anything becomes an all-consuming desire or craving you have crossed the line to addiction.

If you have any doubts about the world promoting greed look no further than a hit Hollywood movie:

"The point is, ladies and gentleman, that greed, for lack of a better word, is good. Greed is right, greed works. Greed clarifies, cuts through, and captures the essence of the evolutionary spirit. Greed, in all of its forms; greed for life, for money, for love, knowledge, has marked the upward surge of mankind." Gordon Gekko, *Wall Street* movie, 1987.

Gordon Gekko and his ilk are not only wrong, but eventually most will pay a heavy price because of the consequences greed has on the rest of their lives. The Apostle Paul is laser clear on this:

"Yes, everything else is worthless (possessions, power, status, fame) when compared with the infinite value of knowing Christ Jesus my Lord. For his sake, I have discarded everything else, counting it all as garbage, so that I could gain Christ." Philippians 3:8.

The Greek translation for the word 'garbage', in the above verse is, "dung." A cow pie! That is the value of greed. It is your choice to pursue the Bible or a life of never ending dung.

Doesn't seem all that difficult when you think of it that way, right?

"The very wealth you were counting on will eat away your flesh like fire. This corroded treasure you have hoarded will testify against you on the day of judgment." James 5:3.

The point is all your hoarding and greed-seeking behavior is pointless, except to prove you are guilty of pride and selfishness. "Survival of the fittest" is a familiar, but egotistical slogan. It is diminishing and, often lonely existence. I have found that friends, groups and teams always achieve more than a greedy, self-serving individual, I know, I was one!

Today's modern world, what many call civilization, is a very substandard human existence. The cure for our "selfish, stingy culture" is love, compassion and generosity. When you are jealous of others, beware, it feeds greedy motives. There is no meaning or wisdom in "Keeping up with the Jones's." Forget about the Jones, focus on the Bible.

"I have seen that every labor and every skill which is done is *the result of* rivalry between a man and his neighbor. This too is vanity and striving after wind." Ephesians 4:4.

Envy is a temporary feeling of want for something another possesses or a resentment of someone else's success. You have no idea what it is like to be that person or how meaningful their life is. So, focus on *yourself* and your financial portfolio. You can bet that person, the one you envy, is envious of someone else, maybe even you.

Comparing yourself to others is a losing proposition - every time. It is a never-ending game that cannot be won. A content and fulfilling life comes from consistently having *your* life compass pointed in the right direction, toward God.

"You must not covet (crave) your neighbor's house. You must not covet your neighbors' wife, male or female servant, ox or donkey (car, boat), or anything else that belongs to your neighbor." Exodus 20:17.

Are you in control or is your money and possessions controlling your life, desires and behaviors? Is your image and status in society really that critical to your self-esteem?

"Therefore, if you have been raised up with Christ, keep seeking the things above, where Christ is, seated at the right hand of God. Set your mind on the things above, not on the things that are on earth." Colossians 3:1-2.

Don't ever let your wealth compulsion cause you to do anything dishonest or hurtful or go into debt to impress someone else.

Not everyone wants to nor will become wealthy. There are many other meaningful personal gifts and ways that bring even more joy, inner peace, contentment and self-worth.

Jesus said it powerfully,

"Beware! Guard against every kind of greed. Life is not measured by how much you own." Luke 12:15.

The antidote for greed is being grateful, content and happy with what you already have. Consider the blessings of a home, health, family, job, meaningful relationships, peace, love and knowing God.

"Don't make your living by extortion or put your hope in stealing. And if your wealth increases, don't make it the center of your life." Psalm 62:10.

So, how much is enough? How do you determine and know if you are greedy or in balance with getting, giving, saving and investing?

When asked how much money was enough, John D. Rockefeller replied: **"a little bit more."**

Rockefeller was right, you will **never** be happy or content if money is the center and measure of your life. I am generous because the Bible commands it and my conscience confirm it is the right thing to do. Obedience to the Bible allows me to feel grateful and useful to God's plan for me. Human nature is not naturally generous. That is why God wrote the Bible; to help us overcome our selfish human nature and transform our lives.

I listen to sermons, take accounting courses, read the Bible and have decades of both good and bad experiences on the topic of greed. Additionally, my wife (a financial wizard) and I lead biblically-based courses from Dave Ramsey on personal finances. Since everyone is unique, there is no one precise answer to the question - how much is enough? Read the Bible and ask God for guidance and wisdom regarding your finances.

Money is not the problem; we all need money. The issue is the 'love of money' that becomes an all-consuming goal. It leads to selfishness, fraud, lying or other corrupt motives and behaviors in order to earn more or avoid paying those you owe. Human greed has led to corrupt politicians, the extinction of animals, child pornography, destroying the atmosphere, slavery, even murder. Greed is powerful!

"For the love of money is the root of all kinds of evil." 1 Timothy 6:10.

Thus, use your spiritual mind, heart and scripture, combined with your budget to pre-determine and plan your financial life. The answer is to personally and honestly balance getting, giving, saving, investing with all the other important areas of your life.

Enjoy your work and accept your lot in life - this is a gift from God. Solomon, the richest man ever says:

"Here is what I have seen to be good and fitting: to eat, to drink and enjoy oneself in all one's labor in which he toils under the sun *during* the few years of his life which God has given him; for this is his reward." Ecclesiastes 5:18-20.

Take Away: If you find yourself always needing more of anything, or never being satisfied, then you are greedy and, maybe, addicted to what controls you. Money controlled me for years until I learned how to invest it for good on earth and eternity.

Read the Bible, put God first in all the financial areas of your life, be generous and don't compare or envy. Learn to congratulate others for their successes. Formulate and manage the monetary areas of your life according to the Bible using your long-term financial plan and budget. Learn to appreciate and be grateful for all that you already have, which will lead to peace and contentment.

Here's the moral and purpose of wealth:

"Here's the lesson: Use your worldly resources to benefit others and make friends. Then, when your earthly possessions are gone, they will welcome you to an eternal home." Luke 16:9.

God, not greed, is good.

Jesus said: **"only God is truly good."** Mark 10:18.

Your Physical Health

"Subway is definitely the healthiest fast food available because they make you get out of the car." Unknown.

Being created by God and born on this beautiful planet is a gift and privilege. We have the opportunity to develop and productively use our complex bodies and powerful minds. It is our responsibility to treasure life and take care of our bodies so we can become all that we are meant to be.

"The first wealth is health." Ralph Waldo Emerson.

While writing this chapter and wanting it to come alive biblically, I soon realized there were not a plethora of verses directly referring to how to improve physical health. How could I illuminate this important area of our lives using the Bible to demonstrate conclusively that being in shape, eating well and quality sleep are *critical?*

It came to me one morning. The entire purpose of the Bible is to instruct us in how to live excellent, complete lives - in every area of our special existence. Because of my detailed and perfectionist personality, I was being too literal and limiting only looking for specific Bible verses. The Bible gives an **all-inclusive** picture for how to live a life of health, purpose, love, meaning and hope.

Here is one example.

"Trust in the Lord with all your heart; do not depend on your own understanding. Seek his will in all you do and he will show you which path to take. Don't be impressed with your own wisdom. Instead, fear (respect) the Lord and turn away from evil. Then you will have healing for your body and strength for your bones." Proverbs 3:5-8.

The premier symbol of health, positive attitude and meaningful lifestyle in the Bible is demonstrated best by Jesus Christ. He walked the earth and endured the hardship of the land, climate, torture and a gruesome death. Very few individuals would have survived the way He did. Jesus had no home and braved the elements of the Middle East from the scalding desert sun by day to the merciless freezing at night for days and months at a time.

Jesus was rejected, called names and ridiculed. He was disappointed by the apostles, often inconvenienced and frustrated by others. He experienced all the positive and negative emotions we do today. Much of what He and the disciples endured is incomprehensible to the average person today, no matter what physical shape they are in.

In addition, there is no indication that Jesus ate heartily. He and His followers lived off the land consuming primarily natural foods like fruit, berries, plants, fish and water. The thousands of miles He walked and the physical carpentry work He did, surpassed any contemporary health club or fitness plan. And, He lived a life of purpose and mental alertness with a positive attitude and drive to deliver His message of hope to thousands. Additionally, He personally cared for and loved everyone, regardless of their social standing, financial status, faith or physical health. He counted on others and God for all His needs.

It is recorded biblically that God sent His Son to earth in John 1:14, with the same body as ours. It is designed perfectly for the physical rigors, challenges and purpose Jesus had to face. He never once used His deity to enhance His stamina or reduce suffering. At the end of His physical life Jesus endured a physical gauntlet none of us could possibly imagine. He was kept up all night and suffered through three unjust trials condemning Him to death. He was stripped of His clothing, verbally belittled and lashed with leather strips tipped with metal.

The soldiers then made Him carry a heavy, wooden cross, for over a mile to a remote area outside the city gates called Golgotha ("the Skull") to be crucified. After reaching the site the soldiers laid Him on the large beams of the cross, nailing Him to it with grotesque spikes penetrating His wrists and feet. Then, as they jammed it into the ground, the huge nails shot thunderous pain to every nerve ending in His body.

Is physical health important? If you want to emulate Jesus or simply be a competent human, the answer is a resounding, YES! If physical fitness was significant to the Son of God how can we settle for obesity or an unhealthy lifestyle?

Fortunately, we are not expected to roam the desert, sleep outside or be crucified. But we are expected to pay attention, respect and care for our complex bodies so we can accomplish our mission in life: to love God, love others and tell everyone about the Bible. To successfully do our job, we must be in the best physical and mental shape to run our individual race to a successful conclusion.

"Let us run with endurance the race God has set before us. We do this by keeping our eyes on Jesus, the champion who initiates and perfects our faith." Hebrews 12:1-2.

This is not a suggestion, it is a commandment.

"Don't you realize that your body is the temple of the Holy Spirit, who lives in you and was given to you by God?" 1 Corinthians 6:19.

Your Healthy Life Plan

When it comes to your overall health, what grade would you give yourself? Try to be honest.

There are two influences that determine our health; **things we can do something about and things that we genetically inherit.** Our family DNA and upbringing carry with them possible health issues such as arthritis, cancer, diabetes, heart disease and so on. On the flip side, our family heritage can give us many positive protections like strong genes and good habits.

Once we get past the genetic issues, the maintenance of our bodies is up to us.

As to **the things we can do something about**, let's face the truth, most of us know what we should do and how we should live to *maximize* our health. But because many of us are lazy, busy and have a penchant for unhealthy food, we don't do what we know we should. If you listen to your mom, hang around healthy friends, read lifestyle magazines, surf the internet and watch a little television, you can't help encounter numerous stories on how to be healthy. Along with the latest scientific discoveries on health and fitness; you have no excuse for ignorance.

In our modern society, the overwhelming availability of good health and medical information is not the problem; it is our lack of motivation and discipline that is missing.

This chapter focuses on healthy opportunities that you can actually do something about. A healthy lifestyle is doable, you just have to care a little about yourself, your family and your future with them. The choice is yours, live a healthy life or live with the consequences. Notice the next verse emphasizes **two qualities you must use** as keys to a safe, fully lived and confident life.

"My child, don't lose sight of common sense and discernment for they will refresh your soul. They are like jewels on a necklace. They keep you safe on your way and your feet will not stumble. You can go to bed without fear; you will lie down and sleep soundly. You need not be afraid of sudden disaster or the destruction that comes upon the wicked, for the lord is your security. He will keep your foot from being caught in a trap." Proverbs 3:21-26.

Let's get to work!

Have a Positive Attitude

"There are basically two kinds of people: positive thinkers and negative thinkers. Did you know that negative thinkers tend to have more health problems than those who think positively? Not only can positive thinking make you healthier, but it can actually help you have a better life." Helen Sanders, Health Ambition magazine.

This is not a hard and fast fact by any means, because a joyful, upbeat person can still get a serious illness. However, a positive attitude and outlook not only helps our physical immune system fight off disease, but carries you through the treatment, as well.

"A positive attitude causes a chain reaction of positive thoughts, events and outcomes. It is a catalyst and it sparks extraordinary results." Wade Boggs, Professional baseball player.

📖 **If you respect and take care of your body long-term your body will take care of you!**

It's not surprising that according to a growing body of scientific evidence people of *faith* have better health. Individuals who attend church, believe in God and pray tend to be healthier. I do believe that better understanding the Bible and following its guidance for my life, contributes to me being healthy physically, mentally and spiritually. Just like healthy eating, exercising, working and family habits, developing biblical behaviors lead to a better life.

📖 **Habits and routines are how we actually live life most days.**

Living a long life is the goal of most people, but that is only *half* of the job. A long life is only enjoyable if you are *healthy and vital*. Quality of life is just as important as the length of your life.

"My child, never forget the things I have taught you. Store my commands in your heart. If you do this, you will live many years and your life will be satisfying." Proverbs 3:1.

Physical Health

The first thing to establish is your current physical condition. Get a physical, do blood work and ask your doctor's opinion of your health. The internet, magazines and books provide a plethora of information about what your healthy weight should be and other key health measures.

Your energy level, a mirror, a spouse, friend and an honest assessment of your eating habits will give you clues to your health.

You are probably not in high school anymore, so don't be unrealistic about your ideal weight or physical capabilities. Each of us is physically *unique*. Learn your body type and make up. Some of us are skinny, others not and there are endless other variations. Enhance who you are, don't try to be a different body type. But, if you are like most Americans, you have a good chance of being out of shape and overweight. Experts in the medical community report that 60% of Americans are overweight or obese. It's time to take a longer-term view to ensure you are doing all you can to have a long, high-quality life.

📖 **"I'm in shape. Round is a shape, isn't it?"** George Carlin, comedian.

The three major components to health.

Part I: Diet

Can you handle the truth?

Dieting is worthless and counter-productive to your goal of a healthy life. If there was one that worked we would all be on it.

Dieting is a short-term phenomenon; not a long-range, permanent success strategy. Most dieters fall back into their old eating habits after a few days, weeks or months. The reasons for giving up on diets are many, well-documented and devastatingly human. It takes discipline and patience over the rest of your life to jettison old habits and create new ones.

📖 **"A recent study has found that women who carry a little extra weight live longer than the men who mention it."** Unknown.

Accept a diet for what it is: A *quick fix* to help you get ready for a reunion, summer, wedding or any situation where you want to look good. Most people will lose a few pounds of water weight in the first few days before they hit the wall. After that, it is a very slow process with a loss of a few pounds a week. Success usually only comes when accompanied by daily exercise. That is a tough regimen that many are incapable of sustaining.

Diets, for the most part, do not work!

"**Dear Diet, things are just not working out between us. It's not me, it's you. You're tasteless, boring, at times painful and I can't stop cheating on you.**" Somecards.com.

If you can be happy losing a few pounds enjoy your new bathing suit or clothing for a little while. But, if you truly want *permanent* health and weight, you need to commit to a Healthy Life Plan, not for weeks or months, but for the *rest of your life*.

You focus on healthy, nutritious foods, not losing weight. If you eat and exercise properly the weight will come off slowly but surely and you will feel better. This plan is not about punishing yourself with restrictions; it is about creating *healthy eating habits* you can enjoy for your entire life.

The results of a balanced diet will pay off in dividends for you: a longer life, more energy, clothes that look great on you, fewer medical problems and less expenses, stress, depression, worry and a significantly better attitude and outlook on life.

No short-term diet can do what long-term healthy eating does.

People are crazy about diets in America; not Health Life Plans. Most want a "magic pill" or a "quick fix" to renovate their bodies. But, over years and years, people have liked their fast food, sodas, sweets, fattening carbs, trans fats, booze, deserts and prepared foods. To give that all up for salads, low fat dairy, lean beef, poultry and fish, prepared at home, mandates a strong will, time and discipline. Change of any kind is hard, but never impossible. The main reason most people consider a Health Life Plan of eating and exercise is when they are confronted by a traumatic medical need to do so or the threat of a severely shortened life span. Don't be one of those.

A guy is standing on the bathroom scale desperately sucking in his stomach.
"That's not going to help," says his wife.
"Yes, it will," replied the man, "It's the only way I can see the numbers!"

For all of you with diabetes, high cholesterol, high blood pressure, hypertension and heart disease out there, here is something to remember,

📖 **"Every time you eat or drink you are either feeding disease or fighting it."** Heather Morgan, singer and songwriter.

Still reading?

Food is more than taste and calories. What you eat sends messages to your body and mind, contributes to wellbeing or ill health - you are and become what you eat! Consider these steps to dietary greatness, which are on most healthy eating lists.

-Educate yourself; read books, Google healthy eating
-Ask your doctor about diet, exercise, stress and sleep
-Learn to decode and understand food labels
-Throw out all your unhealthy foods, sodas and snacks
-Go to the grocery store with a list and re-stock your pantry with only nutritious whole foods, not pre-packaged meals
-Eat three healthy meals a day, slowly, drink lots of water
-Supplement your meals with 2-3 *smaller* nutritious snacks
-Don't eat snacks late at night
-My guess is more people die from being overweight than underweight.

📖 **You can only eat what's in your house. Don't let unhealthy foods into your home!**

Don't be surprised if you don't miss your former way of life because your body has made a new partner in living healthy. My wife and I do everything outlined above and have all but eliminated our unhealthy food addictions. It did require intentional change, reading food labels and new habits, but we now feel the difference every-day.

Enjoy your new Healthy Life Plan eating regimen. You may have to experiment and try different foods to find the right mix for your unique metabolism and taste preferences. You will be on it for a long time, hence the term, "Life Plan". **Read Daniel 1:8-16** to learn what the

Bible says about healthy food and, surprisingly, a biblical vegetarian diet.

"Each morning when I open my eyes I say to myself: I, not events, have the power to make me happy or unhappy today. I can choose which it shall be. Yesterday is dead, tomorrow hasn't arrived yet. I have just one day, today, and I'm going to be happy in it." Groucho Marx, American comedian, film and TV star.

Part II: Exercise

I can't believe I forgot to go to the gym today.
That's seven years in a row now.

Eating healthy is admirable and essential, but it is not enough to create a total Healthy Life Plan. It's time to put down the remote, get off the couch and lace up the tennies.

Growing up, we played with our friends, competed in sports, rode bikes and walked or ran *everywhere*. Friends are key, we have fun together and help each other through encouragement, competition and holding each other accountable. It's time to "play" again. The more types of play the better; **"Variety is the spice of life,"** because eventually everything gets boring.

Play could include:

--Walk, jog or swim every day, take stairs, park far away
--Gardening, mowing, pruning, washing windows, vacuuming
--Join a hiking, running, tennis, pickle ball, dance, surfing club
--Sensible weight training to maintain muscle mass
--Hire a personal trainer or team up with a friend
--Golf, without a cart, train for a 5 or 10k or marathon
--Aerobics, Pilates, Yoga, Tai chi, martial arts, self-defense
--Play baseball, basketball, racquetball, paddle tennis
--Work at a stand-up desk, bike or rowing machine at home
--Consistently stretch to maintain and increase flexibility

If you are not currently physically active, you need to begin *now*. The opportunities are endless. Pick your type of exercise, preferred time of the day and set up a *regular* schedule, it is mandatory for a healthy life! My wife and I alternate hiking, biking, weight training, stretching, yard work and volunteer work. The harder and longer you exercise the bigger the benefits and the better you will sleep.

"I have to exercise early in the morning before my brain figures out what I'm doing." Marsha Doble, author.

The key to exercise is **consistency** supplemented by distance, pace and time. You do your part faithfully and your body will do the rest. You can count on one fact: Your mind will not want to exercise, we are lazy. Live the Nike slogan: **Just *do* it!** Make it a habit, schedule it, hopefully with a partner.

This is where discipline and passion to accomplish your goals comes in. Exercise may not seem appealing at any age, but you will look back when you are 70 and beyond and be enormously thankful you did! Or as the Bible pointedly challenges you,

"But you, lazybones, how long will you sleep? When will you wake up? A little extra sleep, a little more slumber, a little folding of the hands to rest – then poverty will pounce on you like a bandit; scarcity will attack you like an armed robber." Proverbs 6:9-11.

At this point, it is time for me to take a break from writing and take a 3 mile hike up a steep hill, in the great outdoors, to be inspired by nature and the view, with my wife. The fresh air, some huffing and puffing will clear my mind and reinvigorate my writing.

Benefits of exercise are:

1. controls weight, increases muscles and metabolism
2. combats diseases, obesity, diabetes and hypertension
3. improves mood, attitude and boosts energy
4. promotes better sleep
5. puts the spark back into your sex life
6. reduces stress and anxiety.

To help motivate yourself, remember all the benefits of exercise and how great you feel afterward because of the dopamine released in your brain. Exercise, of any kind, "optimizes your genetic potential" and makes every part of life better. You are getting healthier every day.

📖 **"A person without self-control is like a city with broken-down walls"** Proverbs 25:28.

Part III: Sleep

In general, most healthy adults need **seven to nine hours** of sleep a night. However, there are a few individuals able to function with fewer hours of sleep and a few can't perform at their peak unless they've slept ten hours. Everybody is physiologically varied, decide what is best for you and your optimum health! God knows the importance of rest:

"On the seventh day God had finished his work of creation, so he rested from all his work." Genesis 2:2.

A significant number of Americans experience frequent sleep problems. Sleep is just as important as diet and exercise.

Adequate sleep allows the body to recover from a normal day's work, stress, illness and injury. The emotional, physical and mental benefits of sleep are significant. Inadequate sleep is associated with obesity, diabetes, heart disease and depression.

📖 **"If your husband has difficulty getting to sleep, the words, 'we need to talk about our relationship,' may help."** Rita Rudner, comedian.

Here are some excellent suggestions from several sleep experts on how to sleep more consistently.

Set aside time for eight hours of sleep. Go to bed and get up at the same time every day. Limit the *difference* in your sleep schedule on weeknights and weekends. Don't go to bed hungry or stuffed, avoid nicotine, caffeine, alcohol, computer and smart phone usage an hour before bed time. Instead read a book or the Bible, meditate or listen to music. For some, napping is healthy, for others it may make sleeping through the night problematic.

"The LORD replied, 'I will personally go with you, Moses, and I will give you rest – everything will be fine for you.'" Exodus 33:14.

Take Away: Coincidence and luck are not why people enjoy great physical health. They plan and are conscious about eating, exercising, resting and their lifestyle choices. Choose nutritious food, exercises that are fun, social and doable and get adequate sleep. Don't *wait* for a serious medical diagnosis to start your Healthy Life Plan.

The older you get; the more important physical health becomes. Prepare now, whatever your age, begin managing a Healthy Life Plan which will keep you and your quality of life vibrant. It is your responsibility to live the best life you can, choose to be actively loving, kind, generous, compassionate, healthy and have fun. As the Bible says:

"Physical training is good, but training for godliness is much better, promising benefits in this life and in the life to come." 1 Timothy 5:8.

Your Mental Health

"I told my psychiatrist that everyone hates me. He said I was being ridiculous - everyone hasn't met me yet." Rodney Dangerfield, comedian.

Mental health is just as important as physical health. Your mind is the battle ground of life. After all, you are and become what you think about most. Your ever present "Self-talk" eventually becomes your reality. Your mental dreams and beliefs propel you to prophesize your future.

Your powerful mind miraculously guides you toward what you think about most.

Therefore, it is important to think *hopeful, positive thoughts*, always, focusing on what you *want to transpire* and not dwelling on what you *do not want to happen*. Having a positive outlook, upbeat attitude, loving approach and gratefulness are the keys to leading you through a successful life to your destiny.

"Fix your thoughts on what is true, honorable, right, pure, lovely and admirable. Think about things that are excellent and worthy of praise. Keep putting into practice all you learned and received from me – everything you heard from me and saw me doing." Philippians 4:8-9.

Make the biblical choice - fill your mind with truth, beauty, knowledge and goodness, every day.

Additionally, intentionally decide what you let into your magnificent mind because it is a strong influence your well-being and what you inevitably think about. Thus, be *deliberately discriminating* about the books, TV shows, movies, music, internet sites, entertainment and friends you select.

What you feed your mind, like your body, determines your perspective, outlook, attitude and behaviors. An old computer analogy is applicable, **"Garbage in, Garbage out,"** or **GIGO**. Put garbage and trash into your brain and out will come demeaning, hurtful comments, illness, depression, pessimism and a negative perspective.

"A wise person is hungry for knowledge, while the fool feeds on trash." Proverbs 15:14.

The onus is on you to focus on mentally healthy subjects. You choose your thoughts, beliefs and actions. Sure, spontaneous thoughts will pop-into your mind, but you decide how long they stay there. You can't prevent birds from flying over your head, but you can stop them from making a nest in your hair.

"Low self-esteem is like driving through life with your hand-break on." Maxwell Maltz, author.

If you say or think, **"I am weak," "I am stupid" or, "I'll never get that job,"** that will *become* your reality, like a self-prophecy coming true. *Take off the hand-brake.* Rather, purposefully state and believe, **"I am strong," "I am smart", "I am attractive" and "I deserve that job/promotion,"** and that will often be your *reality*. Like anything it takes practice and discipline, but it is essential for your self-esteem, well-being and success.

You have the power to choose empowering, uplifting and encouraging words. You are determining your confidence, self-worth and life outcomes by the thoughts and words you choose to live by. Positive willpower will come from letting the Bible's practical wisdom saturate your essence and seep out into your thoughts. Those thoughts will become your habits, which will determine the direction of your life.

"We become what we think about all day long." Ralph Waldo Emerson.

The same is true for what you say to others. Your tongue is a very powerful tool and therefore critical to control. A few words, used as "weapons," only take a few seconds to utter, but in that short time they can leave an emotional scar on someone long-term. Words said quickly out of pride, anger or hurt, can negatively affect relationships for years, sometimes permanently. Choose your words and tone carefully and intentionally strive to build yourself and others up with your tongue.

"Don't use foul or abusive language. Let everything you say be good and helpful, so that your words will be an encouragement to those who hear them." Ephesians 4:29.

Whether I create a situation or not, I always get to decide how to react to it. Whatever happens to you, from trivial disappointments of missing a party, having a flat tire, not getting a promotion, to serious events like relationship breakups, serious illness or death, *you* get to decide what it means to you and how to react.

Losers let others determine how they feel, whereas winners decide for themselves what they feel and how they will react.

It took me some time to replace my secular world thinking and reasoning with the counter-intuitive certainties of the Bible. The lifestyle described in the Bible, is a worldview. It does not care about your personality, race, nationality, education or secular standing, it is the worldview, perspective and truth of God.

"Those who are dominated by the sinful nature (world) think about sinful things, but those who are controlled by the Holy Spirit think about things that please the Spirit (God). So letting your sinful nature control your mind leads to death. But letting the Spirit control your mind leads to life and peace." Romans 8:5-6.

Determining my attitude and response to any situation or individual, is my choice. Dr. Victor Frankl, was a prisoner in a German concentration camp and author of *"Man's Search for Meaning"* states:

"You can take away my wife, you can take away my children, you can strip me of my clothes and my freedom, but there is one thing no person can ever take away from me – and that is my freedom to choose how I will react to what happens to me!"

Dr. Frankl gives us all an inspiring and powerful way to think about and respond to what happens to us. You can be in control if *you choose* to be. It empowers you to be a leader and not a victim. This attitude and behavior will significantly change your response in any situation.

Happiness

📖 **No one except you can make you happy, content, joyous and at peace. Life is 10% what happens to you and 90% how you decide to respond.**

Consciously decide ahead of time, every morning, to have a great day, be happy and respond positively, kindly and lovingly. The Bible tells you to be happy every moment of every day.

"When people live to be very old, let them rejoice in every day of life. But let them also remember there will be many dark days. Everything still to come is meaningless. Young people, it's wonderful to be young! Enjoy every minute of it." Ecclesiastes 11:8-9.

Ray Chambers, a very successful business owner and investor, decided that in spite of all his worldly success, wealth and accolades, he was not happy. After much contemplation, trial and error he changed his life to align his priorities with the following behaviors because he discovered they made him happy.

-Be of service to others
-Live in the moment
-Better to be loving than right
-Observe your own thoughts and behaviors; learn and improve
-Be grateful every day

Not a bad list for how to be happy. Create your own list!

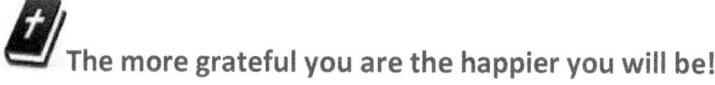

📖 **The more grateful you are the happier you will be!**

I have decided to try and be positive, upbeat and have an attitude of expectancy, which results in goodness for me and others. It is your choice to think positively or focus on lesser options. **We are each as happy as we decide to be.**

📖 **"For the despondent, every day brings trouble, for the happy heart, life is a continual feast."** Proverbs 15:15.

This chapter is devoted to letting the Bible *flow through you* concerning draining mental health issues and learning how to improve your own mental health.

If you fill your mind with the Bible every day, the insidious secular thoughts are less likely to infiltrate your mind. Replace your demeaning thoughts with Bible verses and loving pursuits. Choose to be infused with God every day.

"Joyful are people of integrity, who follow the instructions of the Lord. Joyful are those who obey his laws (the Bible) and search for him with all their hearts. They do not compromise with evil, and they walk only in his paths." Psalm 119:1-3.

Let's look at a few of the major issues many of us face in our quest to improve our mental health.

Controlling Everything

"You must learn a new way to think before you can master a new way to be." Marianne Williamson, author.

Most mental health begins and ends with what you can and cannot control. The expressions of ego, pride and power are at the root of our human existence. It was selfish pride that took Adam and Eve down. God was rightfully in control and determining the rules for the universe and the Garden of Eden. However, Adam wanted to be in control and he plunged the human race into sin. Releasing powerful negative forces on the earth and mankind that will increasingly plague us forever.

"Though the Lord is great, he cares for the humble, but he keeps his distance from the proud." Psalms 138:6.

Adam, just like us, didn't understand how the "unseen" spiritual world works. We must deal with reality according to the Bible. Like Adam, we want to function in *our own or society's false reality*. We want to be in charge of our situations and everyone else's, as well as, make our own rules. We hate to depend on others or ask for help, because we think it is weak or humiliating. That is prideful and short-sighted. If you defy God, you will make bad decisions and flounder in any situation, behavior or effort that differs from His will for you. Adam, ate the fruit for one reason, **he wanted to be God.**

This is also true for most of us. Your biggest battles in life are not finances, health, family, career or death. The major obstacle to God and faith is **you** and your pride - you want to be God. In most cases, it is not more evidence for God that you need, but humility.

Control is the essence of most beliefs and behaviors, which cause most of the pain in the world. Whenever we do not follow the guidelines of the Bible, we believe we are God and are as powerful as He is. Anyone who believes they are in complete control, will encounter numerous problems. You and I are not God and never will be. The only answer is to live as the Bible instructs. Otherwise, you are on your own without God; not a good position to be in.

You will only get frustrated trying to control family, friends, others, the weather, traffic, rude people, coworkers and politics. Control freaks rarely know that they have this issue. They believe that they know best, want to do everything their way and are "helping" people with their constructive criticism, because, *"no one else can do it right."*

Here are a few signs of a controlling individual,

1. You micromanage others to make them fit your (often unrealistic) expectations.
2. You judge others' behavior as right or wrong based on your self-righteous standards.
3. You constantly try to mold those around you in your image of them.

The truth is you are only responsible for you! The path to better relationships *always* starts with you. Rather than attempt to control everyone else, work on becoming a *better version of you.*

Here are a few ideas to help you stop or negate your controlling ways:

-Be more vulnerable, transparent and humble
-Admit when you are wrong. Learn from others
-Accept people as your equals
-Don't be passive-aggressive—speak the truth in love

- Accept that much of life is filled with unknowns
- Embrace honest, truth seeking conversation
- Work on your own improvement and happiness

"Heaven would tell you that it's just a little rain. And it's not the rain that kills you it's the pain of wanting to control the sun." Tessa Shaffer, author and entrepreneur.

Perfectionism

"When you stop expecting people to be perfect, you can like them for who they are." Donald Miller, author.

Mentally healthy individuals learn to accept their limits. Perfectionism is beyond human bounds; it will make you crazy. Perfection is unattainable but can be effectively used to reach the next best thing – Striving for Excellence.

"My biggest fear is that eventually you will see me the way I see myself." Anonymous.

Perfectionists often prevent themselves from taking the first step towards excellence, unless that step is *perfect*, thus, sabotaging their journey at the outset. This is the curse of perfectionism. Everything must be perfect first or it is not worth pursuing. For that reason, perfectionists do not come close to accomplishing much of anything.

"If you look for perfection, you'll never be content." Leo Tolstoy, Russian author.

We were designed and made perfect before the foundations of the world. When we choose to ignore God, and go our own way, we are disrespecting Him. There are two critical truths here; only God is perfect and secondly, only through grace and forgiveness can we be perfect in His eyes. This should cause us to be followers of the Bible, not obsessive believers in our own unattainable, perfection.

"The closest a person ever comes to perfection is when he fills out a job application form." Stanley Randall, Canadian businessman and politician.

Prideful perfectionism is ego-centered, not Bible-centered. As a result, perfectionists are going to be eternally disappointed and forever frustrated in every endeavor and relationship. Humility helps us realize it is only as we strive to follow the direction in the Bible that we can move toward excellence.

"And he (God) gives grace generously. As the scripture says, 'God opposes the proud, but gives grace to the humble.'" James 4:6.

When you work hard at something, do an outstanding job and someone praises you, just say "Thank you!" Being good at what you do is a blessing and should be used to honor God.

"You are allowed to feel messed up inside and out. It doesn't mean you're defective – It just means you're human." David Mitchell, British comedian, actor and writer.

Grace and forgiveness drives healthy effort; perfectionism drives pride and arrogance. The key is an honest self-assessment based on the Bible, not society. It's up to you.

"Because of the privilege and authority God has given me, I give each of you this warning: Don't think you are better than you really are. Be honest in your evaluation of yourselves, measuring yourselves by the faith God has given us." Romans 12:3.

Mental institutions are filled with perfectionists who drove themselves to achieve the unattainable out of pride.

"Perfection does not exist; to comprehend it is the triumph of human intelligence; to desire to possess it, the most dangerous of follies." Alfred de Musset, French poet and novelist.

Worry and Stress

"92% of the things we worry about never happen." This quote was taken from the movie, **"Heat,"** but it has been around for centuries. It makes a strong point about human frailty.

Worry: to give way to anxiety or unease, allow one's mind to dwell on difficulty or troubles; to subject oneself to persistent or nagging attention, agitation or effort.

Do we really need to put ourselves through all that?

The impetus of all this needless worrying is our obsession to be in control, as well as, fear of the future. We want things the way we want them, when we want them and we believe it is possible to achieve our selfish standards. If this is you, can you guess **who** is at the center of that universe?

Here is a clue…it's not God.

In today's world, worry and stress are a normal part of everyday life because most people look at their own foibles instead of focusing on God. It is true that, at times, life's problems can seem endless, that is exactly the time to turn to God.

Why is worry so debilitating to us?

-Science has proven worry and stress are detrimental to our physical and mental health
-Worry never changes anything, it only wastes time
-Worry places a wall between you and God because it is the epitome of a lack of trust

The solution is two-fold; if you want to worry less, take action to resolve the problem, secondly, turn your concerns over to God. The Bible says the primary cause of worry is being world-centered, rather than consistently focused on God. Don't worry, trust God!

"God opposes the proud but favors the humble. So humble yourselves under the mighty power of God, and at the right time he will lift you up in honor. Give all your worries and cares to God, for he cares about you." 1 Peter 5:5-7.

Whenever you start to worry, stop and pray, asking for help and guidance to know how to bring peace to your mind and heart. I have found that praying always helps me to refocus my mind on what I can actually do to resolve the concern. It is a form of meditation and planning, while simultaneously deepening my relationship with God.

"But they delight in the law of the Lord, meditating on it (the Bible) day and night. They are like trees planted along the riverbank, bearing fruit each season." Psalm 1:2-3.

Often, as I pray in detail about my problems and their potential solutions, I soon find new solutions, alternatives or determine that it is not a problem I can resolve. Praying is a form of simply thinking issues through in more detail and opening yourself to other solutions, including supernatural resolutions.

"Don't worry about anything, instead, pray about everything. Tell God what you need and thank him for all he has done, (gratitude). Then you will experience God's peace, which exceeds anything we can understand. His peace will guard your hearts and minds as you live in Christ Jesus." Philippians 4:6-7.

Trying to change the unchangeable or being consumed with controlling something beyond your reach, causes most worry. I find it useful to differentiate between a *real problem or fear* and a *perceived worry*. For me fears, uncertainties and problems fall into one of three piles:

1. Something I am responsible for and can do something about; useful worry.
2. A genuine concern but one I cannot resolve; *worthless* worry.
3. A troublesome thought that only exists in my head; *paranoia*.

I find that a genuine worry is an issue I should *take responsibility for* and do something about which moves me to take action. Whereas, a perceived worry only leaves me stressed and consumed with fear. Continuing to worry about something I cannot resolve or take action on, means I am not trusting God. It is a waste of my time, energy and peace of mind.

"My therapist told me that I over-analyze everything. I explained to him that he only thinks this because of his unhappy relationship with his mother." Michel Templet, humorist.

While eliminating all worry may be impossible, I limit my worries by:

- Not worrying about the **future,** which I cannot yet act upon

- Forgiving myself for **past** errors, God did
- Remember that worrying is **harmful to my health**
- **Telling someone else**; asking for help and advice
- **Live in the present**; the only time I can actually do something
- Continually **reading the Bible** for perspective and wisdom

"**That is why I tell you not to worry about everyday life – Can all your worries add a single moment to your life? – So, don't worry about tomorrow, for tomorrow will bring its own worries. Today's trouble is enough for today.**" Matthew 6:25 & 27 & 34.

In spite of their much smaller, less sophisticated brains, we can learn a lot from our pets. They only live in the moment, don't regret the past and don't worry about the future. Animals have no motives, envy, regret or bitterness and are honest in their behaviors. That is why they are content and spontaneous. As children, you and I had the same mindset. We had an accepting attitude and approach to life before we started taking things into our own hands.

"**Never worry alone. When anxiety grabs my mind, it is self-perpetuating. Worrisome thoughts reproduce faster than rabbits, so one of the most powerful ways to stop the spiral of worry is simply to disclose my worry to a** *friend*... **The simple act of reassurance from another human being [becomes] a tool of the Spirit to cast out fear -- because peace and fear are both contagious.**" John Ortberg Jr., pastor, author.

When you take a moment, you realize you are mostly living in the *future* or in the *past,* rather than right now. We are constantly *fixated* on where we want to go, what will be better in a few days or weeks or we regret the past, wishing we had behaved differently. When our minds repetitively ruminate on anything but the present, it is not useful.

Not surprisingly, **NOW** is the only place and time you can actually live in peace. What are you thinking about right now? Life is experiential and the only time you can actually experience life is *now.*

"**The true definition of mental illness is when the majority of your time is spent in the past or future, rarely living in the realism of now.**" Shannon L. Alder, author.

Appreciate life and be grateful for every moment - blue skies, puffy clouds, green trees, stars, your health, relationships and every blessing around you. If you aren't intentionally grateful, it is unlikely to occur. Just *be* and let the rest of the world be on its own for a little while. It is wonderfully freeing, as Paul reminds us:

"I focus on this one thing: forgetting the past and looking forward to what lies ahead." Philippians 3:13.

One can only imagine God in heaven looking down upon us in our stressful moments of panic, shaking His head, as we struggle.

"Then, turning to his disciples, Jesus said, 'That is why I tell you not to worry about everyday life – whether you have enough food to eat or enough clothes to wear. For life is more than food, and your body more than clothing. Look at the ravens. They don't plant or harvest or store food in barns, for God feeds them. And you are far more valuable to him than any birds! Can all your worries add a single moment to your life? And if worry can't accomplish a little thing like that, what's the use of worrying over bigger things'" Luke 12:22-26.

According to the Indy 100 survey, here are the Top Ten personal *worries* that stress out Americans:

1. Getting old
2. Financial future
3. Low energy levels
4. Diet
5. Debt
6. Job security
7. Facial appearance
8. Physique
9. Rent/mortgage
10. Happiness

These worries can be lumped in to the broad categories of career, health and financial security. It is not a coincidence that those are among the longest chapters in this book.

"This is what the LORD SAYS: 'Don't let the wise boast in their wisdom, or the powerful boast in their power, or the rich boast in their riches. But those who wish to boast should boast in this alone: that they truly know me and understand that I am the Lord who demonstrates unfailing love and who brings justice and righteousness to the earth, and that I delight in these things.'" Jeremiah 9:23-24.

God designed us, knows our psychological issues and how they affect us. Managing life without the Bible's guidance is like attempting to navigate a jet without radar, in fog.

We are complicated creations. We vary in sensitivity, familial background, culture, experiences, genetics, expectations, successes, failures and beliefs, just to name a few. With this in mind, for us to try to resolve all the issues plaguing us or surviving in a chaotic world, without biblical wisdom, is folly. We were never meant to combat anxiety, busyness and stress without knowing the Bible. Jesus said,

"Come to Me, all of you who are weary and carry heavy burdens, and I will give you rest. Take My yoke (teachings in the Bible) upon you. Let me teach you, because I am humble and gentle at heart and you will find rest for your souls. For my yoke is easy to bear, and the burden I give you is light." Matthew 11:28-30.

Time to smile, put your feet up and enjoy the moment!

Doubt, Confusion and Unfamiliarity

"It is better to keep your mouth closed and let people think you are a fool than to open it and remove all doubt." Mark Twain, author.

For many, doubt, confusion and unfamiliarity are negatives that paralyze them emotionally and psychologically. When one or more of these oppressive clamps grabs hold of us we are not going anywhere for a while. However, brave individuals use these unclear, at times scary conditions in *positive* ways, to investigate and learn. Risking uncertainty, they open the door to find new wisdom. This often results in entirely new perspectives on existence itself.

Unfamiliarity does not have to be permanently uncomfortable; it *can* be a launching pad for innovation, creativity and ultimately, greatness. If you are the only person on the seldom travelled road, it is easier to get noticed. There is no greatness in living like everyone else. The status quo leads to boredom and ensuing deterioration. There is great value in venturing out of your comfort zone in search of understanding, discoveries and new relationships.

You choose to be a couch potato or a world-changer every day.

Our choices, in thought-provoking, confusing or disturbing circumstances, contribute to our view of the world and future progress. Our willingness and openness to different ways of observing society opens new opportunities. Whereas, a "know it all", self-righteous or intellectually resistant attitude to the new or different, limits us. You need to leave yourself open to the spirit's spontaneous, supernatural synchronicity and miracles when you venture into the unknown.

"Then Jesus told them, I tell you the truth, if you have faith and don't doubt you can do things like this and much more. You can even say to this mountain (troubles, frustrations), 'May you be lifted up and thrown into the sea', and it will happen. You can pray for anything and if you have faith you will receive it." Matthew 21:21-22.

Let's be honest, the Bible bridges truth, the unknown and the miraculous like nothing else. Do you file your Bible in the *fiction or non-fiction* section of your bookcase and mind?

I am often in a quandary over some aspects of the Bible that are confusing and a few concepts I simply doubt. But, I believe in the overall importance of the Bible's themes and guidance, which is the reason I wrote this book. There are unfathomable, wild and outrageous stories throughout the Bible that I simply take on *faith*. Because of who God is and who we are, there will always be a gap in understanding. Don't let a deficiency of control, a few missing facts or the "majority" impede your relationship with God.

"Just as you cannot understand the path of the wind or the mystery of a tiny baby growing in its mother's womb, so you cannot understand the activity of God, who does all things." Ecclesiastes 11:5.

For example, I didn't even know I needed a revised life, but God did. So, He intervened in my life, through others, and transformed me into a better and ever-improving man. Having now experienced, firsthand, wonderful ways to live and my potential beyond death, I could never go back to the man I was before.

Granted there is much wisdom in, "seeing is believing," but, there continues to be so much we don't understand about a lot of things, including spiritual realms.

"Intelligent people are always ready to learn. Their ears are open for knowledge." Proverbs 18:15.

Lack of knowledge can be a huge anchor for all of us. Does it lead you to be hypercritical or accepting, a pessimist or optimist or to learn more or hide? I choose to believe life will turn out well and that everyone is good. Pessimism is a cul-de-sac of wasted energy and lost potential. Most give up because they don't know enough about a topic or person. I don't think I know enough to expect anything less than the best from everyone.

"There are only two ways to live your life. One is as though nothing is a miracle. The other is as though everything is a miracle." Albert Einstein, theoretical physicist.

Life has so many complex questions?

Even the apostles, who lived with Jesus, were skeptical and often confused about His teachings and behaviors. Then His death devastated their beliefs and doubt crept in. But on the third day, when they saw and spoke to the resurrected Jesus, they believed conclusively. As a result of the miracle, they dedicated the remainder of their lives to teaching others. They came to realize that death was not the end - only the beginning of forever.

"Not until we are lost do we begin to understand ourselves." Henry David Thoreau, writer and philosopher.

Even Moses doubted and argued with God when He told Moses to return to Egypt to lead the Israelites to a new world. John the Baptist and "Doubting" Thomas had concerns, asked questions and observed what Jesus said and did *before* they believed completely. After Thomas saw Jesus, following the resurrection, he believed and proclaimed,

"My Lord and my God! - then Jesus told him 'You believe because you have seen me. Blessed are those who believe without seeing me.'" John 20:28-29.

I have frequently seen miracles in other's lives and the ongoing results in my life from following the Bible's teachings. I have learned that wrestling, arguing and debating with God is pointless. It is a match no man can win.

"Miracles are not contrary to nature, but only contrary to what we know about nature." Saint Augustine.

Is it possible to be filled with faith and doubt at the same time? Absolutely.

I continue to believe the Bible as I ask questions to resolve uncertainties. That is why it is called *faith*. The stronger my faith, the more likely it is that I will be aligned with God's plan, experience positive outcomes and even miracles directly in my life. Doubt should lead to questions, which reveals answers, greater understanding and leads to better choices in life.

"For the word (Bible) of the Lord holds true and we can trust everything he does." Psalm 33:4.

Doubt and confusion are a part of life for all of us. There will be days when we see life clearly and other days that are like looking through a fog bank.

Likewise, unfamiliarity can lead to fear and dislike. If you don't know someone, you can easily reach erroneous conclusions. Prejudice, dogmatic and unfair perspectives are only eliminated by reaching out, attempting to know and understand other points of view and developing relationships with those we don't know or disagree with.

If you need further proof, analyze the followers of Jesus. Look at the famed apostles, stumbling and bumbling their way in the New Testament (Mathew, Mark, Luke, John and Acts). They often strayed from the teachings of Jesus.

These were ordinary men consumed with doubt and confusion more often than not. It was not until they accepted truth that they suddenly became clear-headed and decisive. For without God, we are all as lost as sheep and left to our own hapless ways.

Being a follower of Jesus eventually resulted in a new way of life for all twelve of them, except Judas. Maybe it's time to start doing things you have never tried before. Maybe taking risks and venturing out into unfamiliar territory, in spite of your doubt, is the only way to personally succeed. There has to be a *first* time for everything, right? When was the last time you experienced the excitement and fear of a "first time"? Children experience something new every day and are filled with wonder.

It has been way too long for most of us!

"Take the unpopular route. Use the road no one travels by. Think of doing what is uncommon, but remarkable. You have absolutely nobody to overtake you on the empty road!" Israelmore Ayivor, author.

Unusual, diverse experiences, people and environments become familiar once you know them. When I force myself to talk to a person "different" from me, I overcome stereotypes and am usually enlightened. When I don't profile and muster the courage to talk with a stranger, like a homeless person, a famous/wealthy person or someone with a unique appearance, my fear quickly turns into curiosity. I can learn something new and potentially, make a new friend. This is because at our core we are all the same. It is primarily our fear, ignorance, prejudice, complacency and, at times, politics or cultural traditions, that keeps us bound in our small, vanilla worlds.

Jesus often intentionally hung-out with the destitute, criminals, tax collectors, the sick, different nationalities and ethnicities because He understood that we all need unconditional forgiveness, mercy, grace and love. How many foreigners, addicts, prostitutes or individuals in jail do you know? Do you know anything about your neighbor? Jesus, was brave and non-judgmental, He loved the whole world, not just those like Him.

It is the risk-takers who crossed the lines of fear and unfamiliarity to venture into the unknown, that we remember and often regard as heroes. From the daring explorers on the open seas, colonists who came to new lands, inventors, astronauts, civil rights leaders and scientists that revolutionize technology, changed governments and made our lives simpler, better and healthier. They moved forward in spite of their doubts, unknowns and fears. Be someone's miracle.

Were they mentally healthy? In the areas of **curiosity, courage, decisiveness and hope** they were!

The seven last words of a dying company or church are, "We've never done it this way before." Unknown.

Do you want to be like everyone else or the unique individual you were designed to be?

Only by reading the Bible and applying it, will you find the answers to the important questions about life. There may be safety in numbers and the majority rules, but, on the other side of that old adage, is the unique life spelled out for you in the Bible.

"But those who trust in the LORD will find new strength. They will soar high on wings like eagles. They will run and not grow weary. They will walk and not faint." Isaiah 40:31.

That is God's reward for our obedience to the Bible. Be patient, understanding and open to something new before you judge or reject anyone or new information. The majority is not always right. Only God decides what is right and wrong and the Bible explains His ways.

"Share our similarities, celebrate our differences." M. Scott Peck, psychiatrist and author.

Familiarity and acceptance with those different from you usually results in understanding and communication, which leads to new perspectives and relationships. If doubt leads you to investigation, it has done its job. So, use confusion, doubt and unfamiliar situations with diverse individuals and scary situations as opportunities to expand your life, knowledge and love.

While unfamiliar to most, the Bible provides endless possibilities for expanding and transforming your lifestyle, which can lead you to a new, open-minded, glorious life.

"Don't be afraid, for I am with you. Don't be discouraged, for I am your God. I will strengthen you and help you. I will uphold you with my victorious right hand." Isaiah 41:10.

He loves you unconditionally and is with you – Always!

How to Deal with Failure

"Success is the ability to go from one failure to another with no loss of enthusiasm." Winston Churchill, former British Prime Minister.

Life is not a problem, it is a *gift!* It is an exquisite puzzle to be experienced, enjoyed, cherished and is preparation for eternal life.

"We must be willing to fail and to appreciate the truth that often - Life is not a problem to be solved, but a mystery to be lived." M. Scott Peck, psychiatrist and author.

Think about how movies depict great heroes. The hero always goes through threatening times, failure, betrayal, lies and is often abandoned by others. The hero eventually contemplates their purpose, the people they can trust and what will bring meaning to their lives. Finally, the hero gets focused on the "greater good." They become encouraged and fight for the less fortunate, the "underdog." Heroes always pass through impossible struggles and failures before the battle of good over evil.

"The first man through the wall always get bloody," from the movie, "Moneyball".

The story line for most movie conquerors is formulaic and appeals directly to our mundane lives. The irony is, miraculous, happy endings, great accomplishments and love usually pass through risks, mistakes, hurts, failures and huge struggles before success arrives. Movie executives have figured out how human psychology works and they tap into it to make great movies. We each need to do the same to create our own wonderful, heroic lives.

"Character cannot be developed in ease and quiet. Only through experience of trial and suffering can the soul be

strengthened, vision cleared, ambition inspired and success achieved." Helen Keller, author, lecturer.

Remember, it is not about you, it is all about God. That is how life works. Hard work, problems, mistakes, frustrations and failures always precede success. If, you want to be successful, a great mother or father, a super boss, the best spouse possible, even a hero – put God first, your spouse second, your children third, followed by friends and others. That is how you do God's will and simultaneously, be thought of as a hero.

"So don't worry about these things, saying, 'What will we eat? What will we drink? What will we wear?' These things dominate the thoughts of unbelievers, but your heavenly Father already knows all your needs. Seek the Kingdom of God above all else, and live righteously, and he will give you everything you need." Matthew 6:31-33.

Success and failure are inexorably linked together forever and rightly so. You cannot have one without the other. More importantly, in many cases, one *is* the other. Yes, you heard correctly, one can argue that in most instances, success and failure can be the same given adequate time…How is that possible? If you want to handle failure successfully, you need to understand the truth of this axiom.

Use failure to achieve success.

Let me explain this dynamic principle. Most failures are actually successes and not failures at all! What we consider a setback is, in most cases, a blessing in disguise, given a little *time* and *perspective.*

Take a relationship for example. Have you ever dated someone you thought you wanted to marry because they were the 'perfect one for you'? Looking back, are you now grateful you never married that person?

Seriously, how many boy or girlfriends have we had that were totally wrong? How about a career position you failed to obtain but later landed a much better job? At the time, they appeared to be 'failures', but, in truth they were not only successes, but also effective avoidance of much pain and wasted time.

Now, looking back with 20/20 hindsight, it is easy for me to recognize that a particular relationship, job or decision would have been an abysmal failure. Thus, I actually succeeded when I failed. Avoiding them turned those failures into a *plus* on life's scoreboard. Once I didn't take a high-powered position in Chicago. But, a few months later I landed an even better position and met my soulmate at the same company! Any 'failure' can turn out to be a life-saving or altering success!

So, get out there and fail!

When we are young, we are foolish, trust too easily, are greedy, ill-informed and impetuous. We want success too quickly. Our past is littered with mistakes that posed as 'failures' in the moment but were eventually righted and miraculously turned into needed educational foundations and outcomes. That is how we learn much of what is important.

As you assess poor decisions and superficial reasoning from the past you may find that many of them turned out better than you expected. Given enough time, these "failures" reveal the truth about themselves and you have one success after another to build on, all of which brought you to be the person you are today. We have all dodged bullets that could have put us into a major hole in life, maybe even ended it.

"There's something about being broken at various times in life, that makes you a more complete person." J. Iron Word, poet.

Thank God for stepping in to save you from your silly, prideful self and protecting you from your impulses, infatuations and inexperience in the heat of the moment.

"Though I am surrounded by troubles, you will protect me from the anger of my enemies." Psalm 138:7.

During my career, I made many mistakes and was laid off or let go five times. You wouldn't think that was a recipe for success or retiring early. But, looking back, it was. At the time, each event was hard to take, not to mention, demeaning, stressful and emotional. Yet I somehow persevered, learned about resilience, not to trust companies, nor other worldly enticements. I can now honestly say that those hard-hitting times were for my long-term benefit. I take no credit for those learning opportunities and magnificent outcomes, they were clearly orchestrated by God. Miracles happen every day, we often assume they are a coincidence or luck.

"Those who never make mistakes work for those of us who do." Henry Ford, founder of the Ford Motor Company.

Do you really believe your life was or is mere luck, random or a coincidence? When something doesn't happen in your time frame or at all, it may simply be God helping you avoid serious mistakes or unethical people. He usually has something bigger and better planned for you in the future.

"... I focus on this one thing: forgetting the past and looking forward to what lies ahead, I press on to reach the end of the race and receive the heavenly prize (eternity) for which God, through Christ Jesus, is calling us." Philippians 3:13-14.

Learn to shake off failure and disappointments and soar to heights you never believed existed. Those hard-hitting experiences are often your launching pads.

"If you're waiting until you feel talented enough to make it, you'll never make it." Criss Jami, author.

Contentment, Peace, Happiness and Hope

"Too much of a good thing... can be wonderful." Mae West, American actor and singer.

The goals of mental health are contentment, inner peace, happiness and everlasting hope. This is not to say that you will never experience challenges and trials because that is unrealistic in this world. God created you specifically to be His friend, tell others the truths in the Bible and thrive His way.

He wants you to be *content*,

**"Trust in the LORD and do good. Then you will live safely I the land and prosper. Take delight in the LORD, and he will give you your heart's desires. Commit everything you do to the Lord. Trust him, and he will help you." Psalm 37:3-5.

He wants you to be at *peace*,

"I am leaving you with a gift - Peace of mind and heart. And the peace I give is a gift the world cannot give. So don't be troubled or afraid." John 14.27.

He wants you to be *happy*,

"Come everyone! Clap your hands! Shout to God with joyful praise! For the Lord Most High is awesome." Psalm 47:1.

He wants you to have *hope*,

"I pray that God, the source of hope, will fill you completely with joy and peace because you trust in him. Then you will overflow with confident hope through the power of the Holy Spirit." Romans 15:13.

Contentment is simply being happy with what you have and where you are right now. Lack of contentment is usually the result of comparing yourself or your situation to others, wanting to be somewhere else and believing that having or owning something will make you happy.

"Yet true godliness with contentment is itself great wealth. After all, we brought nothing with us when we came into the world, and we can't take anything with us when we leave it. So if we have enough food and clothing let us be content." 1 Timothy 6:6-8.

When you compare yourself to others, you either feel superior (pride) or you don't compare well (envy) and feel lesser of yourself.

"Pay careful attention to your own work, for then you will get the satisfaction of a job well done, and you won't need to compare yourself anyone else. For we are each responsible for our own conduct." Galatians 6:4-5.

We live in a 'hyped' world of relentless stress, inner conflict and unhealthy pursuits from hedonism to narcissistic behaviors and devastating addictions. Do we really know and understand what real peace and happiness is anymore?

"The best feeling of happiness is when you are happy because you made somebody else happy."

Are most people happy today? My opinion, in many cases is no.

Modern society lives in a constant state of discontentment. We are taught from birth to never be satisfied, to always want to be better, have more and to do just about anything to achieve it. That is a recipe for 'Stress Stew'. The result of society's teachings only ends in frustration and breakdowns physically, mentally and spiritually. We are a very unhealthy culture and clueless about how to stop the slide. We are more in debt, more obese and more dependent on prescription drugs than ever before. That is what happens when man places himself at the center of the universe.

Contentment is being happy with what you have and where you are today.

Gratitude, for all that you do have, will free you to be content. Dissatisfaction comes when your attention shifts from all you have to continuously wanting more. Appreciate your relationships, your job, family and health. Look for moments of joy throughout the day; a beautiful flower, a refreshing drink, an excellent meal, meaningful conversation, a sincere smile and an inspiring sunset. These moments of peace and fulfillment are never to be taken for granted.

Look for opportunities to make others happy through a smile, kindness, friendly comment or act of compassion. Most importantly, tell those you love that you *love* them. Talk to and play with your kids, call your mom, dad, siblings, a friend you haven't seen in a long time. Texting is impersonal and the lazy option when communicating with those you really care about.

Life is not about acquiring and accumulating stuff; those who die with the most toys, *still* dies. Society relentlessly tries to teach us that we must be blissful all the time, but this is insane and unattainable.

Minimize the shiny, new stuff and quick thrills, in favor of following that which gives you a sense of purpose, significance and meaning. Generosity with your time, talents, money, energy and love is the cure for materialism, selfishness, pride, stress, loneliness, and low self-esteem.

"The generous will prosper; those who refresh others will themselves be refreshed." Proverbs 11:25.

Think honestly for a few minutes; what would others say about *your* generosity?

Think of a funeral you attended…how did the mourners remember the deceased? Did they gush over the person's financial assets, fancy car, real estate holdings or did they hold the person in high esteem for what they did for others, their generosity and meaningful relationships?

"The poor wish to be rich, the rich wish to be happy, the single wish to be married and the married wish to be dead." Ann Landers, advice columnist.

This would be hilarious if it weren't filled with so much truth. We have created a culture of "Being #1", competition, multi-tasking and ten cups of coffee to keep you productive. All out competitive individualism is destroying relationships, society, as well as, the environment. But 'busyness' is not going to solve much of anything. Many of us are frantically going nowhere! We are a society of mixed up malcontents.

The only way to be happy and content in life is to help others, be generous and develop meaningful relationships with God and those we love.

I know this sounds counter intuitive, but I tried the selfish-lifestyle for decades and it is a truism. If you are only out for yourself, hoard money or admire possessions you will not be happy.

You see, meaningful happiness does not come from money, success, sex, power, fame or more stuff; as the world tries to tell you. You were made for significance, to make a difference in the lives of others. Surprisingly, the more of your love, time and treasures you *give away*, the happier and more content you will become. You were made to be in meaningful, uplifting relationships.

"Joyful are people of integrity, who follow the instructions of the Lord (Bible). Joyful are those who obey his laws and search for him with all their hearts." Psalm 119:1-2.

Gratitude is a mandate for peace, contentment and serenity. Constantly, chasing after vanity, pleasure and stubbornly refusing to honor God, dooms you to a run-of-the-mill earthly life.

"A peaceful heart leads to a healthy body; jealousy is like cancer in the bones." Proverbs 14:30.

"Make me walk along the path of your commands, for that is where my happiness is found." Psalm 119:35.

These verses tell us to follow the commandments of the Bible because that is *where real, long-term* inner peace, contentment and meaning are found. This is concise direction from scripture and another example of how following the rules in the Bible frees us to enjoy the natural joy we all crave.

Recent scientific studies show that people who volunteer and are generous with others actually live longer, healthier lives.

This is not to say that you should live a completely frugal, bare bones existence or that being wealthy is bad. A successful life is an excellent way to demonstrate how beneficial it is to read, understand and apply the Bible directly in your life. Individuals failing in their earthly lives are not examples of what the Bible teaches. Nowhere in the Bible does it say to live a mediocre or miserable life.

Who would want to emulate or buy into any faith that resulted in a failed life, with nothing to give to others?

Throughout the Bible, God has promised to always be with us, give us a spirit of power, love and a strong mind. But, His greatest gift, one society cannot provide, is peace. Jesus said:

"I am leaving you with a gift - peace of mind and heart. And, the peace I give is a gift the world cannot give. So, don't be troubled or afraid. Remember what I told you: I am going away, but I will come back to you again." John 14:27-28.

Regardless of your situation and what is going on around you, focusing on God's deep and lasting peace will fill you with calm, confidence and power. In every situation, it is your *choice* to focus on God or society's shallow solutions.

Don't let the sun go down while you are still angry, for anger gives a foothold to the devil. Ephesians 4:26-27.

For example, when you become angry at all the injustice, tragedy and lies in the world, you may think the world is falling apart. It's not, the world is actually safer today than in the past. None-the-less, you have a choice to funnel your energy toward revenge and depression or channel your inflated emotions to correct the situation. So, get "positively" mad! Anger can motivate you to lose control or constructively change the world - one friend, person, neighborhood and organization at a time.

"Short-tempered people do foolish things, and schemers are hated." Proverbs 14:17.

Make the wise choice.

"The Lord himself watches over you! The Lord stands beside you as your protective shade. The sun will not harm you by day, nor the moon at night. The Lord keeps you from all harm and watches over your life. The Lord keeps watch over you as you come and go, both now and forever." Psalm 121:5-8.

Peace is often defined as an absence of conflict. God's version of peace is a deep assurance and strength that provides a sense that everything will be just fine regardless of your situation. It is a choice to behave in a way that promotes love, peace, harmony, teamwork and mutually rewarding relationships, rather than conflict, anger or selfishness.

"Search for peace and work to maintain it. The eyes of the Lord watch over those who do right and his ears are open to their prayers." 1 Peter 3:11-12.

The only way to discover and maintain real peace, security and meaning is through a personal relationship with God. We constantly work on our human "puzzle pieces" of wealth, possessions, education, health and relationships, ignoring the "God piece" that makes life worth living. In every area of life, God is the missing piece of life's complex puzzle. Yes, it is a mystery and takes faith – but, there is no alternative.

"The person with a secular mentality feels himself to be the center of the universe. Yet he is likely to suffer from a sense of meaninglessness and insignificance because he knows he's but one human among five billion others – all feeling themselves to be the center of things – scratching out an existence on the surface of a medium-sized planet circling a small star among countless stars in the galaxy lost among countless galaxies. The person with the sacred mentality, on the other hand, does not feel herself to be the center of the universe. She considers the Center to be elsewhere and other. Yet she is unlikely to feel lost or insignificant precisely because she draws her significance and meaning from her relationship, her connection, with that center, that Other." M. Scott Peck, psychiatrist and author.

Take Away: Mental health is an enormous topic, yet crucial to a fulfilled and purposeful life. The Bible is *indispensable* to finding your way in life. Good mental health, without God is an oxymoron; there is no other way. In order to be mentally healthy, you need to be drenched with the Bible from Genesis to Revelation. Otherwise, the Bible will just be another book that you intellectually digest and then resume your earthly ways.

You will never find long-term inner peace, happiness and meaning through purchasing another possession, making more money or conquering another mountain. Control, perfectionism, worry, doubt and fear are potential enemies to your mental health and joy. I appreciate that putting your life and trust in the hands of an all-powerful God seems scary, until you realize - everything else is worse.

Remember, you are worthy because God made you, has a purpose for your life and says you are valued, loved and His child. God wants you to be joyful, content and know you are loved.

Addiction

Addiction: The state of being enslaved to a habit or practice or to something that is psychologically or physically habit-forming to such an extent that its cessation causes severe trauma.

In today's world, there are endless idols, substances, obsessions and ways to be addicted. Alcohol, tobacco, drugs (prescription and illegal), food, gambling, money, work, power and shopping are just a few of the more well-known dependencies. Smart phones appear to be the next big addiction, unless you intentionally control when and how you use it. The Bible simply says that anything that puts distance between you and God is wrong.

"Don't you realize that you become the slave to whatever you choose to obey? You can be a slave to sin, which leads to death or you can choose to obey God, which leads to righteous living." Romans 6:16.

How do you know you are addicted? If something or someone has so much power over you that your life becomes unmanageable and out of your control, you are addicted. The first step of Alcoholics Anonymous (AA) is: Admit that you are powerless over "the addiction" and that your life has become unmanageable.

Symptoms of addictive behaviors include: poor health because of substance abuse; debt because of your spending or gambling habits; divorce because of spending little or no time with your spouse, children; no friends because you are self-centered and not saving or investing for future needs and retirement because of your overwhelming desire to spend for immediate gratification. These are just a few examples. Anything that causes grief in your life, which you cannot stop, is an addiction.

"Do not carouse with drunkards or feast with gluttons, for they are on their way to poverty and too much sleep clothes them in rags." Proverbs 23:20-21.

The ways and tentacles of the world can be overwhelming and powerful. The purpose of marketing is to convince you to make a purchase or do something you would not ordinarily do. Do not let advertisers, celebrities, friends or others run or control your life. Make conscious Bible-based choices that are best for you and your family.

Addictions are more prevalent today than ever. Opioids are the latest addiction to make the national news, apparently caused, to a large extent, by doctors over prescribing powerful drugs for pain.

"Do not be drunk with wine, because that will ruin your life. Instead be filled with the Holy Spirit." Ephesians 5:18.

Looking back, it is clear I was addicted to work, money, sex and power. What finally helped me adjust my priorities was my wife, attending church, a men's group and reading the Bible every day.

Addiction is real! It can cause pain in your life and maybe death. There are many reasons why people become addicted or behave compulsively:

-They may be genetically predisposed
-A trauma in life triggers the addictive behavior
-Escaping reality
-Fear of something emotional or physical
-A compulsive craving for a certain "high" or pleasure.
-Illness requiring the extended use of pain relieving medications
-Peer pressure to experiment with addictive behaviors

And, dozens more explanations.

Recovery from the addiction is, at times, only curing the most obvious symptom. Dealing with the *underlying* cause is just as difficult to resolve. For example, low self-esteem, avoiding reality, loneliness or other thoughts that drag you down, must ultimately be resolved to free you for a new life.

The verse below suggests being controlled by God and reading the Bible will lead you to avoiding poor choices. That is why AA's approach is Higher Power based, because they know you can't recover by yourself.

"So, I say, let the Holy Spirit guide your lives. Then you won't be doing what your sinful nature craves (human desire to do other than what the Bible teaches). The sinful nature wants to do evil, which is just the opposite of what the Sprit wants." Galatians 5:16.

Any addiction or obsession is a form of *idolatry*. When we rely on ourselves, someone or something else to meet our needs for self-worth or meaning in life, we are replacing God as our authority. God has specific direction for idol worshipers:

"You must not have any other god, but me." Exodus 20:3.

God will hold us accountable for all of our choices, addictions, habits and otherwise.

"Yes, each of us will give a personal account to God. So, let's stop condemning each other. Decide instead to live in such a way that you will not cause another believer to stumble and fall." Romans 14:12.

God wants and expects us to help others. There are many ways we can compassionately and lovingly respond to help those who are addicted or simply exhibiting poor behaviors:

-We can live a lifestyle that demonstrates principles and behaviors of the Bible. Others will see our behaviors and the positive outcomes of our life choices, and hopefully, want to emulate you.

-We can encourage them to get help. There are many Bible and "Higher Power" centered recovery programs, like AA and Celebrate Recovery.

-We can lovingly and directly challenge them, through an intervention with family and others important to them.

-We can invite them to church or a Bible study group of other humble, supportive individuals who will listen and be open about their own struggles in life.

-Encourage use of a full-time recovery program.

"Love your neighbor as yourself." Matthew 22:39.

Sometimes the only way addicts will ask for or accept help is when they run out of options and hit *absolute bottom*. Helping them or minimizing the consequences of their choices and behaviors, called enabling, frequently only prolongs their path of self-destruction.

I have personal experience in this area and, as hard as it is to watch someone suffer, the best approach, at times, is to walk away. It is the hardest, most disturbing choice I have ever made. But, the addict must arrive at an utterly dark place where the only choices are death or a decision for them to get well and survive.

"but they did not listen or obey. They stubbornly refused to pay attention or accept my (God's) discipline." Jeremiah 17:23.

We must show mercy and kindness to everyone, including those whose choices have led them into addictive or compulsive behaviors. We would want others to do the same for us, right?

An obvious question is, when should you stop ignoring, accusing or feeling sorry for those who are hurting and take action? My take is to always be kind, respectful, compassionate and love everyone, no matter their situation or choices. I don't know their background, personality or their current "battles". I choose to participate with the hope that they will eventually stop making bad choices, blaming others and take responsibility for their lives. Additionally, I pray that God will make them whole and give them the courage to reach out and seek help.

"For you have been called to live in freedom, my brothers and sisters. But don't use your freedom to satisfy your sinful nature. Instead, use your freedom to serve one another in love. For the whole law can be summed up in this one command: 'Love your neighbor as yourself.'" Galatians 5:13-14.

Balance is good for tightrope walkers and acrobats as well as all areas of our lives. I have found that most activities can be both good and bad for you. For example, one glass of alcohol is fine, but not an entire bottle. A one-hour workout is great, but several hours every day is excessive. Eight hours at work is good, but 12 hours, day after day is obsessive. Shopping for needed items is fine, but out of control spending for "materialistic opulence" is wrong.

Any behaviors you do compulsively, at the expense of yourself, family or friends, could potentially evolve into an addiction. Balance is achieved by allocating appropriate time and attention to relationships, education, physical and mental health, spirituality and work. Living a balanced life is the only productive, logical and long-term successful way to conduct yourself in this chaotic, "me centered" world.

Every day we face choices that lead us toward goodness or disaster, helping or avoiding, love or hate, understanding or ignorance. Honestly assess, "Am I moving toward God and the teachings of the Bible or away from them?" If away, rein yourself in before your life results in less than desirable outcomes.

Before I finish I have to mention the addiction of smoking, which is stupid, ugly, stinky, expensive and life threatening – read the label and get help. Quit now!

According to the Centers for Disease Control: Smoking causes 480,000 deaths per year in the United States, including more than 41,000 deaths resulting from secondhand smoke exposure. This is about one in five deaths annually, or 1,300 deaths every day. On average, smokers die 10 years *earlier* than nonsmokers. Smoking is the #1 cause of *preventable* death.

Take Away: You will never have a successful addiction to any substance, thing or person, except God. Humbly, lovingly and persistently help and support those who are recovering or need to beat an addiction. If you are addicted, God loves you; your family and friends love you. You are not alone. Reach-out and ask for help. You will be surprised how God, your family, friends and professionals will gladly and positively respond.

"Keep on asking and you will receive what you ask for. Keep on seeking and you will find. Keep on knocking and the door will be opened to you. For everyone who asks, receives. Everyone who seeks, finds. And to everyone who knocks, the door will be opened." Matthew 7:7-8.

Your past or current situation does not have to define your future. At times, it actually prepares you for the future. For example, my addiction to work and money has turned in to generosity and teaching a personal financial course. My divorce equipped me to relate with those who are struggling in their marriage.

"I see very clearly that God shows no favoritism. In every nation he accepts those who fear him and do what is right" Acts 10:34.

Loving, honest relationships are the most powerful antidote for addiction. Do not fight this battle alone. You will lose. But, with God, the Bible, family and friends, you can develop hope, courage and strength for your future.

RELATIONSHIPS

Marriage and Family

"Marriage is trying to solve a jigsaw puzzle whose pieces keep on changing shapes every minute." Unknown.

The blessed, committed relationship of marriage is treated very seriously throughout the Bible. It originated with God making woman from man's rib to symbolize their "oneness". Thus, the common need and desire in marriage must be to become "one." God's grand design for us is to be united as husband and wife.

Being "one" doesn't mean that we have to be or think exactly alike or always agree on everything. It does mean we are to be committed to and love one another, live in monogamy and prioritize your marriage ahead of all other human relationships. Marriage is not mandatory, it is a choice. Our marriage vows, made in the presence of God and witnesses, are to be until *"death do us part";* not something entered into lightly or recklessly.

"I love being married. It's so great to find that one special person you want to annoy for the rest of your life!" Rita Rudner, comedian.

Most, including me, completely underestimate our marriage commitments. The concept of, "forever" is apparently beyond human understanding. Marriage is a merger of two imperfect humans, striving to become *one* with each other through their holy union, becoming more than they thought possible, individually and together.

Marriage doesn't create problems and it certainly doesn't solve them, it reveals them. In fact, it has been said that marriage *multiplies* the problems of a romantic relationship between four and ten times! We need each other, whether in marriage, family, work or friendship.

Many married couples who end up divorced or separated are either too selfish or lazy to put forth the effort to build and shape a lasting marriage. Successful marriages are not an accident. They require patience, perseverance, hard work and selflessness to reap the benefits of unconditional love, trust, security, longevity, companionship and bliss. And, it is totally worth it!

There is a reason most TV shows, movies, books, and our personal dreams are centered on romantic love. We each urgently desire to love another and be loved. God designed a man and a woman to be in a loving, marital relationship. The key to a meaningful marriage is **trust**. Without it there is no basis for commitment between two people.

Science has proved that a long-term healthy marriage results in feelings of intimacy, a sense of safety and a bond that is rarely broken. So, here are the ground rules for husbands and wives from God's perspective:

"And further, submit to one another (put your spouse first) out of reverence for Christ.

For wives, this means submit to your husbands as to the Lord. For a husband is the head of his wife as Christ is the head of the church (Christ loves and promotes His church). He is the Savior of his body, the church. As the church submits to Christ, so you wives should submit to your husbands in everything.

For husbands, this means love your wives, just as Christ loved the church (Christ died for His church). He gave up his life for her to make her holy and clean, washed by the cleansing of God's word. He did this to present her to himself as a glorious church without a spot or wrinkle or any other blemish. Instead, she will be holy and without fault. In the same way, husbands ought to love their wives as they love their own bodies. For a man who loves his wife actually shows love for himself. No one hates his own body but feeds and cares for it, just as Christ cares for the church. And we are members of his body.

As the Scriptures say, 'A man leaves his father and mother and is joined to his wife, and the two are united into one.' This is a great mystery, but it is an illustration of the way Christ and the church are one. So again I say, each man must love his wife as he loves himself, and the wife must respect her husband." Ephesians 5:21-33.

No one is perfect, there will be breakdowns in these marital mandates. We all fall short of our own expectations and completely miss the standards of the Bible. Combining two imperfect individuals in to a lifetime union is a challenge from start to finish. You are to be a *team;* working together to help your spouse become all they were created to be. Marriage has to be built equally on the husband and wife. You both win at marriage or you both lose.

It is a partnership of equally unqualified and unprepared individuals pursuing God, accepting His grace and forgiveness and doing the best they know how. It is only through Bible-centered trust, kindness and self-sacrificing love that relationships of any kind can flourish.

"I don't think I'll get married again; every five years or so, I'll just find a woman I don't like and give her a house." Lewis Grizzard Jr., writer and humorist.

Sorry Lewis, no short cuts or easy way out here.

In a successful marriage relationship, each partner must be kind, caring, loving and forgiving and make your spouse the priority. You must strive to become soulmates in order to experience a spirit-inspired and fueled marriage. Bible driven marriages are forever new, exciting and rewarding.

The union of two imperfect individuals also requires continuous character and personal development. It is not a time to say "I made it, now I can stop caring, trying, learning, growing and maturing." Marriage is the time to learn to put your partner ahead of yourself. Your precious marriage alliance must come first. It's time to step-up your game and consciously decide to love each other on purpose.

"But among the Lord's people women are not independent of men and men are not independent of women. For although the first woman came from man, every other man was born from a woman and everything comes from God." 1 Corinthians 11:11.

As is often the case with the Bible, its instructions are counter-cultural, so you will behave differently than most other couples. There is nothing romantically rarer in our *"me first"* culture, than putting your spouse ahead of yourself.

Our society appears to value strong marriages less and less in spite of the fact the family structure is what holds our world together. When you think about it, movies and books about love stories always *end* with marriage. The reason the story stops there is because that is where the real work and change *begins.* Have you ever noticed movies don't show you that part? It makes you wonder how many great Hollywood love stories actually survived!

Like Vivian and Edward in the movie, "Pretty Woman". Really? At least Rhett and Scarlett, in "Gone with the Wind", had an honest ending.

The fairy tale of life, as in, "happily ever after," depicted in fictional works, are, in fact, *fiction.* Marriage is not a Cinderella fairy tale. It is the hardest work two people will ever do; requiring unwavering honesty, trust, respect and commitment to achieve unparalleled bliss.

In the past, marriage and having children were more about survival, running the family farm, producing food and getting the work of life done than it was about Hollywood love. Couples from my parents' and previous generations stayed married because they *needed* each other to survive and be secure. Today's modern world has solved most of life's mundane struggles and safety issues so couples no longer need each other just to stay alive.

There is a far different challenge than economics for today's marriages. In many ways marriage is more real because it is a free choice, not a requirement.

For my wife and I, what started as an earthly, sensual union, has become a *deep spiritual bond* through living according to the teachings of the Bible. While she and I will always be *'a work in process,'* our married relationship has matured into something we cannot completely explain, nor take complete credit for it. It is now *spiritually* inspired. Our relationship, love and companionship are miracles, intertwined in a practical and spiritual bond. Through the grace of God, we, "have each other's backs" every day. We do our best to listen to each other, communicate directly and always remember we are talking to our soul mate.

It is not clear how much of our fabulous relationship is based on our compatibility, mutual respect, the continuous effort to grow our relationship or the power and grace of God. We are partners, for life. Nevertheless, as we continue to learn and apply the Bible to our individual lives and "soul mate" relationship, it just gets better and better in every way. We intentionally choose to improve and excel in our union, rather than looking for ways to belittle or undercut our relationship. We have learned to differentiate between trivial "first world" problems and our true needs.

"Marriage is not that complicated, I just do what she says!" Unknown.

God created marriage, it is between a man and woman (body parts fit perfectly!) and it was meant to be *permanent.* When entered into and conducted as the Bible directs, marriage is perfectly magnificent. I have learned that being married, as the Bible instructs, is quite different from the world's standards and much more spectacular.

Marriage math made simple: **If you have $20 and your wife has $5, she has $25.00!**

Here is a remarkable definition of how the Bible describes the gift of a good wife:

"Who can find a virtuous and capable wife? She is more precious than rubies. Her husband can trust her, and she will greatly enrich his life. She brings him good, not harm, all the days of her life. She finds wool and flax and busily spins it. She is like a merchant's ship, bringing her food from afar.

She gets up before dawn to prepare breakfast for her household and plan the day's work for her servant girls. She goes to inspect a field and buys it; with her earnings she plants a vineyard. She is energetic and strong, a hard worker. She makes sure her dealings are profitable; her lamp burns late into the night. Her hands are busy spinning thread, her fingers twisting fiber. She extends a helping hand to the poor and opens her arms to the needy.

She has no fear of winter for her household, for everyone has warm clothes. She makes her own bedspreads. She dresses in fine linen and purple gowns. Her husband is well known at the city gates, where he sits with the other civic leaders. She makes belted linen garments and sashes to sell to the merchants.

She is clothed with strength and dignity, and she laughs without fear of the future. When she speaks, her words are wise, and she gives instructions with kindness. She carefully watches everything in her household and suffers nothing from laziness. Her children stand and bless her.

Her husband praises her: 'There are many virtuous and capable women in the world, but you surpass them all!' Charm is deceptive, and beauty does not last; but a woman who fears the LORD will be greatly praised. Reward her for all she has done. Let her deeds publicly declare her praise." Proverbs 31:10-31.

If you were wondering what kind of woman is a man's dream, you just read it. If you are a single man, how does this stack up with your criteria for a wife?

"Women are meant to be loved, not understood." Oscar Wilde, playwright.

Now, about a woman's dream...

A devotional called, *"The Theology of Marriage,"* presented a very intriguing interpretation on how men are to love their wife. It is based on Ephesians 5:25, **"For husbands, this means love your wives, just as Christ loved the church. He gave up his life for her."**

Thus, we are to love our wives the way Christ loves His church.

"When you find a guy who calls you beautiful instead of hot, who calls you back when you hang up on him, who will stand in front of you when other's cast stones, or will stay awake just to watch you sleep, who wants to show you off to the world when you are in sweats, who will hold your hand when you're sick, who thinks you're pretty without makeup, the one who turns to his friends and says, 'that's her', the one that would bear your rejection because losing you means losing his will to live, who kisses you when you screw up, watches the stars and names one for you and will hold and rock that

baby for hours so you can sleep....you marry him all over again." Shannon L. Alder, author.

Following are the **10 practical ways** for men to love and treat their wives.

1. **Pray with your wife.** When my wife and I pray together, it is impossible to be upset with each other.
2. **Pray for your wife.** "God, help me to love You more than her, and her more than anyone or anything else. Help me bring her into Your presence today. Make us one. I want to hear her, cherish her and serve her."
3. **Spend time alone with her.** The more common interests you have, the more opportunities there are to grow the relationship.
4. **Intently listen to her without giving a quick reply or any reply.** Listen to learn, understand and respect her. Communication is one of the top three problems in marriages. Women are different from men, they often need to express themselves and do not always want a response.
5. **Touch her.** Successful couples touch each other regularly. Nonsexual touching, holding hands, hugs and loving pats lead to a deeper relationship.
6. **Accept her just the way she is**, unconditionally; and she will do the same for you.
7. **Encourage her with loving words.** Compliment, thank and affirm her often to build her up emotionally.
8. **Take care of her financially**. She must feel secure. Live within your means, work hard and save for the future.
9. **Laugh** with each other.
10. **Make her your top priority;** after God and before all others.

"You are actually the only two in this world together for the rest of your life; everyone else comes and goes." Unknown.

That is a critical statement to always remember. Eventually, in later years, it will be only the two of you, caring for each other, moving toward the end and looking forward to the other side. So, *intentionally* invest in your marriage and one another. Be each other's best friend, soulmate and partners in Christ.

"Wives, submit to your husbands, as is fitting for those who belong to the Lord. Husbands, love your wives and never treat them harshly." Colossians 3:18-19.

Marriage is not all lollipops, hearts and roses. Most weak, lazy individuals don't work at their marriage so life's reality intrudes and they are unprepared. Where reality and the Bible intersect is where God is found and love nourished.

Divorce

Let's briefly discuss modern day divorce. Divorce is just as hurtful, hopeless and destructive today as in the past. God's direction is for every marriage to be a lifetime commitment and for couples to make every effort to forgive, reconcile and restore their relationship. This applies to adultery, irreconcilable differences, verbal and physical abuse, neglect, abandonment, addiction and other reasons for ending a marriage. If abuse and threats are serious, it is appropriate to immediately separate until the abuser can get counseling or recovery help and demonstrate responsible adult behavior.

To stay happily married requires working at it every day. You made a *conscious decision* to always love your spouse: "to love forever, for better or worse, for richer or poorer, in sickness and health, forsake all others, until death do us part." It is an ongoing, *intentional decision* to live your vows, for the rest of your life. Not for as long as you feel like it.

My love for my wife is infinitely stronger and greater than for any other human because it is not based solely on fickle feelings, sexual attraction or my willpower. Sure, there are people who believe it is easier to stay single and go from one relationship to the next or just live together. But, the truth is you will never experience the deep satisfaction from any other relationship as you get from a committed marriage.

I am divorced, so I don't preach or condemn anyone on this topic. I can only you tell the profound negative effects divorce had on me, my ex-wife and my children. My feelings during and since the painful experience are shame, regret and a hurting heart. Forgiveness is the only answer to all I feel, believe and hope for in the future. I never want to hurt anyone like I hurt my ex-wife and two children.

The best antidote for divorce is God, the Bible and putting your spouse ahead of your own desires. The goal is for a husband and a wife to submit to the Bible's plan for their lives individually and as a couple. When you have a spiritual goal bigger than yourself, it is easier to submit to each other in order to accomplish God's larger objectives.

"Didn't the Lord make you one with your wife? In body and spirit, you are his. And what does he want? Godly children from your union. So guard your heart; remain loyal to the wife of your youth. 'For I hate divorce! Says the Lord, the God of Israel.' To divorce your wife is to overwhelm her with cruelty, says the Lord of Heaven's Armies. 'So guard your heart; do not be unfaithful to your wife.'" Malachi 2:15-16.

Fifty percent of marriages end in divorce. We simply get divorced and view it the same as breaking up after a prom date. What are we teaching our children through our poor choices and behaviors? My generation, the Baby Boomers, started this disturbing trend and now the negative consequences are rampant in every age group and economic level of society.

"Since they are no longer two but one, let no one split apart what God has joined together." Matthew 19:6.

So, take care of each other, do something special for your wife or husband tonight. Love them more tomorrow than you did today. You will find that your soulmate is the one you are married to.

Children

"Children are a gift from the Lord, they are a reward from him." Psalm 127:3.

Fully understand the lifelong commitment before you decide to marry or have children. Not everyone should have children. Make sure you are ready, fully able and committed to your children *for the rest of your life*. Committed, loving families create loving, capable children.

"Before I got married I had six theories about bringing up children; now I have six children and no theories." John Wilmot, Earl of Rochester."

The family unit is what holds civilization and the world together. Family should be the first-place children learn right from wrong, how to handle disagreements, success, failure, anger, trust, discipline, compassion and love. A family is where essential values, social skills, fairness, generosity and resilience should be introduced and developed. It is there we should learn how to effectively communicate our feelings, emotions and needs as females and males in relationships. More often than not, home is the only place we learn about God and the Bible. A family is where children are to be protected from society until they are able to understand and reason through life's complexities and make informed choices.

"Get all the advice and instructions you can, so you will be wise the rest of your life." Proverbs 19:20.

Yet children, even in good family settings, are often exposed to lots of murder, guns, violence, sex, drugs and other vices through TV, the internet, video games, movies, books, music and sadly at times, their own parents. It often occurs long before they are able to comprehend the meaning and impact of the emotional damage being done to them. Because of divorce, millions of children are left to fend for themselves without adult nurturing and leadership.

"When a spouse cheats the last thing, they think about is that they are cheating on their *children* too." Unknown.

Sobering and selfish!

Children that get off to a poor start often must catch up and learn how to live and function in a world that can be cold and even cruel. Without a strong support base growing up, many kids are never able to catch up or rebound from an unstable emotional foundation. Our interaction with our parents and siblings are the most important relationships we have before marrying our spouse.

"The Lord is our God, the Lord alone. And you must love the Lord your God with all your heart, all your soul, and all your strength. And you must commit yourselves wholeheartedly to these commands that I am giving you today. Repeat them (10 Commandments) again and again to your children. Talk to them when you are at home and

when you are on the road, when you are going to bed and when you are getting up."** Deuteronomy 6:4-7.

Most of what I learned about important life topics I learned at home and much of it has stuck with me for my entire life. Family interaction and teaching is how I formed my initial world view, values and the criteria I use to evaluate others and circumstances. Families don't have to be perfect, but they need to be **loving, kind, purposeful and safe.**

It is only as I have matured, that I see how vitally important it is to be devoted and competent, taking very seriously the choice to have children and, most important, to raise them well. It is not a part-time responsibility, something you do in your spare time or "farm out" to schools or a nanny. Dedicated, loving parents are priceless.

"Direct your children onto the right path, and when they are older, they will not leave it." Proverbs 22:6.

Children are not an inconvenience or a problem to be solved, ignored or minimized. They are fragile beings and need to be loved, cared for, protected and developed.

"Fathers, do not provoke your children to anger by the way you treat them. Rather, bring them up with the discipline and instruction that comes from the Lord." Ephesians 6:4.

God is serious about parent's responsibility to teach their children about God and the Bible and to lovingly care for them. We are all children of God and must love and treat our children as He loves us. If you do not want to sacrifice your life for your children - do not have any!

"Those who spare the rod of discipline hate their children. Those who love their children care enough to discipline them." Proverbs 13:24.

It is much easier to learn new things when you are young. Thus, teach your children about God and to read the Bible while they are young, open minded and quick learners. This will pay off for the rest of their lives. I know it did for me. If children are not exposed to the Bible early in life, it only becomes more difficult to learn as they get older and more set in their ways. The consequences for neglecting to teach your children about the Bible are serious and each parent will be dealt with directly by God.

"And anyone who welcomes a little childlike this on my behalf is welcoming me. But, if you cause one of these little ones who trusts in me to fall into sin, it would be better for you to have a large millstone tied around your neck and be drowned in the depths of the sea." Matthew 18:5-6.

This is serious business to Him. When God wrote the Bible, He did so to protect you and me, to constantly remind us that He is God and His ways are to be forever honored.

Just because you get married does not mean you must have children. These two important, life changing decisions, are mutually exclusive. Children are a lifetime commitment. They completely consume your life for at least the first two decades and remain in your life, heart and soul for the rest of your life.

Additionally, they require ongoing attention and sacrifice, loads of extra money and time if any child is to have a decent chance in this immoral, chaotic world. Choose and contemplate wisely before bringing a child into the world. **Never** have children because friends think you should, grandparents want grandchildren or any other superficial reason.

Creating a child is easy; it's just procreation or breeding – the plumbing works. It takes no effort and can even occur "accidentally." But, committing and following through to raise your children well is the real test and the obligation of outstanding parents. If you don't want to commit the rest of your life to your children, don't bear any. A child deserves and needs your best effort, as well as, your loyalty and a loving, stable home. Abandoning or marginalizing your children is the worst of human behavior and heartbreaking to their spirit. Let's be clear, "there are no illegitimate children, only illegitimate parents".

This is not a small problem; it is an epidemic. To make it real – in the USA there are approximately **3 million children** who live with neither parent and **20 million** with only one parent.

"Children shouldn't have to sacrifice so that you can have the life you want. You make sacrifices so your children can have the life they deserve." Pinterest.

Today's liberal freedoms, loose morals and self-serving parents are spearheading the breakdown of the family unit. How we will deal with the consequences of temporary marriages, irresponsible parents and abandoned children, is unclear. The government, schools and others, raising our children are not healthy alternatives.

"There is no school equal to a decent home and no teacher equal to a virtuous parent." Mahatma Gandhi, leader in India's struggle for independence.

You are the parent. You are God's designated authority in the home.

"Discipline your children while there is hope. Otherwise you will ruin their lives." Proverbs 19:18.

"Each day of our lives we make deposits in the memory banks of our children." Charles R. Swindoll, pastor and author.

When children are young you may know them well and they enjoy being with you. However, as the middle and high school years come and go, you gradually know them less and less. Most children begin to yearn for independence and the freedom to speak and behave in their *own* way. This is a natural stage of life, where they begin to form their own identity and become their own unique selves. They gradually spend more time with their friends than with family. This process has to happen if they are to become productive, useful, confident adults. Just like you did!

In my case, my biological dad was missing completely and I don't think my mom knew me very well after I went away to college. Likewise, as I learned while writing her life story when she was in her 80's, I didn't really know her as well as I thought.

I recognize that I don't know my kids that well now either. At this point, as adults, they spend much more time with their friends and those they work with. My children are more different than I want to believe.

Parents will always be parents and thus it is difficult to ever view your children, like others are able to, as responsible adults in the real world. They will always be your kids. But, becoming *friends* with our children is what we must do as parents to have a chance of having a meaningful, adult relationship with them.

Because my adult kids are stepchildren to my wife, she has a much more objective view of them than I do. She helps me not only be a better father, but more importantly, to also be their friend. I want to have a meaningful relationship with my children. Any parent, divorced or not, can empathize with me; I want my kids to *like* me.

Jesus loved children and they liked Him. In a Bible story the disciples stopped children from getting to Jesus thinking He wanted time with adults and that the children would be a distraction. Wrong!

"But Jesus said, 'Let the children come to me. Don't stop them! For the Kingdom of Heaven belongs to those who are like these children." Matthew 19:14.

To Children of Mediocre or Missing Parents

There are no perfect parents. We are all flawed and simply did the best we knew how at the time. It is a complex, demanding task to raise competent, compassionate, sensible and loving children. Good parenting requires unconditional love and a plethora of skills most of us only *partially* obtain, develop and use effectively.

Even if your parents were missing, hurtful, abusive or just didn't meet your expectations, you must still *honor* them. It doesn't mean you trust or like them, they must earn the right to be trusted. You must forgive them so you can move on and live your own, unique, unencumbered life.

"Children, obey your parents because you belong to the Lord, for this is the right thing to do. Honor your father and mother. This is the first commandment with a promise: If you honor your father and mother, things will go well for you and you will have a long life on the earth." Ephesians 6:1-3.

There have been millions of irresponsible and hurtful parents throughout the ages. There is no question about that. Perhaps your mom or dad was one of them. **But, you are an adult now.** You are no longer under their influence or control. It is time for you to establish your own identity, confront your own fears and shortcomings in order to become the thriving person you want and were meant to be.

Consciously take responsibility for your life, don't blame your parents or others. Work hard to be the person you want to become. The decisions you make this month and year determine your destinations next year. Ultimately, all *your choices* add up to and determine your life and how your story will end. Be the change you want, transform your family tree going forward for yourself and your children.

Your parents are only *one* aspect of what made you who you are today. Your current friends, work associates and those *you spend the most time with* are much larger influencers. You should not blame your mom or dad for problems you have as an adult. Blaming others is a waste of time and cuts you no slack with God. Remember forgiveness solves a multitude of hurts, regrets, grudges and frees you to move on and live your best life.

"Grudges are for those who insist that they are owed something; forgiveness, however, is for those who are substantial enough to move on." Criss Jami, author.

In the end, it will be just between you and God, no one else.

"Remember, we will all stand before the judgment seat of God." Romans 14:10.

Take Away: Marriage is a lifelong commitment between a man and a woman. No marriage is easy or perfect; it takes effort, perseverance and a daily commitment to each other. Most soulmates are made, not born. If you choose not to work hard and smart on your marriage, everyone suffers. When the Bible is applied to marriage, a soulmate relationship is achievable and eternally rewarding. There is no other relationship like marriage.

Deciding to have children is daunting. Only choose to have children if you want to dedicate the rest of your life to them. God will hold you accountable for how you care for, raise and develop your children.

Friends and Mentors

Friends

"Many people will walk in and out of your life, but only true friends will leave footprints in your heart." Eleanor Roosevelt, First Lady, diplomat and activist.

We are meant to be in relationships as families, couples, teams, friends and other forms of camaraderie. We were not designed to be alone. Most of us are simply looking for honest friendships, but it takes a lot of time and energy to develop a meaningful relationship. Developing deep, *trusted* relationships can only be accomplished through spending lots of quality time together. Relationships are so important to God that the following verse says He would rather you restore and build your relationships before worshiping Him.

"So, if you are presenting a sacrifice (tithe, donation) at the altar in the Temple and you suddenly remember that someone has something against you (disagreement), leave your sacrifice here at the altar. Go and be reconciled to that person. Then come and offer your sacrifice to God." Matthew 5:23-24.

You have a choice of who your close friends will be, who you date, associate with and who you choose to spend your valuable time with. You take a chance deciding to be with a person or group, as you cannot be with someone else. Everyone gets one shot at life and the kind of life you have depends, to a large extent, on your relationships, *particularly those closest to you.*

"Sometimes I wonder how you put up with me. Then I remember how much I put up with you so we're even." Anonymous.

Life is all about *relationships,* not money, accomplishments, fame or possessions. The individuals you spend the most time with will significantly influence your direction in life. If you hang out with honest and positive individuals you are likely to be encouraged. Likewise, if you are around lazy, negative or depressed people, you will likely gravitate to those behaviors and beliefs.

Try to distance yourself from people who constantly complain saying, *"It's not fair"* or *"I can never catch a break!"* They either believe they are entitled or that they are a victim. These low self-esteem individuals do not take responsibility nor think they are accountable for their lives. Instead, they blame former friends, lovers, parents, the government or their boss. They are cowards who tear others down to make themselves feel more powerful. If this describes any of your current friends, it may be time to move on for your own mental health.

You deserve and need better friends than that.

Today, it seems, we value the number of relationships we have more than the *depth and quality* of our relationships. We call many individuals "friends," in spite of not really knowing them very well. Social media is perpetuating the myth that, the more "followers," "friends" or "likes" you have, determines how popular you are and, even more frightening, your worth or stature as a person.

How sad! Quantity does not make up for the quality of your friendships. Meaningful relationships require your time, attention, trust and, eventually commitment. You don't have enough time to be true friends with everyone no matter what Facebook says.

There are skills and information you can only learn in deep, personal, long-term relationships. You learn how to share, relate, trust, forgive, sacrifice and be spontaneous. You learn the skills of carrying on a conversation, responding in real-time, reacting to facial expressions, gestures and visible emotions. Staring at a screen is not the same as looking directly into the eyes of another human.

Technology and social media are not all bad. There is an appropriate time for all forms of communication. Used appropriately, social media can enhance human relationships, but technology has its limits. To learn your identity and how you are perceived, someone you trust must honestly tell you. Without healthy, reliable relationships, you miss much of what life is all about. You need human relationships in order to love. "Screens" cannot do this.

"Don't just pretend to love others. Really love them. Hate what is wrong. Hold tight to what is good. Love each other with

genuine affection, and take delight in honoring each other." Romans 12:9-10.

A few good questions to ask yourself:

Who do you spend the most time with? Are they individuals striving to get ahead, obtain degrees, certificates, relevant experience and gaining knowledge or those who would rather not change? Do your friends watch too much mindless, demeaning television or do they prefer educational shows and read enlightening books? Are your friends happy, joyous and fun or depressed, boring whiners? Are they honest, trustworthy, dependable, nonjudgmental and empathetic? Friends will hold you back if they prefer to take the easy way, are defensive or seldom put forth extra effort. As a 70's rock song proclaimed they have become "comfortably numb".

Does your circle of acquaintances attend church, Bible study groups and read the Bible or are they self-centered, materialistic and think of themselves as the center of the universe? How would you assess your friends living habits? Do your closest friends bring peace or chaos, love or hate, encouragement or negativity into your life? Is the bond mutually beneficial and contributing to your growth, maturity, joy and success? Do your closest friends inspire you?

The quality of your relationships and friends either enhances or limits the outcomes and quality of your life.

You must be intentional and intelligent to identify, nurture and hold on to mutually rewarding friendships. You will, over time, emulate and become like those you spend the most time with. Lifestyle and life outcomes are not random. They are a direct result of those who influences you most. Consider the effect your friends have on you and you have on them.

No doubt you must help others and encourage those who are down or depressed. But, to develop a successful life, change your perceptions and behaviors, you should primarily associate with those with high morals, sterling character, noble values and a positive attitude.

"Brothers and sisters, we urge you to warn those who are lazy. Encourage those who are timid. Take tender care of those who are

weak. Be patient with everyone. See that no one pays back evil for evil, but always try to do good to each other and to all people." 1 Thessalonians 5:14-15.

So, definitely volunteer to help the less fortunate and lovingly encourage those who may be on the wrong path in life. We are called to love everyone. But, not everyone should be a close friend. Reality forces you to judiciously allot your limited time.

For example, you may only email with an acquaintance, whereas, you should frequently *visit* a close friend. You will vigorously help and expend whatever time it takes to help your spouse, children and best friend to be all they are meant to become. And there may be individuals you should limit your exposure to or simply stop seeing.

Consciously set boundaries for those you associate with. Close, beneficial friends deserve more of your time, whereas, those you are helping may only see you occasionally. For example, your *inner circle* should consist of God, spouse, children and a few close friends. If you are not married, it should be God and possibly a couple of very dear friends, relatives or trusted business partners. The next circle of access to you might be parents, or casual friends. As you head to outer circles of relationships, you limit the amount of time and level of detailed, personal information you share. Because your time and energy are limited, this is the only practical and intelligent way to live.

"Walk with the wise and become wise; associate with fools and get in trouble." Proverbs 13:20.

Key assets to look for in close friends:

1. **Integrity**

"Honesty may be the best policy, but it's important to remember that apparently, by elimination, dishonesty is the second-best policy." George Carlin, comedian.

There is no quality more important in a friend than honesty. You must only associate with those who are trustworthy in all circumstances. Lying is a cancer that will eat up the trust in any relationship, so integrity is non-negotiable in any friendship. Not to mention, it is the Ninth Commandment.

"The Lord detests lying lips, but he delights in people who are trustworthy." Proverbs 12:22.

The definition of integrity is the quality of being honest, fair, with strong moral principles. Most people are naturally attracted to individuals that demonstrate integrity. You feel secure around them because they will always tell you the truth and treat you justly.

"The Godly walk with integrity, blessed are his children who follow him." Proverbs 20:7.

Sounds normal, even simple, but how many individuals can you really, consistently count on that demonstrate dependable moral character? Many people, including friends, co-workers and even family members can prove to be unreliable. Every time you behave with integrity you take a step forward; over a lifetime those thousands of honest choices add up to a changed and meaningful life. Individuals with inconsistent integrity cannot be trusted and must be avoided.

"Honesty guides good people; dishonesty destroys treacherous people." Proverbs 11:3.

Every day we encounter opportunities to be honest or dishonest. Many people are able to segment their lives, living with integrity in a few areas, while dismissing honesty in others. If you are serious about exhibiting character, this doesn't work. If you cheat a little on your taxes, take staples from work or gossip, you will gradually be less honest in other areas. "Little white lies" are *still* lies.

"People with integrity walk safely, but those who follow crooked paths will be exposed." Proverbs 10:9.

Eventually, I had to admit I was not capable of living a life of lies in certain areas of my life. It was time for me to clean up my moral act. What a relief! Life suddenly became easier, simpler and less stressful, not having to keep track of stories I had told, information I had withheld and the gray areas I had cheated in. Miraculously, surrendering to complete honesty resulted in my mind being freed to focus on what is really important in life. If you decide to embark on this mission of honesty it will free you from life's compromising issues that erode your integrity and release you to thrive. I expect the same of my friends.

"If you want to enjoy life and see many happy days, keep your tongue from speaking evil and your lips from telling lies." 1 Peter 3:10.

2. **Loyalty**

"I'm very loyal in relationships; even when I go out with my mom I don't look at other moms." Gary Shandling, comedian.

A real friend is dependable. Those who stand by you through thick and thin are indispensable and a relationship to be treasured. Too many "friends" are only fair-weather, good time friends. You need those who will celebrate with you in good times and stand by you in challenging and stressful times. Observe who actually shows up when you're in need and who makes excuses. Actions reveal a person's true character.

"A friend is always loyal, and a brother is born to help in time of need." Proverbs 17:17.

3. **Empathy and Caring**

Empathy: "the ability to understand and share the feelings of another."

A friend who has the ability to empathize with and relate to you is able to listen, be nonjudgmental and supportive. It is a rare individual who is genuinely caring; thus, they will make *your* life more outstanding. Latch onto them when you encounter them. Here is how to live for God and close friends:

"Since God chose you to be holy people he loves, you must clothe yourselves with tenderhearted mercy, kindness, humility, gentleness and patience. Make allowance for each other's faults, and forgive anyone who offends you. Remember, the Lord forgave you, so you must forgive others. Above all, clothe yourselves with love, which binds us all together in perfect harmony. And let the peace that comes from Christ rule in your hearts. For as members of one body

you are called to live in peace. And always be thankful." Colossians 3:12-15.

In today's troubled society it is easy to get discouraged and ask: "Am I doing any good in the world? Is being kind and helping others making any difference?"

It often appears that rude, derogatory, joking, sarcastic and condescending comments and behaviors are the norm. It should not be your acceptable way of treating others. If the friends you keep reflect society's stereotypes and vulgar worldview, it is time to cut the cord and move on. There are more than enough haters in the world. So, stop making excuses and judging others. Decide to be the help, support and hope we all need and crave. Be the healer, the restorer for the most "messy", undeserving of humans. You can be someone's 'life line'; you can be their hero!

I believe you get back what you give to others. I don't know if we are born to be self-centered or we develop selfishness while dealing with the harshness of modern society. But, as I look at our deteriorating world, the majority is not always right.

Make a decision to be in the moral, loving, kind minority.

"And now, dear brothers and sisters, one final thing. Fix your thoughts on what is true, and honorable, and right, and pure, and lovely and admirable. Think about things that are excellent and worthy of praise." Philippians 4:8.

The old saying "Never judge a man until you've walked in his shoes" is still true today. You don't know where a stranger is mentally, physically, spiritually or emotionally; thus, compassion, understanding and mercy should always be our first reaction.

Everyone is "fighting battles" of some kind to create their one and only unique life or just to survive. If the waitress/waiter, cashier or government employee (DMV) is rude or distant, consider maybe their child is ill, their spouse left them or they have other huge struggles. Don't let them bring you down, forgive and encourage them, then smile.

They don't need our judgment; they need *kindness* and *hope*.

As followers of the Bible, we are called to a much higher standard. We must avoid conflicts, always seek to make peace and look for opportunities to be kind and help others. When someone starts to gossip, criticize or demean others, rather than take part or sit there silently, ask how you could help, forgive or pray for the person. Love is always the antidote for hate, prejudice, meanness and sarcasm. There is no doubt this is hard work, takes courage and you will stand out. Your bravery will cause some to commend you, others may ridicule you for being a 'do-gooder'. Do it anyway.

"I trust in God, so why should I be afraid? What can mere mortals do to me?" Psalm 56:4.

Be aware that many are privileged in one or more ways. Your advantage might be health, intelligence, wealth, special talent, appearance, family history or some other trait that gives you an advantage in life. So, don't overlook how your worldview, judgment and evaluation of others is impacted. Recognize, understand and control your arrogance. I have caught myself judging others, only to quickly realize I know *nothing* about them. Then I actually meet them and find out how absolutely wrong I was. I now try to use my smile and fortunate life to become more compassionate, loving and generous with everyone.

I view others as strangers rather than the way I view my family and friends. I have noticed that my perspective changes dramatically when I view others through the *same lens* I use for family. And, remember to: "Do unto others as you want them to do to you."

The Bible provides guidance and a few rules in this area but leaves the choice of how to respond to us. Why does it seem easier to be judgmental than compassionate? As you can tell I am a little perplexed and regretful of how I judge others but being *aware* of my faults is the basis for improvement.

"And don't forget to do good and to share with those in need. These are the sacrifices that please God." Hebrews 13:16.

In my close relationships I am able to forgive and overlook many condescending comments and behaviors. When I am arguing or debating with someone close to me I catch myself now thinking; "Do I need to win this discussion or gracefully end it on good terms?"

When someone I love hurts or insults me I can forgive them and move on, rather than be sarcastic or mean, as I tended to be in younger years. I learned these new ways to think and behaving from a godly man I met in a men's group, who was kind to me in spite of my sarcastic comments. We are now close friends.

"Do not withhold good from those who deserve it when it's in your power to help them. If you can help your neighbor now, don't say "come back tomorrow, and then I'll help you." Proverbs 3:27-28.

I will be working on being merciful and kind until I die. My hope is that others will show me that same compassion in spite of me being me.

"Get rid of all bitterness, rage, anger, harsh words and slander, as well as, all type of evil behavior. Instead, be kind to each other, tenderhearted, forgiving one another, just as God has forgiven you." Ephesians 4:31-32.

4. Moral Character

People who consistently do what they say and always strive to be morally good are individuals you want in your personal life. We all live by a set of rules and values. It is a matter of deciding whose rules, morals and laws we are going to consistently follow. Choose the laws and commandments of the Bible that free you to live a meaningful and peaceful life.

"Don't copy the behavior and customs of this world, but let God transform you into a new person by changing the way you think. Then you will learn to know God's will for you, which is good, pleasing and perfect." Romans 12:2.

There must be fair laws and punishment in a civilized society, to maintain peace, justice and equality. If everyone lived by their own rules it would be anarchy. Thus, we each adopt our own set of values, standards and morals we believe in and use to manage our way through the world. A Thoreau like alternative is to become a hermit and live alone in the woods, but that is not possible for most of us, besides even nature has rules.

"If you look carefully, into the perfect law that sets you free and if you do what it (the Bible) says and don't forget what you heard, then God will bless you for doing it." James 1:25.

This verse, written by James, Jesus half-brother, says that if you investigate and understand the Bible's rules and actually follow them, God will bless you. It seems God is enticing you to follow the ways of the Bible. When I think of instructions, laws and commandments, I often think of them as limiting or keeping me from having fun. However, I found that the Bible's proven ways are actually the opposite. Following them results in living a rewarding, joyful life and protects me from society's sketchy temptations. Scripture does not promise to eliminate all trials and earthly problems; rather it gives us directions on how to successfully confront everyday challenges.

"If you want to enjoy life and see many happy days, keep your tongue from speaking evil and your lips from telling lies. Turn away from evil and do good. Search for peace, and work to maintain it. The eyes of the Lord watch over those who do right, and his ears are open to their prayers. But the Lord turns his face against those who do evil." 1 Peter 3:10-12.

5. Constructive Criticism

As an imperfect human, I, like you, need spiritual and earthly counsel to point out our flaws and help to eliminate them. A real friend will balance love and honesty to confront you. It will not be easy for them to point out areas where you need help, correction and guidance. Listen to them, accept their sincere comments and do the same for them.

"Instead, we will speak the truth in love, growing in every way more and more like Christ, who is the head of his body (group of trusted friends), the church." Ephesians 4:15.

A great friend is passionate about the Bible. Stay close to them and their zeal can rub off on you.

"As iron sharpens iron, so a friend sharpens a friend." Proverbs 27:17.

Men and women who help build a "spiritual barrier" around you and protect you from society's temptations are *rare*. Appreciate their courage, counsel and effort, as your life will be free from many of the problems that plague others who lack friends who look out for them. Life is difficult and can, at times, be an all-out battle. Don't go it alone.

"Plans succeed through good counsel; don't go to war without wise advice." Proverbs 20:18.

The Bible details many great relationships that honored and pleased God. Here are a few.

David and Jonathan

Jonathan, King Saul's son, became friends with David. So much so, that even after his father started a campaign to kill David, Jonathan remained loyal to David, not his father. This relationship was based on their mutual faith in God.

"After David had finished talking with Saul, he met Jonathan, the king's son. There was an immediate bond of love between them and they became the best of friends." 1 Samuel 18:1.

Ruth and Naomi

Ruth was married to Naomi's son. He died and Ruth graciously and lovingly decided to stay with Naomi in spite of Naomi urging her to go live her life and find a new husband. Naomi and her beloved daughter-in-law Ruth, challenged and inspired each other to follow God, demonstrated faithfulness in friendship and unconditional love to the end. The book of Ruth reveals their story in detail and is an excellent example of following God, loving others and loyalty.

"But Ruth replied, "Don't ask me to leave you and return back. Wherever you go I will go; wherever you live, I will live. Your people will be my people, and your God my God. Wherever you die I will die, and there will I be buried." Ruth 1:16-17.

Paul and Timothy

In the beginning, Paul was a father figure and mentor to young Timothy but, as time passed they became close friends and eventually ministry partners. A truly remarkable relationship as Paul wrote here to his beloved partner in Christ:

"But, you, Timothy, certainly know what I teach, and how I live, and what my purpose in life is. You know my faith, my patience, my love, and my endurance." 2 Timothy 3:10.

Pray that God will bring committed friends to you. You must do your part by looking for honest friends that are in tune with the Bible. Finding and developing transparent, spiritually rewarding relationships will inspire and restore your life forever.

"Let us think of ways to motivate one another to acts of love and good works. And, let us not neglect our meeting together, as some do, but encourage one another especially now that the day of his return is drawing near." Hebrews 10:24-25.

Mentors

A mentor is an experienced and trusted adviser, like Yoda to young Luke or Mister Miyagi to the Karate Kid. We all need mentors in our lives.

Mentors are everywhere in history. Great leaders, Presidents, kings and queens, business leaders, athletes, celebrities and ordinary people have benefitted from trusted mentors. They can be supervisors, close friends, co-workers, parents, spouse, teacher or a new acquaintance who cares enough to counsel you.

The greatest biblical example of mentoring is Jesus with His apostles. Meeting the apostles for the first time (John 1:35-51) was the beginning of a truly special relationship that eventually launched the First Century Church. It was the quiet, honest and consistent mentoring He performed, over a 3 ½ year period, that prepared the apostles for ministry greatness. What Jesus did for these men is a classic example of a leader or trusted friend coaching his close friends.

The definitive example of master mentoring was found in the relationship between Jesus and Peter. In working with this impossibly impulsive apostle, Jesus exhibited the perseverance of Nehemiah, the wisdom of Solomon and the patience of Job! To say Peter was a handful to work with is like calling the Grand Canyon a pot hole.

Time after time, Jesus had to step in and mentor Peter to save him and his reputation from embarrassment. It was Peter who believed he had the faith to walk on water with Jesus. Read **Matthew 14:24-32.** It was Peter who tried to take control of Jesus transfiguration and create a man-made memorial. His intentions were good, but his ideas were rash and not well-thought through. Read **Matthew 17:1-4.** It was career fisherman Peter who informed Jesus that he had been fishing all night long and that there were no fish to be found. Tired, he initially resisted Jesus idea to throw his nets over the other side of the boat. But when he did, so many fish were in the net they had to bring in a *second* boat to hold them all! Read **Luke 5:4-11.**

Peter was as consistent in his faith as a fickle leaf blowing every which way in a windstorm. But, the mentoring paid off. Peter not only became a man of God; but the leader of the early church! Jesus had changed Peter's life by patiently bearing with him and believing in his potential. I, like many of us, can identify with Peter as we have all struggled with faith and our misguided egos.

Mentoring through the Bible, can accomplish similar miracles in your life and the lives around you. Pray for spiritual and life mentors who can take you beyond that which you can do on your own. These mentors will expand your knowledge, deepen your faith, help you live a successful life and challenge you to achievements you never imagined.

Both my wife and I continue to be in touch with several of our excellent career mentors, as well as, new mentors. They each help us in different areas of our life. We mentor others by leading a financial class and guiding others with their lifestyle choices. Using our talents and experience to help others is a blessing for us. There is no greater feeling or way to serve God than to love, help and mentor others.

A Little Help from My Friends

"The instruction of the wise is like a life-giving fountain; those who accept it avoid the snares of death (temptations of the world)." Proverbs 13:14.

We all need *help* getting through life successfully. Modern society is tough, complex, frustrating and, at times, demoralizing. We all need support and advice navigating life. No one can ever be completely successful in life without the help of others.

Regardless of your definition of success, the help of good people always provides new perspectives, fresh ideas, sharper understanding and sometimes an opposing opinion or vision. Help and wisdom from an intelligent, trusted friend is priceless.

Feedback, of any kind, may cause you to rethink a topic through a different lens and data points. After getting over the frustration of listening, I find that a discussion with a person who disagrees with me can be totally enlightening. I am always thankful for anyone who **cares about me** and is brave enough to be completely honest with me.

"If you listen to constructive criticism, you will be at home among the wise. If you reject discipline, you only harm yourself; but if you listen to correction, you grow in understanding." Proverbs 15:31-32.

Smart individuals identify, build and nurture a cadre of trusted helpers and advisors throughout life. These relationships are often mutual. Influence is the power to affect how someone develops, acts or thinks. An important purpose for our lives is to be an influence for good and peace in the world.

"Plans go wrong for lack of advice; many advisers bring success." Proverbs 15:22.

I appreciate all the advice and help I have received and try to do the same for others. You can't help everyone, but you can help someone.

"One person can make a difference, and everyone should try." John F. Kennedy, 35 President.

Everyone is different. Some people appreciate good advice, a few don't and some just give you a goofy smile as proof they have no idea what you're talking about! Nonetheless, we must do what we can to ease the burden of others.

"Be yourself" is sometimes the worst advice you can give to some people.

The direct feedback from a trusted, patient and knowledgeable person able to present their views on your predicament in a loving and informative manner is a *blessing*. Most individuals tell you what they think you want to hear, rather than the truth. Honest, forthright, courageous life helpers are rare. You never know when you will encounter a friend or stranger that will be life changing.

"The godly give good advice to their friends; the wicked lead them astray." Proverbs 12:26.

Fortunately, you occasionally encounter an individual gifted with the sensitivity and knowledge to intuitively sense your situation and offer up options you would never think of or consider. The trouble with individuals giving me advice is that I need to be *looking* for new wisdom or at least have an open mind. If you are not open to advice no one will be able to help you.

"If you ignore criticism, you will end in poverty and disgrace; if you accept correction you will be honored." Proverbs 13:18.

We must be willing to put ourselves out there, be vulnerable and take a chance to receive the candid advice we need. Much of the time we only have superficial conversations, talking about irrelevant topics; think weather, sports, fashion, politics. Avoiding asking hard questions and talking with those different from us only results in lost opportunities for personal growth. It is vital to openly communicate with those who disagree with you, have different backgrounds and points of view to learn new perspectives and ways to live.

Finally, regardless of the source, I must intentionally *apply* the new information or it is just meaningless input. If I use new information to change, I can hopefully avoid becoming stuck in my ways and evade turning into an irrelevant 'grumpy old man'.

I have experience with both sides of this equation - giving and receiving advice. It is never easy. Both individuals must be genuine and have the best in mind for the other if advice and wisdom is to effectively pass from one to the other.

Not expecting much, I attended my first men's group at church in 2011. I was surprised by this diverse group of men because they were tremendously helpful in making sense of life. Seems we have all had or soon will experience the same problems, regrets, doubts, successes and failures.

Their ability to be open, honest, humble, supportive and even motivational, changed me. The opportunity to be among other honest, straight-forward, selfless men was new for me and an amazing blessing. For years I had missed out on the benefits of good men honestly talking to each other about meaningful life topics.

"Everyone has scars, hurts and regrets, they just aren't all as visible." Unknown.

Finding and developing "agenda free" relationships is difficult. When you do, grab on to them, nurture and keep them growing. Until I experienced this group of extraordinary men of God of various ages and backgrounds, I had no idea what camaraderie was like among men. They were jointly and unselfishly looking to find greater meaning and a new appreciation of life in the Bible. Most men are afraid or simply don't know how to conduct a meaningful conversation on topics of personal relevance. They usually limit conversation to the superficial topics of sports, cars, work or other *safe* topics. Thus, most of us men remain isolated, alone and miss out on what others can do for us.

These men, who each voluntarily joined the group, were reliable, trustworthy, high integrity, God fearing men. We watched each other to see if, "we did what we said we would do," showed up every week and were the real deal. As trust developed, the artificial walls came down, masks came off and the real men were revealed. We all began to feel comfortable and safe being our genuine selves (faults, warts, regrets, weaknesses and all) and openly shared more of our uniquely imperfect lives. We honestly started to give ourselves to each other. I learned that the process of exposing myself opened the door to self-enlightenment.

"Jesus said, 'You like to appear righteous in public, but God knows your hearts. What this world honors is detestable in the sight of God.'" Luke 16:15.

Many of us became friends outside of our study group, sharing our lives and helping each other stay on track living as the Bible teaches. We became accountability partners in everyday life and we still are. We helped each other defy the status quo, avoid sinful male traps and countered society's selfish ways through truth, discipline, courage and living the Bible.

There were 6-8 regulars in this diverse study group. While I learned from everyone in our weekly forum, I continue to stay in close touch with three of them. It is amazing to me how much I value and cherish these relationships, given how different our backgrounds are. Jacob (not his real name) is a retired farmer from California's central valley. He is always positive, self-depreciating, honest and there to help. I can count on him. When I say "good men" in this book, I always think of him.

Bartholomew is also married, no children, had a career in sales, very intense, outgoing, loud, a wild jokester and always entertaining to be around. He, like me, had only found God in the last few years.

Matthew is married, has two sons and is a Bible expert. He was wounded in Vietnam, but that has not held him back one iota. He has advanced degrees, a successful career and a loving family. While volunteering together, we learned I was left-brained and he right, so we complemented each other, enjoyed our differences, and vigorously challenged each other.

I simultaneously admire and count on these guys. If I had not encountered them in the men's group I know I would never have befriended them, because they are so different from me. But, since we are all Christians there is a bond and trust that cannot be broken. If you let Him, God can do amazing work through ordinary, fallible guys.

I am blessed to have them in my life.

"The righteous choose their friends carefully, but the way of the wicked leads them astray." Proverbs 12:26.

I don't have lots of friends, but the ones I trust are very important to me and hold a high priority in my life. I now have high standards for my true friends. I am a better man because of my close friends. Hopefully, I add something useful to their lives too.

"There is joy for those who deal justly with others and always do what is right." Psalms 106:3.

As flawed, inconsistent human beings we all carry extra baggage. It is just a matter of how much. Our bag may contain pride, insecurities, regrets, shame, grief, confusion, doubts, failures, broken relationships and a plethora of other human afflictions. This is normal over a lifetime. If anyone says they don't have a 'bag,' they are lying, in denial or naive. I am not sure you can ever completely empty your bag. But you can significantly *reduce* the emotional and physical toll it takes on you through forgiveness, talking with other like-minded individuals and getting counseling when needed. Of course, communing with God, reading the Bible, being involved in church and small faith groups helped me dramatically lighten my load going forward.

Take Away: Godly friends and mentors are required to provide help navigating life's tricky, ever changing and, at times, slippery paths. Nurture friendships so a mutually rewarding connection can evolve for everyone's benefit. There is no replacement for trusted, honest and caring individuals who sincerely put your best interests first. Relationships matter. No one builds a meaningful life by themselves.

"Here on earth you will have many trials and sorrows. But take heart, because I (God) have overcome the world." John16:33.

The best friend you can possibly have is God.

Relationships at Work

"Work brings profit, but mere talk leads to poverty!" Proverbs 14:23.

Co-workers

This is an important chapter because, generally, at least one-third of your weekdays are at work. It is time to address that large body of activity and time, make it enjoyable and understand what the Bible says about it.

"Work hard so you can present yourself to God and receive his approval. Be a good worker, one who does not need to be ashamed and who correctly explains the word of truth." 2 Timothy 2:15.

Co-workers are the individuals in your department or project team you work most closely with. Their skills, behaviors and attitudes run the gamut from excellent to exasperating. Whether they are an inspiration or an ongoing frustration, they are an important influence.

Having enthusiastic, talented co-workers is a joy in your career. Encourage them and learn from them. Conversely, working with negative, lazy individuals can make your job difficult. The ability to work with others is a key aspect and skill in everyone's life! These relationships impact your emotions and life both at and outside of work.

The "co-workers" of Jesus were His disciples and He was their supervisor most of the time. They frequently made His life frustrating. Jesus was able to rise above the fickleness and foibles of these twelve, ordinary men and mold them into an effective working unit. This demonstrates that with patience, guidance and education, almost any co-worker has potential.

"Do you see any truly competent workers? They will serve kings rather than working for ordinary people." Proverbs 22:29.

Helping others is counterculturaI, but a great skill and attitude to have regarding everyone, not just people at work. The focus is on *your* behavior, not the individuals around you.

"How people treat you is their karma; how you react is yours." Wayne Dyer, author.

Your co-workers may have deficiencies in their ability to work effectively or possess annoying behaviors that affect you. Laziness is common in America, the land of plenty. There are millions out there that really don't want to work; they just want to get *paid*. They want success but are not will to invest the time, be disciplined and put forth the effort to achieve it. As a result, they are dead weight and frustrating to have on your team. A few things you can do are praise them when they accomplish something, compliment them on their good traits and ask how you could be a better co-worker. Likewise, when appropriate, humbly and lovingly give them advice on how they could be a better co-worker. Team work is always more productive than individual performance.

"Let us think of ways to motivate one another to acts of love and good works." Hebrews 10:24.

You may run into a co-worker who talks behind your back, gossips or betrays you. That kind of individual has low self-esteem and maybe fearful. The fact they have gone out of their way to demean you says a lot about them, not you. You need to take the high road. Attempt to kindly talk with them to help resolve their issue and encourage them.

"So don't make judgments about anyone ahead of time-before the Lord returns. For he will bring our darkest secrets to light and will reveal our private motives." 1 Corinthians 4:5.

Remember, Jesus was also betrayed by one of His "co-workers," Judas Iscariot. This backstabbing apostle focused solely on himself.

It is frustrating when you are partnered with someone who lacks the ability or expertise to do a good job. This is where you need self-control, patience and understanding.

"And don't forget to do good and to share with those in need. These are the sacrifices that please God." Hebrews 13:16.

Do all you can to train and guide co-workers to more excellent heights. Take them under your wing, inspire them and show them techniques they may never have seen before. You will feel better; the company will benefit and that person may go on to become more than they imagined.

"We who are strong must be considerate of those who are sensitive about things like this. We must not just please ourselves. We should help others do what is right and build them up in the Lord. For even Christ didn't live to please himself." Romans 15:1-3.

"The Blame Game" is an unfortunate staple in the workplace. With a competitive environment, it is fertile ground for workers to point fingers away from themselves. As a woman or man of God you don't need to follow suit. Always take personal responsibility for your mistakes and congratulate others success. You are God's creation and need to please Him, not man.

Here is a maxim to always remember, **"Hurt people, *hurt* people."** Rick Warren, pastor, Saddleback Church.

When someone lashes out at you they may be coming off a bad day or a bad *life*. They cannot handle their personal pain so they use you as an emotional dumping ground. Don't take it personally. They are reacting to their own failures, someone else who hurt them or they don't know how to emotionally cope with or resolve their anxiety. Instead of reacting to a co-worker's hurtful words, pray for them and help where you can.

"The earnest prayer of a righteous person has great power and produces wonderful results." James 5:16.

Here is a sobering fact about co-workers. Did you know that the #2 reason why missionaries come home prematurely from the mission field? *Because they cannot get along with other missionaries!*

This is beyond sad, especially since it involves the work of *Christian* ministry. So, if Christian missionaries have difficulty getting along doing God's work, our careers and lifestyles are also vulnerable. Work hard, do your part, be a team player and a good example for others.

"For we are God's masterpiece. He has created us anew in Christ Jesus so we can do the good things he planned for us long ago." Ephesians 2:10.

Having great co-workers does not have to be a coincidence. Many of us can make that happen by mentoring others, demonstrating work excellence, infinite patience and pointing them toward the Bible.

Supervisor or Boss

"I don't know how you got to be the boss, but I know how you've been able to stay the boss. Your amazing employees make you look good." Unknown.

What is your attitude towards your boss or supervisor? Do you respect them? Do you struggle with your supervisor's inconsistencies? We are commanded to respect our boss because of their *position* of authority, which may have little to do with your *personal* views of them. Everyone has a boss, pray for them.

"I urge you, first of all, to pray for all people. Ask God to help them; intercede on their behalf, and give thanks for them. Pray this way for kings (president, politicians, boss) and all who are in authority so that we can live peaceful and quiet lives marked by godliness and dignity." 1 Timothy 2:1-2.

Your priority at any job is to work diligently, be ethical, fair, encouraging, obedient to authority and excellence in performance. You are working for and representing God every hour of every day. That means no cheating, no slacking off and no negative attitudes or behaviors. If your boss asks you to do something immoral, illegal or unethical respectfully decline and suggest an alternative. Remember, whether your earthly boss is around or not it doesn't matter, God is always there watching.

The first chapter of Daniel tells the story of how Daniel handled a difficult "employment" situation in a respectful way to preserve his religious beliefs and everyone else's responsibilities. Daniel was taken prisoner because of his talents and was selected to serve in the Kings palace. However, he did not want to eat the food King Nebuchadnezzar was serving because of his faith. He didn't become angry, condescending or lie, rather he humbly and respectfully asked if he could have a diet of vegetables and water. This worked out well for Daniel, his supervisor and the King. Read the book of Daniel to learn how to handle challenging life circumstances.

"Work willingly at whatever you do, as though you were working for the Lord rather than for people. Remember that the Lord will give you an inheritance as your reward, and that the Master (boss) you are serving is Christ." Colossians 3:23-24.

You need to develop *"Eternal employee eyes."* This means that your perspective goes far beyond what your boss might say or do because God is your boss at work and in life. If you have a great boss, you are blessed. Tell them they are great, support them and help make them successful.

"Always work enthusiastically for the Lord, for you know that nothing you do for the Lord is ever useless." 1 Corinthians 15:58.

This perspective changes everything. Now, you need to work harder, be more careful with the details, follow through on everything, be a reliable team player and perform your work in its finest form. You are accountable to the Creator of the Universe from Monday through Friday as well as on Saturday and Sunday.

"And may the Lord our God show us his approval and make our efforts successful." Psalm 90:17.

If you are the boss, your job is to lead, inspire, value and develop everyone. Regardless if you are a project supervisor, manager, director, vice president or the top person, remember who your ultimate boss is.

"Leadership is practiced not so much in words as in attitude and actions." Harold Geneen, businessman.

Entrepreneurs

"Your *smile* is your logo, your *personality* is your business card, how you *leave others feeling* after an experience with you becomes your trademark." Jay Danzie, author.

We live in a world that is rapidly becoming more entrepreneurial. People want to work for themselves and control their own business and financial destiny. This is a tribute to the concept of personal responsibility and a key strength of America. But, being an entrepreneur brings a bundle of problems not encountered by the nine-to-five crowd.

Running your own show can mean longer hours and more responsibilities. You are obligated to create your own brand, build and sell your product and serve your customers. Your cash flow suddenly becomes a major issue since you are not getting a company pay check. In fact, there may be months when you will not be paid at all! You must please shareholders, banks, employees and customers.

"From my very first day as an entrepreneur, I've felt the only mission worth pursuing in business is to make people's lives better." Richard Branson, entrepreneur.

You will be dealing directly with your customers. There is no buffer here. Your business success is all on your shoulders. The good news is that no one can fire you. The bad news is you can go bankrupt all by yourself.

Here are biblically-based suggestions for how to treat your customers.

1. Serve them

Remember that you work for them. They are your boss and you must respectfully defer to them no matter their demands, unless illegal, immoral or unethical. Having a client is not something to be arrogant about; it is a privilege. Show them honor, respect and truth.

"Since God chose you to be the holy people he loves, you must clothe yourselves with tenderhearted mercy, kindness, humility, gentleness and patience. Make allowance for each other's faults, and forgive anyone who offends you." Colossians 3:12-13.

2. Apologize when you're wrong

Because of our pride, it is hard for us to admit when we are wrong. It is even more problematic to tell that to the person we wronged. But, your clients deserve your grace, humility, as well as, the truth. Face up to your mistake and make it right. Humility is a choice. Being humble is not weakness. It is recognizing reality and doing what is right. It takes great courage to admit when you are wrong, apologize and behave in a manner that honors you, your customer and God.

"Don't be selfish; don't try to impress others. Be humble, thinking of others as better than yourselves. Don't look out only for your own interests, but take an interest in others, too." Philippians 2:3.

3. Never Lie

A worldly business maxim states, **"The end justifies the means."** This maxim is not in concert with the Bible. Never lie or cheat to accomplish any earthly goals. As a business leader and a human, truth is always worth standing for in your dealings with others. If you deceive a client you have lost them forever. Not only that, you have lost all his partners and friends, too. Or as a renowned writer put it:

"A lie can travel half way around the world while the truth is putting on its shoes." Mark Twain, author.

Dishonesty has been the downfall of more marriages and business partnerships than anything. No deception or manipulative behaviors here. Tell the truth 100% or say goodbye to your business not to mention your reputation. Trust is paramount in personal and professional matters and once it is broken, it is difficult to re-earn.

"The Lord detests lying lips, but he delights in those who tell the truth." Proverbs 12:22.

4. Always help customers succeed, even if you must refer them to someone else

You want your client to succeed, however, sometimes you are not the best person to help them. Instead of trying to make a profit off them, be honest and find someone who might be a better fit. Your client will appreciate your honesty and likely tell others about your behavior and company. We are not experts in everything and we shouldn't pretend to be.

"Is there any encouragement from belonging to Christ? Any comfort from his love? Any fellowship together in the Spirit? Are your hearts tender and compassionate? Then make me truly happy by agreeing wholeheartedly with each other, loving one another, and working together with one mind and purpose." Philippians 2:1-2.

5. Praise them in public

Everyone loves to be complimented, especially in public, verbally and using social media. Let others know how much your client means to you and speak highly of them wherever you go. This will not only cement your relationship with them, but will enable them to flourish in their business, which, in turn helps you.

Jesus was constantly lifting up individuals with words of praise. He was gracious even with many of His enemies. Apostle Paul says:

"Don't use foul or abusive language. Let everything you say be good and helpful, so that your words will be an encouragement to those who hear them." Ephesians 4:29.

Having your own business is an awesome privilege and responsibility. You are the judge and jury of your fate. When you worked for others, you were an employee with limited power and control. Now, it is all on you. Your customers will make or break your business. Be certain to treat them and others as the following verse says:

Golden Rule: "Do to others whatever you would like them to do to you. This is the essence of all that is taught in the law and the prophets." Matthew 7:12.

Here's another perspective from King Solomon as he looked back reflecting on his life. His point is to balance work with all the other important aspects of life.

"I observed yet another example of something meaningless under the sun. This is the case of a man who is all alone, without a child or a brother, yet who works hard to gain as much wealth as he

can (workaholic). But then he asks himself, "Who am I working for? Why am I giving up so much pleasure now? It is all so meaningless and depressing". Ecclesiastes 4:7-8.

Take Away: In order for you to succeed with co-workers, bosses and as an entrepreneur you must be mindful of several key points.

1. You may spend one-third of your life with co-workers and supervisors. Make it meaningful for everyone.
2. Treat everyone with honesty, compassion and respect no matter how they treat you.
3. Find ways to encourage and help everyone to succeed.
4. Respond with patience and kindness to mean, hurting individuals.
5. Treasure your clients and customers.
6. God is your ultimate Boss at work and in life.

Now, go out, have fun and a productive work week knowing you work for God!

Note: While I did not specifically name 'parenting' as a career, it is the most honorable, selfless and important profession of all. Being a great mom or dad is the highest calling, most impactful and provides the maximum long-term return for your valuable time. Much of what we have discussed applies equally to the occupation childrearing. I respect and admire devoted, competent parents more than any other vocation or leader. Being a competent parent is difficult enough, but not good enough; children must know they are loved, unconditionally.

Sex

"Your marriage is in trouble if your wife says, "You're only interested in one thing," and you can't remember what it is." Oscar Levant, author and comedian.

Society and Sex

Speaking of being interested in only one thing: Our contemporary society is obsessed with S-E-X.

Sex is everywhere today, it is inescapable and in your face. The primary reason for this saturation is because *sex sells!* Many companies exploit sex to sell cars, burgers, beauty products, jeans, perfume, beer, tools, vacations, prescriptions and sports. Everything! From teenagers to Baby Boomers, we are all vulnerable to Madison Avenue's influence and their use of sex in advertising.

Sex itself is not inherently evil. The Bible says sex is only bad when it is *not* exclusively between a husband and wife. Sex before marriage breeds mistrust in your marriage for years to come. Adultery can ruin a marriage forever. There are not only biblical reasons for monogamy there are also many social ones; out of wedlock pregnancy and sexually transmitted diseases, such as herpes, gonorrhea, HPV and AIDS. And don't forget abandon, hurt children.

"But, the man who commits adultery is an utter fool, for he destroys himself. He will be wounded and disgraced. His shame will never be erased. For the woman's jealous husband will be furious and he will show no mercy when he takes revenge. He will accept no compensation, nor be satisfied with a payoff of any size." Proverbs 6:32-35.

Maybe the Titanic sank because Jack and Rose had sex before marriage. Okay, just a thought!

Here are a few statistics regarding sex in America:

-The average male loses his virginity at age 16.9; females slightly older, at 17.4.

-Two-thirds of college students have been in a "friends with benefits" relationship.
-According to a survey of adults aged 20 to 59, women have an average of four sex partners during their lifetime; men have an average of seven.
-One in five say they've looked at porn websites. 47% of Christians say pornography is a major problem, 10% of adults admit to an internet driven sexual *addiction*.
-The vast majority of Americans are monogamous and happy about it. Most, by far, prefer marriage to single life.

There is a lot to contemplate and work to do on the influence of sex. Christian or not, your approach to sex must be guided by the Bible.

"So, you also should consider yourselves to be dead to the power of sin and alive to God in Christ Jesus. Do not let sin control the way you live, do not give in to sinful desires. Do not let any part of your body become instrument of evil to serve sin." Romans 6:11-13.

Major Sexual Temptations Today

Social Media

Bantering with the opposite sex at work, sending private messages behind your spouse's or committed partner's back, looking up old flames to see if the spark is still alive or exchanging phone numbers with attractive strangers are all signs of trouble. You need to diligently manage your social media world or its seductive tendencies will sink your marriage or warp your dating life. "Sexting" is stupid, just ask Anthony Weiner.

A few suggestions for managing the use of social media:

-Freely share all your passwords so there will be no secrets
-Married or single; set up your browser to block X-rated sites
-No pornography
-No intimate electronic conversations with anyone except your wife or committed partner
-If you feel a temptation coming, turn off the computer or phone
-On dating sites, be honest in your profile

Work-related flirting

This practice may seem harmless at first; just a way to get through a long workday. But, if your fellow employee is the *opposite* sex, end it. The latest top news stories about the fall of powerful men and their behavior around women should be enough to scare or motivate both men and women to behave appropriately.

Sexual temptation is like a frog in water that is slowly being heated up, eventually burning the unsuspecting reptile to death. Recognize the fatal heat before it traps and scorches you.

"But I say to you that everyone who looks at a woman with lustful intent has already committed adultery with her in his heart." Matthew 5:28.

Pornography

It is estimated that pornography is a $4 billion-dollar industry. This is composed of internet sites, publications and on-demand television via cable or satellite, movies, phone sex, strip clubs, sexual toys and clothing. You can't have this large an industry without an extraordinary number of individuals involved. If you want porn in the USA it's as easy to find as a cheeseburger.

This solo sexual practice is done in secret usually after the spouse has gone out for the day or retired for the night. If single, you do this home alone. It primarily attracts males, although females are showing an increasing interest in pornography. This visual buffet of sexual excitement is power-packed with fantasy, beauty, out of this world eroticism *and is seductively designed to be addictive.*

"Keep watch and pray, so that you will not give in to temptation. For the spirit is willing, but the body is weak!" Matthew 26:41.

The porn industry is psychologically ingenious in playing to male viewers:

-Porn allows a constant supply of new woman rather than the woman they are married or committed to every day.

-Men love young, new women who "adore" them on the screen. An addict begins to believe a porn star is the girlfriend he could never date or marry in real life.

-Some men don't want to take the time, nor experience the hassle that real-life relationships and marriage require. Porn provides them an easy, selfish option, with no effort or commitment. Of course, there is no meaning, love and eventually your physical love making capabilities will be diminished.

The best way to resolve a pornographic addiction is to tell your partner or trusted friend, get professional help or find a 12 Step Program.

"Run from sexual sin! No other sin so clearly affects the body as this one does. For sexual sin is a sin against his own body." 1 Corinthians 6:18.

The Ultimate Betrayal: Adultery

Infidelity is one of the Ten Commandments. Yet after repeatedly hearing about famous, wealthy and seemingly "good" people who commit adultery, along with cheerful depictions of it in movies and books, the conclusion could be that it is normal.

It is not.

It has become much too common, acceptable and quickly forgiven in today's liberal society. It is a home-wrecking devastation in Hollywood fantasy form which wreaks havoc on trust, respect, self-esteem, loyalty and health.

Consider not only the stimulating moment, but the longer-term consequences and downside. The collateral damage to others in your life, including your precious and innocent children, is disastrous and could emotionally scar them forever. What appears to be so exciting, freeing, powerful and stimulating at the time actually results in exactly the opposite outcome: divorce, disease, bitter children, mistrust, guilt, regret or unwanted pregnancy are all lurking in the wake of infidelity.

Sadly, selfishly I had an affair during my first marriage. While I know God forgives me, the memories still hurt, demean my self-esteem and are shameful. Take it from my personal experience; nothing can insulate you from the guilt and disgrace caused by your egotistical poor choices and behaviors. Imagine explaining your behavior to your children. I also betrayed myself and became a person I did not want to be. Guilt inescapably shows up to haunt you until you humbly ask for forgiveness as King David did in **Psalm 51**. The only, somewhat, positive from this dreadful episode is when I use my experience as a testimony to counsel others to avoid adultery at all costs.

"So, it is with the man who sleeps with another man's wife. He who embraces her will not go unpunished." Proverbs 6:29.

If you have sinned sexually, God still loves you, so sincerely ask for forgiveness, demonstrate genuine regret, turn away from your sin and stop the behavior.

"We waste time looking for the perfect lover, instead of creating the perfect love." Tom Robbins, novelist.

Attributes of Perfect Love

Here are some attributes that set up the foundation for romance, enduring relationships and great sex.

Communication:

Without honest communication trust can never develop and without trust love is impossible. It is imperative that a man and a woman completely relate intellectually, spiritually and emotionally to each other. But, where do you begin to understand a woman?

"The most important sexual organ of a woman is her mind." Josh McDowell, evangelist and author.

Men are often fooled by this truth believing that the sexiest aspect of a woman are her *physical* attributes. Not true. If a man wishes to truly ignite the woman of his dreams he must begin with her mind. If a woman is confused, angry, irritated, afraid, or preoccupied, she is *not* going to feel sexy.

Before she can be in the mood for any sexual activity she must first be freed up of the issues that are flooding her brain and feel safe. Once she is relaxed mentally she is then more likely to engage in the physical realm of sexual activity. It is absolutely critical that a man connect emotionally with his wife before any physical engagement. There needs to be understanding at the deepest intellectual and emotional levels or there is little possibility of pleasing a woman physically.

As far as communication goes, most women use twice as many words as men in the average day; 25,000 vs 12,500. As men, we tend to physically and materially *show* our love and affection not verbally express it. Hence, when a husband arrives home after a day of work he has used up *most* of his words. His wife is only halfway done with hers! Guess who talks more from that point on.

"You cannot truly listen to anyone and do anything else at the same time." M. Scott Peck, psychologist and author.

She wants to talk; her man wants to mindlessly doze, have a beer, watch sports or obsess on the TV remote. This can lead to major communication gaps and set a dangerous trend in relating to each other. In addition, women tend to communicate emotionally while a lot of men favor the analytical and factual approach. This puts each partner in completely different arenas of dialogue, arguing and understanding.

When it comes to your wife actively and intently listening is more precious than gold.

"Every time you talk to your wife, your mind should remember that this conversation will be recorded for training and quality purposes." Unknown.

What does this have to do with sex?

Since it all goes back to a woman's *mind;* the answer is *everything.* A wife is capable of impeccably recalling every word and event when she felt disrespected or ignored. Husbands, work on the quality and quantity of your communication skills. What you say, how you say it and how you behave will determine the quality and quantity of your love-making.

"A gentle answer deflects anger, but harsh words make tempers flare. The tongue of the wise makes knowledge appealing, but the mouth of a fool belches out foolishness." Proverbs 15:1-2.

Appreciation:

Honor each other 24/7 if you want a great sexual relationship as a married couple. When you cherish your partner, you are laying the groundwork for not only a great marriage, but awesome physical sex, too. Husbands, you are to compliment your woman, put her on a pedestal, make her feel safe, provide for her, protect her and always be faithful.

In return, she will love, respect, spoil, look after you and be sexy too! Appreciation works both ways. She will more than reciprocate.

"For husbands, this means love your wives, just as Christ loved the church (Christ died for His church). He gave up his life for her to make her holy and clean, washed by the cleansing of God's word. He did this to present her to himself as a glorious church without a spot or wrinkle or any other blemish." Ephesians 5:25-27.

Honesty:

If you want to lose a partner, friend or business associate; lie to them. The #1 marriage breaker is dishonesty. Once trust is broken, it is almost impossible to piece back together. Yes, honesty is like Humpty Dumpty. He had a great fall, remember? Good luck with repairing the damage and making it whole again.

"An honest answer is like a kiss of friendship." Proverbs 24:26.

A recent study involving couples who have been married more than 30 years revealed a staggering truth as to why they succeeded. Can you guess what behavior, word or phrase was the secret to their ability to stay together?

First, here are some logical guesses: *financial stability, communication, fulfilling sex, unconditional love, being best friends and having wonderful children.*

While all of these concepts are critical to a great marriage none of these were the #1 reason. Give up?

The successful married couples surveyed revealed that the *main* reason they remained married was because, **their partner made them feel safe.**

That reason resonates with logic when you think about it. When you are in a committed relationship, as powerful and passionate as marriage, where you are giving everything you have and putting the other person first, you are vulnerable. Knowing you are *safe* is vitally important with all the temptations and dangers out there in this treacherous world.

What made it possible for these couples to always feel safe with each other? The answer is *honesty.* Their foundation is that they always trust each other and never doubt the love of their partner. Honesty must undergird every moment and aspect of love.

Common Interests:

This category includes shared activities, fun, goals, and dreams; two people, as one, inspiring and encouraging each other to greater meaning, joy and accomplishments!

One of the main reasons that a man and a woman marry is because they believe they can accomplish more *together* than they can alone. Not to mention, that one-of-a-kind feeling, experience and explosion of emotions that gives you the "anything is possible" attitude.

It begins with common interests. What do you have in common and enjoy doing together? Without specific search criteria how will you know when you find the treasure? Heck, even Google is only as accurate as the search criteria you enter. So, here is a starter list, in no particular order, for you to look over and tailor-make for your partner search.

-Religious beliefs and habits; relationship with God
-Life priorities, financial goals, career objectives, values, morals
-Family, relative and children expectations
-What makes you joyful, happy and content
-Types of recreation, hobbies, outdoor activities, travel

-Indoor pleasures (TV, movies, reading, games, hobbies, music)
-Entertaining others, social needs (how, whom and frequency)
-Food and beverage favorites, health goals, exercise preferences
-Dreams, fantasies, long-term goals
-Generosity, who or what are you inspired to support
-The "spark" that allows you to put the other person first?

This will get you started toward understanding your own needs and priorities, as well as, those of your potential life partner. Now, *refine* it for your personal needs as a couple. The goal is *shared love* and joy, not perfection.

Are things you do together sexy? Very much so! Sex is the bonding of a man and a woman in every area of life. These bonds are more than physical; they are daily activities and habits that you imprint upon each other's hearts.

For example, my wife and I are well matched in the areas of family, finances, outdoor activities, health, Christian faith, food, travel and overall priorities. We are less well aligned on tidiness, emotions, and I have children from a previous marriage and she never wanted kids of her own. We are a great team and complement each other, which makes our relationship much happier and forever meaningful.

The Ability to Argue:

Nothing stops love or great sex in a marriage than an ugly argument. Couples need boundaries and guidelines for conducting useful debates, problem solving and disagreements.

Resolving conflicts and problems is an important skill to develop. It requires hard work, discipline and love. Here are some tips on how to argue with your spouse or friend to minimize emotional damage and reach a speedy, mutually beneficial conclusion.

Remember that most arguments are about ego; not major issues. Be willing to swallow your pride and compromise. Even better, let it go; don't even bring it up in the first place.

Never attack *personally*. Keep the argument impersonal and factual. Reconciliation and understanding is the goal, not *winning*.

Remember you are debating with the person you treasure most in your life. The goal is to grow closer together.

If the argument is about either one of you lying there is NO argument; just apologize and promise not to lie again. Trust is impossible without absolute honesty.

It is each person's responsibility to completely tell the other what they don't understand or need. Then the other person is responsible for saying what they can and cannot do to help meet the other's needs.

Listen more than talk. Let your spouse finish their statement before you launch your rebuttal. Be respectful and value each other's thoughts, opinions and emotions. If you end up in an argument with your spouse who refuses to be respectful and truthful, don't participate until they can.

Stay within the *boundaries* of the subject; don't bring up issues from the past. Stay on topic. Resolve one argument at a time. Additionally, you are only qualified to say how you feel and what you believe, not what the other should believe, feel or do according to you.

Once you both begin to repeat your main points the argument is officially over. Time to kiss, lovingly reach out, make up and have some ice cream.

"A hot-tempered person starts fights; a cool-tempered person stops them." Proverbs 15:18.

There are millions of married couples who have great marriages, but simply argue too much. Consciously ask yourself, "Is this disagreement worth an argument?" Does this issue really matter or should I just let it go? Many disagreements are not worth the time and potential downside of an argument.

Fun:

Never stop having fun together! Be teenagers, do silly and spontaneous things as creatively as you can muster. Be unpredictable, poetic, daring, goofy, childlike, inventive and crazy when the occasion calls for it. Couples who have fun are not only special, but also happy!

Go to amusement parks, have picnics, take long drives, watch sunsets and rises, hike, bike, walk in the rain, kiss under the moon, sing songs, take a dance class, make out at the movies, don't limit sex to the bedroom, wear crazy outfits in public, hold hands everywhere, do all your favorite things and do them *often.*

Is having fun together *sexy?* You bet it is!

Physical Sex:

God created sex and told us why, "Be fruitful and multiply." Sex as the Bible describes it is unbeatable. You see physical sex is not simply inconsequential entertainment or a momentary feeling of exuberance. It is much deeper and long lasting than most understand. The physical act creates a bond, intimacy and connection that should last forever.

You don't need Hollywood fantasies, affairs or pornography to enjoy great sex. Romance between two people who are truly in a committed marriage is the key to fantastic sexual intimacy.

How many happy, proud and fulfilled prostitutes have you met? Why do men brag about their sexual conquests, yet inevitably state they are looking for that one special person? How many stories have you heard about devastated individuals who have been hurt deeply by relationships that were based only on sex? The teachings of the Bible are the only way to achieve a meaningful, lifelong and fulfilling sex life – between a married man and women. You will never outthink or outwit God on this topic.

"Drink water from your own well – share your love only with your wife. Why spill the water of our springs in the streets, having sex with just anyone?" Proverbs 5:15-16.

The Bible warns of the consequences of inappropriate sex throughout the Bible, here are a few to check out: **1 Corinthians 6:9, 2 Corinthians 12:21 and Galatians 5:19-23.** There is no doubt in my mind that the Bible is correct.

What do you believe?

Fortunately, for those of us who have sinned sexually, there is the grace and forgiveness of God. I now follow the Bible's teachings on marriage and sex.

"He is especially hard on those who follow their own twisted sexual desire, and who despise authority. These people are proud and arrogant, daring even to scoff at supernatural beings without so much as trembling." 2 Peter 2:10.

You can successfully create a marriage and a sex life that the rest of the world will envy and is relentlessly looking for. Sex in marriage is important because it increases bonding, imprinting and closeness. Following society's formulas for relationships, marriage and sex is based on Hollywood, lust and humanism - all dead ends.

"Give honor to marriage and remain faithful to one another in marriage. God will surely judge people who are immoral and those who commit adultery." Hebrews 13:4.

Thus, if you are married, God *expects* you and your spouse to enjoy sex. If you are not married, then you must abstain from sex or unpleasant consequences will follow. Sex inside of marriage was designed by God; sex outside of marriage is disastrous in emotional, psychological, spiritual and physical ways. Admittedly, this is a tough commandment so why even try?

Because the Bible tells us to obey,

"God's will is for you to be holy, so stay away from all sexual sin. Then each of you will control his own body and live in holiness and honor – not in lustful passion like the pagans who do not know God and his ways. Never harm or cheat a Christian brother in this matter by violating his wife, for the Lord avenges all such sins, as we solemnly warned you before. God has called us to live holy lives, not impure lives." 1 Thessalonians 4:3-7.

God created sex, which proves He knows how to make something fantastic, irresistible and completely satisfying. It's like nothing else on earth! Who said God is boring, constraining or uncreative?

"Sex without love is as hollow and ridiculous as love without sex." Hunter S. Thompson, journalist and author.

Take Away: We have become a society based on free, uncommitted, meaningless sex. Instead of enjoying fantastic, unconditional love, romance and sex; we have settled for instant gratification, lust and short-term liaisons with virtual strangers. It is imposter sex, fool's gold, empty, throw-away sex. We must focus on committed, long-term, happily married couples who love each other and show it. Enjoy sex God's way and both of you will be much more secure, content, joyous and together for eternity.

"Let there be no sexual immorality, impurity, or greed among you. Such sins have no place among God's people. Obscene stories, foolish talk, and coarse jokes – these are not for you. Instead, let there be thankfulness to God." Ephesians 5:3-4.

You and your spouse are in a "one of a kind relationship"! Believe it and use your marriage to live a blessed and sexy life, honoring each other in and out of the marriage bed.

The Power of Love

The boyfriend grabbed her hand and held it tightly, and *she* thought, "He finally admits that he loves me!" And *he thought*, "Wow, this sidewalk is really slippery!"

"Love" is the most misunderstood word in human expression. Understanding it is like *learning* calculus, *achieving* it is like climbing a glass mountain in steel cleats and *trusting* it is like walking along the rim of the Grand Canyon blindfolded.

Most of us have little idea what love is. One thing is for sure, there can be no true love without humility, honesty, trust and respect. You must also be vulnerable, commit to faithfulness and risk rejection to discover true love with another person.

There are no guarantees or warranties when you honestly and completely give yourself and your heart to another individual. You risk humiliation and a broken heart in the hope of finding that one soul mate who will change your life forever.

"A soulmate is someone who has locks that fit our keys, and keys to fit our locks. When we feel safe enough to open the locks, our truest selves step out and we can be completely and honestly who we are; we can be loved for who we are and not for who we're pretending to be. Each unveils the best part of the other. No matter what else goes wrong around us, with that one person, we're safe in our own paradise." Richard Bach, author.

Fully comprehending and explaining love is difficult, if not impossible. In our modern culture the word "love" has many meanings, fantasies and lots of baggage.

In an average day we might use the elusive word several times and none of them are remotely related to each other:

> **I love chocolate!**
> **I love reading a good book!**
> **I love Super Bowl parties!**

I love my cat!
I love walking on the beach.
I love you, honey!

See my point? We completely debase and obscure love by using it universally to describe everything.

Everyone wants true love often chasing it wherever it takes them. Those who say they don't need love or have given up on it are lying, bitter, hurt or naïve. They have never experienced unconditional love.

Honest love is not easy. Thus, people frequently settle for a less satisfying and hazardous substitute for true love. Genuine love can only be initiated by a brave, self-assured, humble person willing to put another person *first,* hoping that first risky step and the ones that follow will result in that rare encounter of unconditional love between a man and a woman.

"Money cannot buy love, but it can put you in a good bargaining position." Evan Esar, humorist.

"And we are never too old to study the Bible. Each time the lessons are studied comes some new meaning., some new thought which will make us better." John D. Rockefeller, businessman and philanthropist.

The Apostle Paul penned the epic "Love Chapter" in **1 Corinthians 13**; clearly defining the true nature of love. I have read it over and over and gain new perspectives, understanding and insight every time. I strongly urge you do the same. Here is an excerpt from that infinitely beautiful set of verses.

"If I gave everything I have to the poor and even sacrificed my body, I could boast about it; but if I didn't love others, I would have gained nothing." 1 Corinthians 13:3.

Love is not mere feelings or a temporary, off-the-chart dopamine rush; it is consistently and selflessly helping the one you care for to be all they can without expecting anything in return. It is an uninhibited journey all about intentional giving. Love of this type is infrequent in today's *"Me first"* society. Real love is effortful, it is not a fantasy relationship you fall in to and live happily ever after.

As the Beatles sang, **"And in the end, the love you take is equal to the love you make."** The sentiment expressed in this song is exactly right. It is more purely expressed than the majority of the desires expressed in most sex-dominated and "happy ever after" love songs!

"Love is the will to extend one's self for the purpose of nurturing one's own or another's spiritual growth ... Love is as love does. Love is an act of will – namely, both an intention and an action. Will also implies choice. We do not have to love. We *choose* to love." M. Scott Peck, psychiatrist and author.

So, if you don't learn and develop your capacity and skills to give love fully, you are missing the indispensable and best part of life itself.

The purpose of life is to love God and love others.

Unconditional love is supernatural, surreal and only from God. Perhaps love can't be explained, only *experienced.* Thus, it is truly most often *"The Road Not Taken,"* as poetically expressed by Robert Frost. The poems closing line is *"I took the one less traveled by, And that has made all the difference."*

Or, as this quote so eloquently puts it: **"Missing you is my hobby, caring for you is my job, making you happy is my duty and loving you is my life."** Anonymous.

Merely thinking of love doesn't convey love to anyone. If you want to truly love others, your attitude and personality must be clearly and repeatedly revealed through loving *words, choices* and *behaviors.* I have learned that what is in my heart only counts when I express it through actions and words.

"Dear children, let us not love with words or speech but with actions and in truth." 1 John 3:18.

Love is as love does. Love can be inconvenient, requiring trust and work. We all want to experience unconditional love, but very few are willing to do the *hard work* that true love requires to follow through on that dream, hence, our 50% divorce rate. When two individuals do step up and love unselfishly, the reward is astonishing. Everyone notices because we so seldom actually see or experience selfless love in action.

God's love for us is unconditional. However, most human love is conditional, we all want something first or in return. Love must be a top priority to excel and last. My experience is that if you have a spouse and family you quickly run out of time and energy. And, we all know that "new love" is all consuming. You are forced to set priorities for who you can love. If you don't, you will have a mediocre marriage, neglected kids, upset friends and/or a life of loneliness. Because, no one can honestly love everyone - you don't have unlimited energy or time.

You cannot truly love everyone because *selfless love is simultaneously inspiring and exhausting.* It takes all out physical, mental and emotional effort and, thus, must be reserved for only a few people in your "inner circle". You need to: hug; listen intently; care for; surprise; perform mundane tasks without being asked; tell her she is beautiful without make-up or when he hasn't shaved; consistently call, text or email for no reason except to say I miss you.

You may, at times, wonder why bother. But, the ongoing exuberant sensation and rewarding relationship will be mutually fulfilling as nothing else can be. I have found that the more I do in loving my wife, the more I want to do. Your partner will be so blessed that they will return the love *multiplied.* Over time, the synergy, of both your actions, will create a relationship much bigger than either of you. And, you can't fully understand or explain it but, you don't need to. It's love.

"The heart has its reasons, which reason does not know at all." Blaise Pascal, French mathematician.

In reality, true love is a choice and an action. The world has, in its usual distorted, shallow, immediate gratification way turned it around to be a selfish, perverse act of only brief excitement for oneself; an egotistical, one-sided version of selfish pleasure. While physically enjoyable, it is a counterfeit. Love is much more than feelings, a sexual urge, a few well-chosen words or red roses. The contemporary phrase, "falling into love" implies it is out of your control, thus the love could end outside of your control. It is a modern myth.

Dependable love is not an accident, you don't 'fall into it', you intentionally initiate loving actions. Honest love is best demonstrated when you choose to serve and help another in meaningful, giving and completely unselfish ways. It is a relationship where you always want joy and success for the other person. Authentic love purposely decides to take action, expressing your love for the other person. If you are not spending a lot of time with and paying undivided attention to your spouse, children and close friends, you don't love them. Do you give your spouse undivided attention, do you play with your children, are you developing deep friendships?

All relationships, romantic or otherwise, will be significantly better when you intentionally put others first. Magically others will like you more for helping and treating them so well. Society preaches love is about you and what you can *get* from a relationship. The Bible is clear that love is about you serving another person.

"For you have been called to live in freedom, my brothers and sisters. But don't use your freedom to satisfy your sinful nature (self-indulgence). Instead, use your freedom to serve one another in love." Galatians 5:13.

If you believe you can explain love, you have most likely never genuinely experience it. Matters of the heart and faith require no proof. Purely human experiences, like love, morals, judgement and faith are exactly what make us human. We know, feel, express and experience significantly more than any other life form. Love is unique to humans.

What is your understanding of love? How have your "loving" relationships worked out?

Four types of Love

It's time to see if we can make a modicum of sense of what love is and the numerous variations of love. So, let's go back to the beginning and examine the original types of love brought to the world by God through the Greeks. There are four types of love: **Eros, storge, phileo and agape.**

Eros love is named after the mythical Greek god of love and is based upon sexual and physical desire. In contemporary terms, it is known as Hollywood love, the kind of attraction we see in romantic movies, television shows and romance novels. It represents a sensual feeling and is physically based.

The words, "erotic" and, "erotica" come from this root word. These definitions relate more to sex, lust and pornography, than the healthy love we need as human beings.

Eros "love" is all about self-centered lust, infatuation and satisfaction. It is not really love at all despite what Hollywood portrays to the world.

Hooray for Hollywood. (sense the sarcasm here?)

We are often willing to sacrifice moral principles and use others in order to selfishly experience that brief, physical excitement. Today many have downgraded love to a physical act no different than a thrill ride at a carnival. Erotic's say, "Let's make love." The truth is you cannot make love you can only give love. Erotic love often leads to emotional hurt, distrust, disease and it never lasts.

Storge, the 2nd type of love, is the love a parent has for a child. **It is a deep family affection** that comforts us and helps us feel connected to our immediate family and all our extended spiritual family.

Of course, I love members of my immediate family. This is expressed primarily in two ways: I love my children because they are my kids; I can also love them, in a deeper way, because of who they are as individuals. The first is instinctual; the second is a choice I make to love them for the unique individuals they are.

Phileo love, is a deep, abiding love between **friends.** The Old Testament relationship between David and Jonathan is a perfect example of phileo love.

"After David had finished talking with Saul, he met Jonathan, the king's son. There was an immediate bond between them, for Jonathan loved David. From that day on Saul kept David with him and

wouldn't let him return home. And Jonathan made a solemn pact with David, because he loved him as he loved himself." 1 Samuel 18:1-3.

I experienced this type of love after moving to a new city, attending a new church and men's group. I met one of the men from the men's group, the first time, to have coffee. After a great conversation, we walked to the parking lot and my car did not start. My new friend unselfishly spent the next two hours helping me diagnose the problem, get a new battery and install it. He is my image of phileo love.

Agape love, the final Greek word for love, is the most powerful and the most prevalent in the Bible. **God's love** for us is agape love. It is the most self-sacrificing love there is. This type of love was displayed by Jesus Christ. Agape love involves faithfulness, giving, commitment and an act of the will.

Unconditional love is beautifully described in 1 Corinthians 13.

"Love is patient and kind. Love is not jealous or boastful or proud or rude. It does not demand its own way. It is not irritable, and it keeps no record of being wronged. It does not rejoice about injustice but rejoices whenever the truth wins out. Love never gives up, never loses faith, is always hopeful, and endures through every circumstance. Prophecy and speaking in unknown languages and special knowledge will become useless. But love will last forever!" 1 Corinthians 13:4-8.

Agape is a sacrificial love that voluntarily serves others, endures inconvenience, discomfort and even death for the benefit of another without expecting anything in return. We are called to love others in the same way as Christ loves us.

"Imitate God, therefore, in everything you do, because you are his dear children. Live a life filled with love, following the example of Christ. He loved us and offered himself as a sacrifice for us, a pleasing aroma to God." Ephesians 5:1-2.

Agape love does not depend on your love interest; it is contingent upon you, the giver of love. It is *not* a bargain we make expecting something in return, rather a gift we freely give expecting *nothing*. Jesus said:

"This is my commandment: Love each other in the same way have loved you. There is no greater love than to lay down one's life for one's friends. You are my friends if you do what I command." John 15:12-14.

The Greeks were so overwhelmed by this type of love they had to coin an entirely new word for it. Describing sexual, friendship and family love was easy for their genius intellect, but agape love was beyond the range of their intellectual scholarship.

How can anyone comprehend unconditional love, especially to the point of dying in someone else's place?

Regardless of the type of love, it is the universal glue, link and expression that connects everyone. Love is the only way to develop sincere relationships, help people and really live.

I have been amazed by what happens when I pay attention to someone and love them unconditionally. It has frequently led to great outcomes that I cannot adequately explain. The initial shallow **Eros** love that led to **agape** love with my wife continues to surprise, encourage and humble me. The **storgy** love I experience with my children is rewarding beyond understanding. The **phileo** love I have with a handful of friends is amazing. God's Agape love for me is beyond comprehension.

Love is the most powerful force on earth. When I first read this, it struck me as an exaggerated and hyped up statement. But, this is the real deal. Meaningful love is greater than a simple friendship or causal relationship. Love is more important than power, achievement, acquisition and popularity. It is much greater than any physical or mental experience. Agape love leads the way.

"For love is as strong as death, its jealousy as enduring as the grave. Love flashes like fire, the brightest kind of flame. Many waters cannot quench love, nor can rivers drown it. If a man tried to buy love with all his wealth, his offer would be utterly scorned." Song of Songs 8:6-7.

God loves us not because we are lovable, but because God *is* love. If it were any other way, God's love would be conditional. If you were nicer or performed better, would God love you more? No, of course not! God's love for us is not based on our performance, but on *His* character and love. Therefore, we can never lose His love under any conditions.

"Then Christ will make his home in your hearts as you trust in him. Your roots (understanding) will grow down into God's love and keep you strong. And may you have the power to understand, as all God's people should, how wide, how long, how high, and how deep his love is. May you experience the love of Christ, though it is too great to understand fully. Then you will be made complete with all the fullness of life and power that comes from God." Ephesians 3:17-19.

I only have agape love for my wife, children, brother, mom and in-laws. I try to love others that way as well, but it takes a lot of time, effort and discipline and I quickly run out of all three. It is up to me, not the other person. Love is intentional and effortful!

Only you can decide to love someone. The freedom to love or not love another individual is the ultimate human choice. We are the only living creatures that actually love as the Bible defines love. You have the power to choose, with every thought and interaction, how much love to give.

True love is premeditated, an act of the *will* that you consistently do deliberately; not accidentally. Smart individuals knowingly think through all important choices, including who to love and how to love Eros, storge, phileo or agape. They love as the Bible instructs, not the world.

Ultimately, God's love offers the greatest rewards of forgiveness, grace, a meaningful life on earth and eternity. To avoid love or only give conditional love is to miss your purpose for being alive.

A recent daily devotional from "The Upper Room," talked about the transforming power of Agape love. The Bible says there are *three* ingredients that are essential to knowing God personally.

First, sense and accept that God's love always accompanies us.

Second, love ourselves, knowing that we are loved, thus, liberated from self-doubt, fear and filled with hope.

Third, we then have the courage and capacity to offer and give unconditional love to others.

The devotional went on to describe how we all experience acts of love and kindness daily through smiles, hugs, encouraging comments and service. We have opportunities every day to make a difference in others' lives. If enough of us share unconditional love with others, all the world's people will know that they are valued. A simple smile, a little sympathy, mercy or generosity will ricochet around the world or at least through your neighborhood, place of work and family.

The devotional closed with, *"Where do I see opportunities to love my neighbors?"* It was a new mindset for me, to think in terms of how I can *intentionally* search for opportunities to not only be nice, but overtly love and encourage others. I have tried this and when I express love with a simple smile or a kind deed, the experience is always overwhelmingly positive and, occasionally, transformational. That is because kindness is love in action! Be someone's hero, encouragement and inspiration today.

"Most important of all, continue to show deep love for each other, for love covers a multitude of sins." 1 Peter 4:8.

Your smile is the most powerful expression and communication tool you have. Smiling is the best first impression you can make. I have seen a smile and kind word change the outcome of a tense situation. Additionally, studies show that people who smile are healthier, happier and more successful.

Are you smiling?

Here is another interesting description of love from the novel, ***"Corelli's Mandolin"*** by Louis de Bernieres. He wrote about a dad talking to his daughter about the love between he and her mother.

"Love is a temporary madness. It erupts like an earthquake and then subsides. And, when it subsides you have to make a decision. You have to work out whether your roots have become so

entwined together to the point where it is inconceivable that you should ever part.

Because this is what love is. Love is not breathless, it is not excitement, it is not the promulgation of promises of eternal passion. That is just being "in love," which any of us can convince ourselves we are.

Love itself is what is left over when being in love has burned away and this is both an art and a fortunate accident.

Your mother and I had it, we had roots that grew towards each other underground and when all the pretty blossoms had fallen from our branches we found that we were one tree and not two."

I like how de Bernieres describes their initial love, *"Love is temporary madness,"* and eventually *"subsides"*. Also, how he defined love as a *"decision."* Love is not *"being in love"*, rather *"what is left over when being in love has burned away."*

Also, that love is *"both an art and a fortunate accident"* that we do not completely understand. And, how *"roots grew towards each other,"* implying that you decide to love and move toward each other. Even after *"all the pretty blossoms had fallen from our branches,"* saying after our physical beauty leaves us, long-term love continues to grow, like roots; part mystery and goes on forever, eventually becoming oneness, *"one tree and not two."* Louis understands love!

While, I don't claim to fully understand unconditional love, it has forever changed me in powerful, significant and meaningful ways.

How else can I explain the exuberant sensation of being totally consumed, joyful, content and alive, when I am with my spouse? It is joyful, spontaneous and effortless. I just know I love her unconditionally and I wouldn't want it any other way. I look forward to every morning and inventing our day together. It is not possible to be together too much. I am getting so much out of our relationship that even though I do a lot for her, I look forward to doing more. I want her to grow into all she is meant to become.

"Love doesn't make the world go round; love is what makes the ride worthwhile." Franklin P. Jones, humorist.

Other couples and individuals have told us they see love in our behaviors, expressions and words. Of course, that is exactly what love produces – choices in the form of words and behaviors that help and encourage spouses and others to thrive. I can't fully express how euphoric it feels to have someone tell me they can actually see the love between my wife and me!

"To be happy with a man, you must understand him a lot and love him a little. To be happy with a woman, you must love her a lot and not try to understand her at all." Helen Rowland, writer.

"Be on guard. Stand firm in the faith. Be Courageous. Be strong. And do everything with love." 1 Corinthians 16:13-14.

Victor Hugo, a French poet and novelist wrote *"Les Misérables"* and *"The Hunchback of Notre-Dame"* and proclaimed, **"To love another person is to see the face of God."**

Take Away: Jesus expressed His deep love for His disciples and the entire world by dying on the cross. If Jesus can do this, it seems obvious that we can love unconditionally, be kind, merciful and compassionate to help those in need. No service or expression is beneath you when you understand the meaning and impact of unconditional love. Regardless of who the recipient is, it's best demonstrated through acts and words of kindness, service and attention.

"Don't just pretend to love others. Really love them. Hate what is wrong. Hold tightly to what is good. Love each other with genuine affection and take delight in honoring each other. Never be lazy, but work hard and serve the Lord enthusiastically." Romans 12:9-11.

The Power of Love. Believe it.

Your Life Purpose

You Are Unique

"YOU are one of a kind. You are lucky enough to have something that makes you different from everyone else. Embrace your individuality. You are amazing just the way you are." Melchor Lim, author.

Nice quote. Here is God's version of it, as stated by King David.

"Thank you for making me so wonderfully complex! Your workmanship is marvelous – how well I know it." Psalm 139:14.

While we each create our own, special unique lives, much of what we experience is very similar. Consider we all encounter the same never-ending series of: surprises/disappointments, successes/failures, relational problems/closeness, opportunities/road-blocks, health/illness, grief/joy, hate/love and numerous encounters with both friendly and unfriendly people.

"It is only because of problems that we grow mentally and spiritually." M. Scott Peck, Psychiatrist and author.

In these everyday circumstances, we are hardly unique. What demonstrates our uniqueness is how we *choose* to react to each life situation. Our individual responses to ordinary occurrences are ultimately what matters most and expresses our individuality. We have a choice to respond negatively, apathetically or with kindness and compassion. We are each responsible for our lives and choices, which ultimately determines who we become, what we accomplish and how others perceive us.

When I read a memoir or talk with someone, what is most interesting and informative to me is not so much what they experienced, but rather how they assessed and responded to each encounter. How did they manage themselves through both good and difficult times? Three people presented with the same circumstances are likely to each respond *differently*. We have all heard about individuals presented with life-changing situations - a few persevere and end up on the high road, while others fail utterly or languish in uncertainty.

We continuously calibrate our evaluation and judgment "antennae" based on our parents, siblings, friends, work associates, the media and social influences throughout life's evolution. Because we have powerful brains, we get to make dozens of choices every day. The discernment we use to interpret and then decide how to respond to life determines the depth or shallowness of our accumulated wisdom.

"This foolish plan of God is wiser than the wisest of human plans, and God's weakness is stronger than the greatest of human strength." 1 Corinthians 1:25.

For some reason, most people are obsessed with trying to be normal, to fit in and not stand out in an effort to downplay their uniqueness. Why is this? Are we not *all* special in our own way? You were created to stand out, not blend in!

We all start out as originals. But, from the time we are born we *observe, compare* and *copy* our parent's, friend's and society's mannerisms, speech and opinions. We learn how to behave in various situations, what to say and all the other expectations for "normal" people. Some of this is good because "mirroring" the majority of society keeps us out of trouble, but it can also limit our unique, delightful and beautiful individuality. The key is to balance both finding your place in society, while simultaneously developing your uniqueness.

The *social trinity* of our existence is **conformity, image and fitting in**. If your uniqueness disappears into a morass of other people's expectations, you miss your calling and others won't benefit from what you bring to them. This was not what God intended for your life.

 **"For we are God's masterpiece."** Ephesians 2:10.

A masterpiece would never be mistaken for a cookie cutter or a copy of the ordinary. Looking, dressing, talking and behaving like most people around us is not an acknowledgement of God's hand-crafted creation; but a rebuke of it. Unfortunately, too many of us bring a memorable bumper sticker to life:

"You are *Unique*; just like everyone else." Bumper Sticker.

Being unique is not a limitation; rather a blessing for you and others.

Our desire to improve on ourselves in order to impress the world through our own machinations regularly ends in distortion and disaster. History has shown us this time and time again. Famous individuals and actors often sabotage their careers by not being satisfied with their physical uniqueness.

Jennifer Gray was popular having starred in, ***"Dirty Dancing"*** and, ***"Ferris Bueller's Day Off."***

But, she didn't like her nose. So, she underwent rhinoplasty and had it "fixed." It radically changed her unique look. It also dramatically affected her acting career and not in a good way. She lost her signature appearance and resembled thousands of other, "look alike," actresses who had "normal" noses and unmemorable physical features. Jennifer has not had a hit movie since her surgery.

Being unique is not limited to individuals, the corporate world is vulnerable, too. The 1955 Ford Thunderbird was considered one of the world's most unique cars ever made. However, they kept "normalizing" its unique signature looks right out of existence. It was no longer extraordinary. It evolved into being rather bland, ordinary and unremarkable, just like every other vehicle.

Coca-Cola, the most prestigious and popular soft drink in the world, made the same mistake. In 1985, the company decided to stray from the unique taste that had established them and invented something called, *"New Coke,"*. It was a disaster. Within months, the executives at Coca-Cola were scrambling to return to the original flavor that had made them famous. They realized, when it came to the public, that Pepsi was not their problem, *they* were the problem.

Whether you are an individual or corporation, **be proud of who you are.** Continue to grow and develop your unique self, learn throughout your life and as a result, unless you're a serial criminal, you will love who you are.

"So God created human beings in his own image. In the image of God he created them; male and female he created them." Genesis 1:27.

God created you exclusively, possessing a one-of-a-kind mix of personality, physical, emotional, talents, treasures and potential, unique to *only* you. You can only fulfill your purpose when you accept and leverage your exceptional, authentic self. Attempting to be like anyone else only limits you, your potential and God's plan for your life.

That doesn't mean you shouldn't learn from others, just don't emulate, envy or attempt to behave exactly like them. God specifically created you to be yourself and He has a magnificent plan for your life which can only be accomplished by you; no one else. You will never be successful by being the authentic, genuine *somebody else*!

"Envy is ignorance, imitation is suicide." Ralph Waldo Emerson.

Trust God, be who He says you are.

"Popularity isn't just something that happens. You have to give something in exchange for it, and that's the dangerous part of the process." Robert Bringhurst, Canadian author and poet.

Sharing your genuine inner self is a gift only you can give to others. The more you are able to share your one-of-a-kind beliefs, hopes and talents with those around you the more you will realize how amazing and useful you are to the world. On the other hand, the more you pretend to be someone else, the less growth and more frustration you will experience.

Why do we naturally possess an image of ourselves, yet try to conform to society or others demands? It is because we think everyone else is a normal, full functioning, happy adult, when in fact, they have the same or more insecurities and anxieties than we do. We are all a little "crazy" in our own unique way. Individuals who make pleasing others a priority can end up with mental disorders because their true self-image is in conflict with their external behaviors.

"To be yourself in a world that is constantly trying to make you something else is the greatest accomplishment." Ralph Waldo Emerson, essayist and poet.

Everyone is insecure! I have been insecure my entire life. In younger years I hid my insecurities. Now I admit them so I can learn, grow and help others do the same. It turns out that exposing your insecurities, weaknesses and worries is the beginning of enlightenment.

When you look in the mirror and believe you are ugly, you may not realize it, but it is an indictment against your Creator who carefully made you. God did not make a mistake, but you might be making one. Never criticize yourself. Rather be grateful, smile at who you are and be at peace and confident in your uniqueness.

"Since everything God created is good, we should not reject any of it but receive it with thanks. For we know it is made acceptable by the word of God and prayer." 1 Timothy 4:4-5.

You and I are individually blessed by God and the Bible. Think about that for a moment. There is nothing about us that is a "mistake." We are intentionally and fearfully made by the same loving God who designed the magnificent universe.

"For God has not given us a spirit of fear and timidity, but of power, love and self-discipline." 2 Timothy 1:7.

Success and blessings come from applying your uniqueness to developing distinctive relationships with others. There are individuals and situations in your life and neighborhood that *only you* and your special combination of personality, appearance, experiences and talents can reach to provide hope.

Society's short-term, quirky lifestyles and trends may at times be fun, but don't rely on them to determine who you are, nor to find purpose for your life. There is no better source than the Bible to learn about how to interpret life and discover your exceptional self. The entire Bible, especially the book of **Proverbs**, is filled with wisdom on how to productively live the life God "shaped" you for.

I don't have to conform to the world to understand reality. Rather acquiring and developing a divine perspective reveals the meaning of life. It does require continuous study, obedience and effort, but it is the only genuine and meaningful way to live.

If you twist or deny reality, to justify your behavior, you are living in fantasy land. Attempts to escape or avoid reality never lead to meaningful outcomes. Many try to evolve by changing their geography, job, appearance and relationships, only to find out that what really matters has not changed at all. That is because wherever **you** are, whatever **your** situation, *you* are still there! To live a meaningful life, **you** must change. You succeed being your genuine self and reading the Bible.

When you rely exclusively on yourself, someone or something else to meet your needs for self-worth and meaning in life, you are replacing God. It is only as your expectations and plans are in alignment with earthly realities and the Bible's truth, that life is actualized.

"Reality is merely an illusion, albeit a very persistent one." Albert Einstein, Theoretical physicist.

Take Away: We were individually created and the Bible was written to direct you in how to make the absolute most of your special life. Only you can be *you!* You can only achieve God's special plan for you by being the genuine person God created you to be. You are not just rare, but "one of a kind". Use your uniqueness to live a blessed life, honor God and inspire everyone you encounter. Study the Bible daily and apply it directly to the issues and opportunities in your life. The Bible holds the truths that can release meaning and purpose in your special life.

"Our identity crisis cannot be resolved without accepting the truth that we are created in the image of God." Catherine Skurja, author.

Who do you trust to learn and know who you are and what you are meant to become? Do you trust the Bible, yourself or society?

Why are You Here?

"We are here on earth to do good for others. What the others are here for, I don't know." W.H. Auden, poet.

Even those of us who are only marginally introspective, have speculated what the point of life is all about. The question of why we are on this earth is a valid one and cannot be satisfied with a glib response. It is a powerful, potentially life-altering revelation and deserves our full attention to honestly answer the probing questions.

Why am I here; do I have a purpose for existing?
Is there any meaning to life?
Is there a specific plan for the earth and, specifically, me?
Is life, earth and the universe just a huge, random accident?
Are we simply here to live a few years and die?

These are a few of the biggest, most perplexing and often unanswered questions for each of us. Unfortunately, most people are simply apathetic, too busy or see no value in understanding life. Maybe a lot of folks believe they are the point, the center of everything.

"It's the simple things in life that are the most extraordinary; only wise men are able to understand them." Paulo Coelho, author.

What are the two most important times in your life? Most would say birth and death but, I learned a more insightful proposition: when you are born and when you discover the *purpose* of your life.

Once you know your primary purpose it will become your worldview and foundation for making everyday decisions and rationale for judging everybody and everything. All your smaller day-to-day choices, as well as, other aspects of life will be clarified.

"Once you find your meaning and commit yourself to it, there is no other meaning to you. So, get it right the first time or at least before you die. Your purpose in life is going to make or break you from here to eternity." Anonymous.

Airplane pilots use instruments to fly, sea captains use charts to navigate, hikers use a compass and topographical maps and drivers use maps on their smartphones. Some use our perceived *purpose in life* to guide us, but an untold number of wanderers simply "ad-lib, improvise or fake it." Like GPS, the Bible is the divine code for leading a purposeful life.

What authority, compass or tool do you base your purpose for life upon? Is it a human philosophy, worldly idol, religion, inner sense, belief in nature or do you just wing it?

Rick Warren, the renowned pastor from Saddleback Church in California, says our purpose is not about us, it is all and only about God. God designed and created us, in His image, put us here to have a relationship with us, for His enjoyment and purposes, not ours. Warren's famous line from his book **"A Purpose Driven Life,"** succinctly states, **"It's not about you."**

Similarly, Paul was powerfully terse, **"...everything was created through him and for him."** Colossians 1:16.

"For everything comes from him (God) and exists by his power and is intended for his glory. All glory to him forever!" Romans 11:36.

Warren adds, "All of our *'I'* questions not only reveal our shallowness, but completely miss the point. What do *I* need to become or achieve, how can *I* discover real love, what will allow *me* to possess real wisdom? The way to find your way to a deeply meaningful life is to look upward not inward and ask: *"what does God want me to do to fulfill His plan for me on earth?"*

This is difficult for most to accept and even harder to live by.

"'For I know the plans I have for you,' says the Lord. 'They are plans for good and not for disaster, to give you a future and a hope.'" Jeremiah 29:11.

I have tried self-help books, DVD's, made New Year's resolutions and experimented with an endless array of society's shiny trends. I had a successful career, made money, travelled the world, tried a few drugs, enjoyed sex and rock & roll in the turbulent 60's and productively saw a psychiatrist for a year. Nothing stacks up to the Bible.

At this point it is more difficult to fool me, as I have experienced most of the world's options from the ridiculous to the sublime. I know their meaningless endings. All along, I knew there must be more.

I am not saying to ignore or not take advantage of every learning opportunity. Many worldly activities can make your life better and provide some insight and direction. They provide needed ideas and support to cope with earthly life. However, man-made solutions are usually short-term and of this world only. They cannot take you to your destiny.

I repeatedly discovered that all earthly pleasures, experiences and worldly successes were not enough to satisfy my soul. I knew there had to be *more*. You can reach this conclusion when you hit bottom, at the top of a mountain possessing everything, as well as, every other destination in between. It was not until I discovered that God is the only genuine, complete answer to all my searching and started reading the Bible that "wisdom lights begin to illuminate."

This became even clearer to me when I randomly attended an out of town church service. "Coincidentally," that Sunday, the pastor was concluding a long series of messages on **the purpose of life.**

He began his revelation by summarizing the four life goals he had covered over the previous weeks:

1. Initially meeting God and accepting Jesus as your savior
2. Getting to know God by reading the Bible, praying, attending church and hanging out with other Christians
3. Growing as a Christian by living according to the truths in #2
4. Use your God-given time, talents, resources and influence to serve others and introduce them to Jesus Christ.

Thus, he concluded:

The ultimate purpose of life and why you are here, is to believe there is only one God, to love Him, love others, live by the principles of the Bible and help others to know God.

"There is one God, the Father by whom all things were created, and for whom we live. And there is one Lord, Jesus Christ, through whom all things were created, and through whom we live." 1 Corinthians 8:6.

There was no mumbo-jumbo, no ethereal philosophy, no intellectual wandering and no confusing theology. For the first time in my life God and the Bible began to make a little more sense.

"Today I have given you the choice between life and death, between blessings and curses. Now I call on heaven and earth to witness the choice you make. Oh, that you would chose life, so that you and your descendants might live! You can make this choice by loving the Lord your God, obeying him, and committing yourself firmly to him. This is the key to your life. And if you love and obey the Lord, you will live long in the land the Lord swore to give your ancestors Abraham, Isaac, and Jacob." Deuteronomy 30:19-20.

Notice the choice is yours. Not even God will force you to trust Him. An additional result of your choice, is spending eternity in heaven with God, rather than being eternally separated from Him. Eternity is difficult to grasp, even the Bible says we cannot possibly understand what God has planned for us.

"No eye has seen, no ear has heard, no mind has imagined what God has prepared for those who love him." 1 Corinthians 2:9.

Shortly thereafter, another pastor at Seabreeze Church confirmed our purpose in a similar fashion:

"The great treasure in life, the search for the meaning of life, can *only* be answered by and through God."

When I look back at my life, most of my time had been spent striving to obtain power, wealth and an endless array of earthly possessions. Of course, if you live long enough, you eventually discover, through trial and error, that all your earthly "getting" and all your "inward looking" fail to provide a path to your purpose in life.

The simplest way I can state this dynamic theology is,

📖 The purpose of life is to love God, love others and help everyone to know God. If you perceive, "There's got to be more to life!", than read the Bible because it tells you what that "more" is and how to find it.

You accomplish this by nurturing a one-on-one personal relationship with God and accepting Jesus as your savior. Then, as you read, understand and live your life according to the Bible, you will have a meaningful life. Your long-term reward or bonus for living life God's way is spending eternity with Him.

📖 "But, my life is worth nothing to me unless I use it for finishing the work assigned me by the Lord Jesus – the work of telling others the Good News about the wonderful grace of God." Acts 20:24.

We all need to make sense of our story. All us fragile humans are searching for is to know we are loved, that our life has purpose and how to make a difference in our lifetime. The truth is, there is no other way to find real meaning and purpose in life, except through a personal relationship with God. But, that is *not* how most of the world thinks. From birth, we are relentlessly taught to define and validate our existence through any means possible that does not include God.

"My people are foolish and do not know me, says the Lord. They are stupid children who have no understanding. They are clever enough about doing wrong, but they have no idea how to do right!" Jeremiah 4:22.

We believe we are the 'Center', the purpose of life. We persist at trying to find meaning through our never-ending *earthly* goals, accumulated treasures, self-absorption and pop-psychology, which consistently fails to provide a path to long-term meaning or contentment. We search everywhere, except in the Bible to determine why we are here. Each one of us is a living portal to God and get to choose to "open the door" to Him or ignore Him. It is a choice to live an earth-bound life or aspire to live eternally.

Let's think like a lawyer for a minute. It is called the, "What THEN?" logic for the average person's life in today's society.

You begin by asking the typical young person questions about their life goals:

"Why do you want to graduate from high school?"

"So, I can get into college."

"What THEN?"

"Then, I will get my college diploma."

"What THEN?"

"Then, I'll find a well-paying job, meet my soul mate, get married and start a family."

"What THEN?"

"Then, I will enjoy financial stability, buy a nice house, send my children to college and eventually become a grandparent."

"What THEN?"

"Then, I will eventually retire, travel with my companion and draw Social Security benefits and returns from my investments."

"What THEN?"

"Well, uh...then, I'll die!"

"What THEN?"

"Uh, what do you mean?"

This is the dead-end of life's journey for non-believers if they do not read the Bible and trust God. If you are that person, who never placed God at the center of your life, you are not only out of answers, you are out of options. Only God can reconcile a life, make it whole and give you eternity.

You see there are actually two lives to consider - your *short* earthly life and your *eternal* life. The choices you make during your brief earthly life, determine the destination for your second, forever life. If you have not read the Bible, don't have a relationship with God and Jesus Christ is not your personal savior, you will not spend eternity in heaven. It will not matter how rich, powerful, accomplished or nice you are.

"And what do you benefit if you gain the whole world but lose your own soul? Is anything worth more than your soul?" Matthew 16:26.

As a humanist, atheist, agnostic or any person who does not believe in God, *you* have been the center of your universe and that is going to stop you far short of your earthly destiny, eternity, heaven or whatever you choose to call it; whatever follows death. There is a certain hopelessness that arises from basing your purpose and life's meaning on yourself and worldly authorities.

If your definition of the meaning of life is – **You**, then God has a very direct message for you.

"If you cling to your life, you will lose it; but if you give up your life for me, you will find it." Matthew 10:39.

What are the odds that **You** can power yourself to eternal life?

None and NONE!

If you have made the choice to worship yourself, an idol or someone else, then God will honor your earthly decision on your day of reckoning. God will not be condemning you to hell, He will step back and respect your choice.

"For the word of God is alive and powerful. It is sharper than the sharpest two-edged sword, cutting between soul and spirit, between joint and marrow. It exposes our innermost thoughts and desires. Nothing in all creation is hidden from God. Everything is naked and exposed before his eyes, and he is the one to whom we are accountable." Hebrews 4:12-13.

Therefore, it is imperative that you not only understand your purpose for this life, but also, your eternal life. It is critical that you read and apply the Holy Bible, trust God and accept Christ as your Savior to ensure your place in the next life - eternity with God.

📖 The Blues Brothers were right about one thing, "We're on a mission from God."

Your Earthly Mission

The Great Commandment and the Great Commission tell you all you need to know about God's **plan and purpose for your life.**

The Great Commandment

"You must love the Lord your God with all your heart, all your soul and all your mind. This is the first and greatest commandment. A second is equally important: Love your neighbor as yourself. The entire law and all the demands of the prophets are based on these two commandments." Matthew 22: 37-40.

The Great Commission

"Jesus came and told his disciples, 'I have been given all authority in heaven and on earth. Therefore, go and make disciples (believers) of all the nations, baptizing them in the name of the Father and the Son and the Holy Spirit, (the Trinity). Teach these new disciples to obey all the commands I have given you (in the Bible). And be sure of this: I am with you always, even to the end of the age.'" Matthew 28:18-20.

The Great Commandment and Commission are the specific instructions for how to find purpose and meaning in life. It is why you are here. That is why my first priority, in the Life Priorities and Plans chapter, is My Relationship with God.

Amazingly, more than anything else, God wants a relationship with you on earth and to spend eternity in heaven with you.

"Do not let your hearts be troubled. Trust in God and also in Me (Jesus). There is more than enough room in my Father's home (Heaven). If this were not so, would I have told you that I am going to prepare a place for you? When everything is ready, I will come and get you, so that you will always be with me where I am." John 14:1-3.

Take Away: Now, you know *why* you are here. In a nut shell, you are here to love God and others, share the wisdom of the Bible and make a difference in others lives. But, God lets you make the final choice to choose Him or some other earthly authority as your life's purpose. Choose wisely!

"Serve the Lord alone. But if you refuse to serve the Lord, then choose today whom you will serve. ... But as for me and my family, we will serve the Lord." Joshua 24:14-15.

Partnering with God

Mount Everest is 29,029 feet high. It is the most intimidating peak in the world. 280 people have died trying to scale it. Every year there is at least one fatality among those who believe they can conquer it. It is the ultimate climb.

The best chance to reach the summit is to enlist local native guides, called Sherpas. They are renowned for their knowledge, climbing skills, superior strength and endurance at high altitude. To have any chance at all of reaching the summit, it is wise to enlist the service of a Sherpa. Be wise and let the experts guide you to the top.

Succeeding in life is nothing like climbing Mount Everest. It is harder, more complex and infinitely more important! So, doesn't it make sense that we enlist the supreme expert in how to live a meaningful and successful life?

God is the Ultimate Sherpa.

"The Lord says, "I will guide you along the best pathway for your life. I will advise you and watch over you." Psalm 32:8.

Almighty God actually wants us to work hand-in-hand with Him, to create the one and only life He envisions. But, there is a problem. While most have thought about God and many believe there is a God, they don't think He has much, if anything, to do with their *everyday* lives. Nothing could be further from the truth. Our Creator has no intention of leaving us halfway up the mountain. He is going the distance with us, to our final breath and beyond.

You not only have an expert guide; you have an unconditionally loving, all-knowing and powerful Partner! And, He documented how the partnership works in the Bible!

Let the collaboration begin.

A *partnership* is a relationship between individuals that is characterized by mutual cooperation and respect, for the achievement of a specified goal. There have been many notable partnerships in politics, business, entertainment and sports:

-The Founding Fathers partnered to create the United States
-The U.S. partnered with our Allies to win World War II
-Bill Gates and Paul Allen brilliantly conceived Microsoft
-Entertainment gave us Lucy and Desi, Sonny and Cher, Faith Hill and Tim McGraw and Elton John and Bernie Taupin
-Great sports alliances included, Bill Belichick and Tom Brady, Michael Jordan and Scottie Pippen and the legendary Muhammad Ali and Angelo Dundee

We achieve more together, then individually. Partnerships are powerful, in what they can accomplish.

"Two people are better off than one, for they can help each other succeed." Ecclesiastes 4:9.

"Teachers call it copying, we call it teamwork!" Unknown.

When you partner with God you get several built-in assets in the deal; holiness, patience, omnipotence, omniscience, sovereignty, eternal perspective, unconditional love, wisdom, and forgiveness, to name a few.

With God as your Partner, it is a slam dunk. Hitch your wagon to a Star! Look at His track record with ordinary human's.

-He tapped Abram to become Abraham, the father of Israel.
-He began a partnership with Moses through a burning bush that led to the Israelites' freedom from slavery in Egypt.
-He led an unknown shepherd boy, David, to not only slay the giant Goliath, but made him one of the greatest kings in history.
-As a result of partnering with God, Joshua conquered Jericho, Esther became a renowned Queen, Peter and the Apostles established the greatest church in history and the Apostle Paul, once an aggressive critic of Christianity, became the greatest writer and theologian, writing half of the New Testament.

Why Partner with God

Our close human partnerships are important, especially as we influence each other to know God and understand the Bible. It is imperative that we help each other look to God and make a commitment to follow His wisdom and direction in the Bible.

"... wisdom is sweet to your soul. If you find it, you will have a bright future, and your hopes will not be cut short." Proverbs 24:14.

If we play god and rely only on ourselves or other humans for our happiness, business decisions, marriage success, raising children, psychological well-being, financial security and meaning, we are at risk for failure in every category of life.

"Trust in the Lord with all your heart; do not depend on your own understanding. Seek his will in all you do and he will show you which path to take. Don't be impressed with your own wisdom. Instead, fear the Lord and turn away from evil." Proverbs 3:5-7.

In truth, God is knowable and genuinely wants to have not only a partnership with you, but also a personal friendship. He desires to help you live a wonderful life, guide you to implement His plan on earth and take you to eternity with Him. You are His physical arms, legs and voice on earth. He gives you direct access to Him through prayer and the Bible so you can competently represent Him to others.

"And whatever you do or say, do it as a representative of the Lord Jesus, giving thanks through him to God the Father." Colossians 3:17.

You are His ambassador to everyone you come into contact with. You represent God, thus must walk the fine line between the earthly "empires" of pride and secular society and what the Bible teaches. Your primary purpose is to do His work and view every one and every circumstance through the wisdom, morals and standards of the Bible. You must not only work diligently to truly know and understand Him and His plans, but to also do your part to execute His plan and explain it to others.

"Oh, how great are God's riches, wisdom and knowledge! How impossible it is for us to understand his decisions and his ways! For who can know the Lord's thoughts? Who knows enough to give him advice? And, who has given him so much that he needs to pay it back? For everything comes from him, exists by his power and is intended for his glory." Romans 11: 33-36.

To all of you out there, God doesn't simply want us to believe and love him, He expects us to humbly partner with Him to accomplish His plans on earth for His glory. In a sense, we are His envoys and our earthly lives are a test to see if we trust Him or will go our own way. It is not enough for us to simply know and believe, we must also take *action*, using our time, talents and resources to do our part to fulfill God's earthly mission. God fully expects us to be His partner to implement His grand strategy for the world.

Why should you collaborate with God, trust the Bible and give up control of your life?

Because God designed you, knows you *personally*, as well as, what is best to significantly enhance your life. Just like the watchmaker knows the intricate designs of his timepiece, a sculptor is intimately familiar with his piece of art and the potter, knows the unique shapes and textures he has formed.

"They (we) know the truth about God because he has made it obvious to them. Forever, since the world was created, people have seen the earth and sky. Through everything God made, they can clearly see his invisible qualities, his eternal power and divine nature. So, they have no excuse for not knowing God." Romans 1:19-20.

Simply look at the beauty, complexity, intelligence and the synchronicity of humans, nature and the universe to gain an understanding of what God is like. Like an experienced Sherpa, who better to trust and rely upon to scale the summit of life?

"For I know the plans I have for you," says the LORD, "plans for good and not for disaster, to give you a future and a hope." Jeremiah 29:11.

His plan is found in His enduring, **User Manual for Life**, the Bible. It is critical that you read and act on it. The Bible never becomes obsolete!

"Study this Book of Instructions continually. Meditate on it day and night, so you will be sure to obey everything written in it. Only then, will you prosper and succeed in all you do." Joshua 1:8.

Life is Difficult

The most obvious reason to partner with God is because life is *tough*. Life as we know it, all started when Adam and Eve disobeyed God and ate from the "tree of knowledge". They could have obeyed God and eaten from any other fruit trees in the Garden of Eden. But Adam and Eve chose to disobey God and the "original sin" ushered in an entirely different and difficult world. Read Genesis 3 for how the fall of humanity came about.

The world has been a persistently challenging place to live. God's powerful gift of "free will" allowed Adam and Eve the freedom to choose. Consequently, it is never going to be easy to live the good life that God originally planned for us. Partnering with God gives you a second chance, it is the only smart way to manage your life. There is no greater opportunity than to participate in God's design and creativity for your life. His love, grace, forgiveness and power are there for everyone.

"Every child of God (you and I) defeats this evil world, and we achieve this victory through our faith. And who can win this battle against the world? Only those who believe that Jesus is the Son of God." 1 John 5:5.

How to Partner with God

The **first step** is to admit you have not lived up to God's standards outlined in the Bible. So, simply ask for forgiveness, accept Jesus is your savior and live your life according to the Bible.

"If you openly declare that Jesus is Lord and believe in your heart that God raised him from the dead, you will be saved. For it is by believing in your heart that you are made right with God, and it is by openly declaring your faith that you are saved. As the scriptures tell us, 'Anyone who trust in him will never be disgraced.'" Romans 10:9-11.

"For all have sinned and fall short of the glory of God," Romans 3:23

This simple step *ensures* that you will have more than just a meaningful life, it goes way beyond that. You are guaranteed a forever life in heaven.

Definition of saved: keep safe or rescue (someone or something) from harm or danger. In the Bible it means spending eternity with God because you are saved from hell. Also called salvation, born again and everlasting life.

Secondly, read and learn the basics of the Bible. It is **"Your Life User Manual"**. No one expects you to be a biblical scholar or a know it all; just make the Bible the basis for how you manage your everyday life, one day at a time!

The goal is to be patient while you are learning, practicing and applying the Bible every day. Few of us are naturally patient but obeying the teachings of the Bible is the only way to learn and experience the unchanging truths of the Bible. Simply knowing and reciting the Bible is not enough, it is information only. You must actually *do* what it says in every area of your life. You need actual behavior change to accompany your knowledge of the Bible.

If your logic, thinking, habits and behaviors don't change, then all your learning and knowledge is pointless. If you don't do what the Bible teaches it means you don't believe it.

"All Scripture is inspired by God and is useful to teach us what is true and to make us realize what is wrong in our lives. It corrects us when we are wrong and teaches us to do what is right." 2 Timothy 4:16.

Your challenge, through knowledge and practice, is to gradually turn everything, all parts of your existence, every choice, relationship, career, finances, marriage, children, sex, etc. over to your Partner by living according to the only book authored by God, the Bible.

Thirdly, you have direct access to God. When you need to hear directly from your Partner, you can personally consult with Him by reading the Bible, praying and listening for the "small, quiet voice" (God speaking to your conscience) to guide you. When praying, I have discovered that the more specific my requests and questions, the more likely it is that I hear and understand His answer. Talking with other Christians also helps me interpret God's will. And, of utmost importance have faith and confidence that God is with you and will help you. Here is an amazing promise:

"You can pray for anything, and if you have faith, you will receive it." Matthew 21:22.

I admit it is often a dilemma to be patient while looking and waiting for direction. But, He is there, not to worry. God is persistent, omnipresent and all-powerful so He will always answer.

"Be still (quietly listen) in the presence of the Lord, and wait patiently for him to act." Psalms 37:7.

God is often counter cultural and often answers with solutions very different from what I would normally do. But remember, He only provides "good news", unlike the persistent "bad news" in broadcasts, newspapers and internet posts. He uses the Holy Spirit, the Bible, others, as well as, pain, confusion and success to move each of us to change.

Every day, I listen for direction by praying, reading the Bible, studying devotionals from the internet, as well as, going to church on Sunday and attending a weekly men's group. I pray specifically for direction (often with my wife), patiently waiting and fully expecting His answer. Patiently waiting for God, is not easy and often frustrating. However, that is what happens when someone else, specifically an all-powerful and sovereign God, is in control. But, all other human options are futile.

Sometimes He answers no or not yet, but that is just as good for me as yes. I have often avoided problems by just waiting and observing. As my honest, all knowing Partner, He is always truthful. I trust my Partner.

"We can make our plans, but the Lord determines our steps." Proverbs 16:9.

The plan is for us to trust completely, knowing His answers will arrive at exactly the right time and place to guide us. I have learned that answers usually show up most often after I take the first step toward an objective or choice. God doesn't steer a parked car or a boat dead in the water, it must be moving first! We are expected to move *forward*, demonstrating unfailing faith as described in Hebrews 11, rather than sitting around waiting to first see a miracle or a clear sign. You can't find a job, budget your finances, raise great children, make new friends or start a company by sitting on the couch.

So, don't demand, pout, sulk or snarl if the answer is slow in coming or not what you expected. Create your best, Bible inspired idea and begin moving towards it and He will direct you *to or away* from it. And, certainly don't think you know better than God. Patiently trust and obey.

Most want to see God act first or get an obvious spiritual signal before they take action. That is not how it works. If God made it crystal clear that He existed, then you wouldn't need faith. You don't develop faith by simply going to church, attending a Bible study group or reading the Bible. No doubt learning and knowledge is important, but faith is like a muscle, if you don't use, develop and stretch it, the muscle atrophies.

Many never try God, some give up when they encounter problems or after a few half-hearted efforts. They conclude that God cannot be found, doesn't exist or has no interest in personally partnering with them.

"Dear brothers and sisters, when troubles of any kind come your way, consider it an opportunity for great joy. For you know that when your faith is tested, your endurance has a chance to grow. So, let it grow, for when your endurance is fully developed, you will be perfect and complete, needing nothing." James 1:2-4.

God partners best with those who are consciously looking, working and testing their faith. God will show up to help, but you need to first take *action* so God can assist you. The more you trust God and persistently move forward expecting Him to be present, the greater your faith will be, the more you will experience and accomplish.

"Pray like it all depends on God, but work like it all depends on you." Dave Ramsey, author, radio host.

Your faith grows in direct proportion to your ability to take risks and trust Him in spite of doubt or confusion. Trust God to show up and intervene in ways you cannot anticipate. **Faith, trust and belief** are one in the same; God promises to be with you always. You can count on Him.

"Faith is the confidence that what we hope for will actually happen; it gives us assurance about things we cannot see." Hebrews 11:1.

Faith is relentlessly doing God's will without knowing exactly what to do, nor completely sure where it might lead. Ask God, "What do I need to do today?" As long as you are aligned with God's will and live according to the Bible, nothing is impossible. God's instructions to us are:

"Keep on asking and you will receive what you ask for. Keep on seeking and you will find. Keep on knocking and the door will be opened to you. For everyone who asks, receives. Everyone who seeks, finds. And to everyone who knocks, the door will be opened." Matthew 7:7-8.

Finally, just like developing human relationships, it takes much time, practice, effort and unwavering trust to build your partnership with God. You will get better at it over time. Your ability to understand Him will be much more pronounced as a mature ambassador than as a new one. With enough practice partnering will become a valuable habit.

It is only through dedicated time and effort that relationships develop, mature and trust is eventually secured. God wants nothing less than a personal, trusting, loving relationship with you. Faith pleases God. It is the currency He trades in. As the next verse clearly states,

"It is impossible to please God without faith. Anyone who wants to come to him must believe that God exists and that he rewards those who sincerely seek him." Hebrews 11:6.

So, how will you know that you are partnering with God?

It is seldom dramatic, rather subtle and steady. A few symptoms or clues I have noticed in my own life, are as follows:

-I finally **surrendered**, realizing I would never be able to learn, understand or live up to the requirements in the Bible. I had to forcefully and persistently put my ego and pride aside to partner with God. According to some, **EGO** stands for **Edging God Out.** It does take relentless attention and practice to turn control over and trust Him completely. The more I do this, **the more straight-forward life has become.**

-I naturally view others, even strangers, through the lens of kindness, compassion and love, rather than suspicion. I began to recognize that we are all are fighting battles and only want someone to care, even a little. I started to **put others first**; spontaneously helping those in need and wanting to tell others the "Good News" in the Bible. We are only as good and useful as how we treat others. If you don't logically view the world differently, behave, reason and treat others with love, mercy and compassion, you are not partnering with God.

-I realize how far I have come and how good it is to be on the right path, with God as my partner. Peace has come over me in a confident, freeing and empowering ways, whether I am struggling or successful. God is with me always; my eternity is secure and everything is going to be alright. **I am at peace regardless of my circumstances.** It became clear that putting others first is the only meaningful and lasting human behavior that matter.

-When partnering with God, **your new adapted behaviors will cause you to stand out** from today's uncaring, self-absorbed, secular culture. People around you will notice you are different. Brave people will ask questions, a few will admire you, the weak will ridicule you and many just won't care. So, get ready to honestly tell them your story and simply be kind and helpful to everyone.

"And if someone asks about your hope as a believer, always be ready to explain it. But do this in a gentle and respectful way." 1 Peter 3:15-16.

-A clear sign you are partnering with God is when you are driven to **tell others about your new life**, because it is so much better and eternity is in the balance. Only Christians can tell others about their faith and there are some individuals only you can reach. This is after all the Great Commission given to us by God. Think about individuals coming up to you in heaven and saying, "you are the reason I am here!"

"Let your light shine before men in such a way that they may see your good works, and glorify your Father who is in heaven." Matthew 5:16.

"Stand firm in the faith. Be courageous. Be strong. And do everything with love." 1 Corinthians 16:13.

-I discovered that, contrary to most male reasoning, the key to partnering with God and living a spectacular life is to **be humble**. Pride makes you fake and hard to know; humility makes you real, knowable and loveable. Without humility you are alone, arrogant and constantly sabotage yourself, with it, doors are opened to wisdom, new relationships and God. Many believe it is weakness, but my experience is that it's the gateway to breakthroughs. Humility allows you to put God first so He can refine you and lead you to your destiny.

"God opposes the proud but gives grace to the humble." James 4:6.

-I am not good at consistently putting myself into the hands and control of someone other than me. But, it does little good to read the Bible, then ignore it. God wants and expects fully engaged partners, who are "all in" with His ways of living. I will always be a "work in progress," steadily growing. **I realized that reading and applying the Bible in every area of my life is the only answer.** I know I can never go back to my self-serving ways.

"As God's partners, we beg you not to accept this marvelous gift of God's kindness and then ignore it." 2 Corinthians 6:1.

-As I trust God more, His amazing miracles multiply in my life, at times, in ways I never anticipated. However, remembering to **"Let go and let God,"** after years of running my own life, is a huge undertaking of trust and behavior modification.

Honestly, it is not easy to always understand God or the Bible, nor to consistently know if I am aligned with His ways. The following interchange, between God and an ordinary man, demonstrates God's infinite wisdom and our lack of understanding.

"God, how long is a million years?"
God answered, "To me, it's about a second."
"God, how much is a million dollars?"
"To me, it's a penny."
The man paused then asked, "God, may I have a penny?"
God smiled, "Sure, give me a second."

The struggle to follow God instead of doing things my or the world's way is a monumental one. Even after witnessing Him caring, guiding and loving me, often, in colossal ways, it is still a surprising struggle. This verse sums it up well.

"If any of you wants to be my follower, you must give up your way, take up your cross (living God's way) and follow me. If you try to hang on to your (secular) life, you will lose it. But, if you give up your life for my sake and for the sake of the Good News (the Bible), you will save it (preserve your life for eternity). And, what do you benefit if you gain the whole world, but lose your own soul? Is anything worth more than your soul?" Mark 8:34-37.

This gradual, but persistent change forced me to recognize and admit how empty and pointless much of my life had been and, most importantly, that there is a better way. Now, contentment, gratitude, peace and hope fill each day, rather than the stress of endless competition, trying to outdo others and the never-ending need for more.

I wish I could do a better job of explaining what it is like partnering with God, but I suspect it is like love, it has to be experienced. And, let's be candid here; much of how God works is an infinite mystery. Us "smart" humans prefer specifics and absolutes, but there are no formulas with God. Science continues to struggle with God because they cannot pin Him down or comprehend His brilliance. No human will ever contain God. Nonetheless, I persevere, wanting a partnership and all the help I can get from the One who created me.

I could never climb Mount Everest alone. Likewise, we were never intended to "conquer" life by ourselves. We are to partner with God and live life His way.

The Bible is my natural, trusted "go to" lifestyle guide and **Life User Manual**. Trust your Partner, if you want a life that only an all-powerful and knowing God can create. Here is what Jesus says,

"Jesus looked at them (the disciples) intently and said, 'Humanly speaking, it is impossible. But not with God. Everything is possible with God.' Then Peter began to speak up. 'We've given up everything to follow you,' he said. 'Yes', Jesus replied, 'and I assure you that everyone who has given up house or brothers or sisters or mother or father or children or property, for my sake and for the Good News, will receive now in return a hundred times as many houses, brothers, sisters, mothers, children, and property – along with persecution (from society). And in the world to come (eternity), that person will have eternal life.' But many who are the greatest now (on earth) will be least important then (in heaven), and those who seem least important now will be the greatest then." Mark 10:27-31.

What an unbelievable privilege it is to be God's partner on earth, getting to co-create my life with God each day. It is a win-win, just like He designed it to be. Life will never be easy or perfect, but through our collaboration, I am better equipped to handle life's endless challenges.

"The Lord will guide you continually, giving you water when you are dry and restoring your strength. You will be like a well-watered garden, like an every-flowing spring." Isaiah 58:11.

Me and my awesome Sherpa.

Time to reach the highest elevations in Life and forever in eternity!

Take Away: God is already "all in"! He sent His Son to die for your sins, loves you unconditionally and provided the Bible to give you direction. The only question is: Are you "all in?" He created us to be His ambassadors and use every part of our being to partner with him.

"For God was in Christ, reconciling the world to himself, no longer counting people's sins against them. And, he gave us this wonderful message of reconciliation. So, we are Christ's ambassadors;

God is making his appeal (to the world) through us." 2 Corinthians 5:20.

It is your choice to trust God, yourself or secular society to manage your life. Decide to develop your relationship and partner with God to achieve His plans and, simultaneously, create your own special life. Will you allow the All-Powerful to be your partner?

"So, humble yourself before God. Resist the devil (temptation) and he will flee from you. Come close to God and God will come close to you." James 4:7-8.

Here is an intriguing question posed by Greg Laurie:

"If you were arrested for being a Christian, would there be enough evidence to convict you?"

How to Live Forever

Most of this book has been about how to use the Bible to make your earthly life better. Now is the time to honestly and openly discuss God, Jesus, the Holy Spirit and how to achieve eternal life. This chapter is my best understanding on what the Bible says about Christian faith. If you are already a Christian enjoy the chapter, I hope it strengthens and expands your faith. If you are a nominal Christian, I hope it reignites your faith. If you are not religious I encourage you to read it with an open mind and heart. My hope is that, while the earthly benefits of aligning your life with the Bible can be great and immediate, the real reward is eternity with God.

I believe this chapter is the most important one in the book because it highlights what you need to do to live forever. I have done my absolute best to present what the Bible says, but please read the Bible and do your own research to honestly, intentionally and completely form your own belief and judgement.

Religion vs Relationship

Religion is a "loaded" word, containing many "man-made" interpretations and requirements.

Religion: "the belief in and worship of a superhuman controlling power, especially a personal God or gods". The definition of Christianity is "the religion based on the personal teachings of Jesus of Nazareth".

The primary difference between Christianity and other religions is that Christianity is based on **what Christ did, not what you do**. Christianity is Christ centered, other religions are man centered. Christians believe Jesus died for our sins and if we put all our faith and trust in Him we are forgiven and will spend eternity with God.

To live forever, God must be your friend, Jesus your role-model and the Bible your 'How to Manual'. Christianity is a personal relationship with God, not following a list of man-made rules.

So, how do you initiate and develop the most significant life transforming relationship of all, your relationship with God? You must invest time to get to know His nature, ways, values, likes and dislikes. This only happens by interacting and spending time together. With God this means praying, attending church, interacting with other like-minded believers, reading and doing what the Bible says, confessing your sins, asking for forgiveness and listening for God's response.

God wants to spend time with you more than anything else. However, God gives you the final choice. He will never force you into a relationship with Him. My advice is to intentionally reach out to God, spend time with Him and watch Him transform your life.

"I want to know all Gods thoughts; all the rest are just details." Albert Einstein, theoretical physicist.

Christianity is not about earning your way to heaven. It is sincerely accepting Jesus as your savior and developing a personal relationship with God that allows you to live forever with God.

"To fall in love with God is the greatest romance; to seek Him the greatest adventure; to find him, the greatest human achievement." Saint Augustine.

Now I will simply and directly describe the major beliefs of Christianity and how to live forever. This will take a few pages, but hang-in-there, it will be well worth your time - now and forever.

GOD

So, who or what is God?

He is known as Yahweh, Father, supreme being, the perfect, all-powerful creator, moral authority and ruler of the universe. When Moses asked God His name, God replied **"I Am Who I Am"**, Exodus 3:14. This appears to indicate that there are no words or names that can adequately describe God. He has always existed, never changes, is all powerful, all knowing, holy, merciful, righteous, just and sovereign. Most of all God is love, as demonstrated by His unending grace, forgiveness, compassion and patience to give us time to find, know and build a relationship with Him. He created the universe, earth and us for

His own pleasure and glory. All of which is, for the most part, incomprehensible to mere humans. That is why you need faith.

God is Jesus father. He sent His son to earth specifically to die so we can be forgiven for our sins and spend eternity with Him. That is how serious God is about loving us and having a personal relationship with each one of us. I know how much I love my children and certainly would not give them up for anyone, let alone a bunch of immoral, self-centered individuals. This is only possible through the grace of God.

Grace according to Webster is: "unmerited divine assistance given to humans for their regeneration or sanctification."

Comprehending grace is a challenge. You and I have done nothing to deserve God's grace. He sent His son to die for us, offers us unconditional love, mercy and forgiveness. And, God actually wants to spend eternity with us. This is supernatural, over the top and hard to believe. It is too good to be true, but it's not. This is what you get when you put God first in every area of your life. God's desire to have a relationship with you and I isn't logical and can't be captured in a few words or mathematical formula.

In addition, He is forever patient and accepts all types of individuals, no matter your background or earthly circumstances. However, the choice to develop a meaningful relationship is completely yours. If God is who the Bible says He is, you have a critical decision to make. Put your faith and trust in God or rely on yourself and the ways of the world. There is no more important decision and it is left to you!

"He (God) is so rich in kindness and grace that he purchased our freedom with the blood of this Son and forgave our sins. He has showered his kindness on us, along with all wisdom and understanding." Ephesians 1:7-8.

The Bible doesn't really spend a lot of words trying to prove that God exists. Rather, all of creation, the universe and earth, all of nature, the beauty of a sunrise and sunset are all overwhelming proof of His existence to me. The Bible provides insights into what He is like, what is important to Him, His perspective on us and understanding of life and death. Additionally, God's son, Jesus, through the way he lived and the stories he told, provides more insights about God's nature and character.

In **Psalms 19** King David describes how God reveals Himself through nature, scripture and the Bible.

"Christ is the visible image of the invisible God." Colossians 1:15.

As mere humans, we continually underestimate God! God is eternally epic.

"Oh, how great are God's riches and wisdom and knowledge! How impossible it is for us to understand his decisions and his ways! For who can know the Lord's thoughts? Who knows enough to give him advice? And who has given him so much that he needs to pay it back? For everything comes from him and exists by his power and is intended for his glory. All glory to him forever!" Romans 11:33-36.

Many, including the secular press, who have not studied the Bible, think of God as primarily limiting, judging, condemning, punishing or a myth. I suspect some preachers have gotten carried away with their "fire and brimstone" sermons believing the best way to change people is to scare them. Other ministers focus only on love, forgiveness and mercy without any judgement. Some ask "How can a loving God let bad things happen to good people?" Numerous individuals contemplate God as an inspirational fairytale or entity that has nothing to do with their everyday life. The answer is in balancing both the mercy and judgment of God.

If you read the Bible you will discover that God has life, death and 'forever after' figured out. My God is actually loving, forgiving, merciful and desires to spend eternity with me. He is also just, ethical and righteous. God is actually all of the above and more. Because He is God, He can balance judgement and grace perfectly. There is mystery in how we are free to interact with God. For example, God is all-powerful, yet He gave us free will so we can say no to Him. Fortunately, he is also patient and provided the Bible to give us time and wisdom to make the right choice. We can and should ask questions, as well as, search for answers and discernment. But I am sure we cannot understand God's ways this side of death; that is why faith is required.

Think about it, good parents are merciful and judgmental all the time. They love, discipline, reward and provide direction to their children simultaneously. Parents do their absolute best to raise and equip their kids to succeed in life. Eventually children become adults and are free to make their own choices; including whether to following their parent's advice or not. If skilled parents can effectively balance punishment, rewards, love and advice with their children, certainly God is more than capable.

Read **Hebrew 4:12-16** for an example of the critical balance between judgement and punishment verses mercy and grace.

God provided the Bible specifically to guide you to Him, describe your purpose, educate you, transform your earthly life and take you to eternity. God is not mean, God is good.

"Give thanks to the Lord, for he is good!" Psalm 107:1.

In the beginning

So, let's use plain talk and start at the beginning: The Garden of Eden.

"Then God said, 'Let us make human beings in our image, to be like us. They will reign over the fish in the sea, the birds in the sky, the livestock, all the wild animals on the earth, and the small animals that scurry along the ground.' So, God created human beings in his own image. In the image of God he created them; male and female he created them. Then God blessed them and said, 'Be fruitful and multiply…'" Genesis 1:26-28.

You may already know the story of Adam and Eve from Genesis 2 and 3. God formed Adam first "from the dust of the ground" and gave him a clear and specific command,

"The Lord God placed the man in the Garden of Eden to tend and watch over it. But the Lord God warned him, 'You may freely eat the fruit of every tree in the garden – except the tree of the knowledge of good and evil. If you eat its fruit, you will surely die.'" Genesis 2:15-17.

The reason God gave Adam this command is because He had also given him "free will", the autonomy to choose. God knows that without choice there is no freedom, humans would be like marionettes.

God wants us to obey Him, but He wants it to be our choice. Forced love is not love at all. The freedom to "pull our own strings," is a key part of God's plan. However, it proves to be risky for us prideful humans.

"Then the Lord God said, 'It is not good for the man to be alone. I will make a helper who is just right for him.'" Genesis 2:18.

"So the Lord God caused a deep sleep to fall upon the man and he slept; then he took one of his ribs and closed up the flesh at that place. The Lord God fashioned into a woman the rib which he had taken from the man, and brought her to the man. At last! The man (Adam) exclaimed. This one is bone from my bone, and flesh from my flesh! She shall be called 'woman', because she was taken from 'Man'." Genesis 2:21-23.

The first man and woman were joined together and humanity was in God's perfect place, the Garden of Eden, ready to multiply and reign over the perfect earth - God saw that it was all good.

Then into the Garden came the devil disguised as a serpent.

"The serpent was the shrewdest of all the wild animals the Lord God had made. One day he asked the woman, 'Did God really say you must not eat the fruit from any of the trees in the Garden? Of course we may eat fruit from the trees in the garden.' The woman replied, 'It's only the fruit from the tree in the middle of the garden that we are not allowed to eat.' God said, 'You must not eat it or even touch it; if you do, you will die.'" Genesis 3:1-3.

The serpent replied,

"You won't die! the serpent replied to the woman. God knows that your eyes will be opened as soon as you eat it, and you will be like God, knowing both good and evil." Genesis 3:4-5.

The phrase, "you will be like God," is the impetus for sin. By eating fruit from the tree in the middle of the Garden, God knew that man would be ambitiously trying to become greater than Him, hence His command to not eat from it. In spite of our powerful brains, free will and societies unrelenting "have it your way" mantra, we will never be God.

"The woman was convinced. She saw that the tree was beautiful and its fruit looked delicious, and she wanted the wisdom it would give her. So she took some of the fruit and ate it. Then she gave some to her husband, who was with her, and he ate it too." Genesis 3:6.

At that instant "original sin" entered the world preventing humans from spending eternity with God. The Garden of Eden was no longer a perfect place and we live in a corrupted world today.

"When Adam sinned, sin entered the world. Adam's sin brought death, so death spread to everyone, for everyone sinned." Romans 5:12.

This is the event that brought sin into the world. God is completely holy and cannot allow any sin. So, he required a sacrifice to annul sin. God's response to sin in the world was to send His son, Jesus Christ, to be crucified as payment in full for everyone's sins. It was the necessary action of a Holy God that His son would take on all sin and die on the cross to reverse the death sentence on all mankind. This may seem unfair and extreme, but we are not God.

"Yes, Adam's one sin brings condemnation for everyone, but Christ's one act of righteousness brings a right relationship with God and new life for everyone. Because one person disobeyed God, many became sinners. But because one other person (Jesus) obeyed God, many will be made righteous." Romans 5:18-19.

Adam and Eve were not wrong in wanting to become *like God*, but they blatantly disobeyed God's command attempting to achieve the goal. They chose to *be God*, rather than wait for God's direction on how to work toward being more *like God*. They took things into their own hands, unilaterally disobeyed God's command and ate from the tree that provides "the knowledge of good and evil".

Today, God expects us to have faith, read the Bible, obey it, accept Jesus as your savior and work toward becoming like Jesus.

"Fear (worship) of the Lord is the foundation of true wisdom All who obey his commandments will grow in wisdom." Psalm 111:10.

Jesus

Like the Adam and Eve story, many also know about the birth of Jesus Christ, but they don't think His teachings apply to their lives. His birth is why we celebrate Christmas. Although, today it is getting harder and harder to recognize the original purpose of Christ-mas.

The virgin Mary, already engaged to marry Joseph, was made pregnant by God. The angel Gabriel came to Mary and told her she was blessed by God and would give birth to His son. An angel also appeared to Joseph and told him the child was conceived by God and that he should name him Jesus. It is a mind-boggling story that is only possible if you believe in an all-powerful God. The book of John is a good place to start to understand Jesus and salvation. But, also read Mathew, Mark and Luke, to get different perspectives on the story of Jesus birth, life and purpose.

"**The Word (God) became flesh (Jesus) and made his dwelling among us. We have seen his glory, the glory of the one and only Son, who came from the Father, full of grace and truth.**" John 1:14.

Names for Jesus include Christ, Messiah, Son of God, Son of Man, savior, lamb, wonderful counselor and prince of peace. For thirty-three years, Jesus lived on the earth, established His ministry, created the church and explained how to know God. His purpose was to give us mortals the opportunity to know and trust God completely. Yet, all the parables Jesus told, all His healing and miracles and all the challenges He overcame were but a prelude to His real mission on earth; **to die for each of us.** Most misunderstand who He is and what He represents – He is the greatest man who ever lived.

"**For there is only one God and one Mediator who can reconcile God and humanity – the man Christ Jesus. He gave his life to purchase freedom for everyone. This is the message God gave to the world at just the right time.**" 1 Timothy 2:5-6.

Jesus was fully human and fully God.

"Christ is the visible image of the invisible God. He existed before anything was created and is supreme over all creation, for through him God created everything in the heavenly realms and on earth." Colossians 1:15-16.

Adam's sin had to be erased so sinful men could be reconciled with God. If you have not spiritually given your life to Jesus Christ, then sin is still with you. It must be forgiven before you can have a meaningful relationship with God.

"For all have sinned and fall short of the glory of God." Romans 3:23.

"For the wages of sin is death, but the gift of God is eternal life in Christ Jesus our Lord." Romans 6:23.

Let's put this in human terms.

Imagine you got into trouble with the law and you went to court and the judge is your dad. As a judge he asks you, "Do you wish to pay a $25,000 fine or spend a year in jail?

You chuckle to yourself because you believe him to be joking with you. He is, after all, your *dad*. You play along with him, "Uh, well your honor, I happen to be broke, so give me the jail time." With that statement, your father the judge announces, "The court finds you guilty and sentences you to jail for no less than one year." Suddenly, you realize there are two people sitting at the courtroom bench, your loving father AND a lawful judge.

You made the mistake of appealing to the *judge*.

The judge side of your dad is going to punish you. You quickly change your approach. You ask your loving father to step in and save you, "Dad, I have no money. I don't want to go to jail. Please help me. I did wrong and I am truly sorry." The judge stands up and removes his court robes and comes down from the bench and stands next to you. At that moment, he is no longer a judge, he is now your **father**.

He pulls out his checkbook and writes you a check for $25,000. Smiling warmly at you he says, "Give this to the judge. I will be back up there in a minute. I love you." He hugs you and returns to the bench, puts his robe back on and you hand the "judge" your check. He announces, "You are free to go."

As a judge, he has sentenced you. As a father, he paid the sentence for you.

Jesus died on the cross for you – He is your $25,000 check! He is the ransom for you to be free of sin and able to live forever.

"He (Jesus) has paid a full ransom for his people. He has guaranteed his covenant with them forever. What a holy awe-inspiring name he has!" Psalm 111:9

"You were dead because of your sins and because your sinful nature was not yet cut away. Then God made you alive with Christ, for he forgave all our sins. He (Jesus) canceled the record of the charges against us and took it away by nailing it to the cross." Colossians 2:13-14.

Our debt is paid by Jesus. Adam's sin and all of ours have been removed. Your case is dismissed.

"So you see, just as death came into the world through a man (Adam), now the resurrection from the dead has begun through another man (Jesus). Just as everyone dies because we all belong to Adam, everyone who belongs to Christ will be given new life." 1 Corinthians 15:21-22.

Why Jesus? Why can't we reconcile ourselves to God through our own effort?

You may be a nice person, go to church, love your family and do wonderful things in your community. You are not a murderer, rapist or criminal of any kind. But, God does not judge on a sliding scale; He does not have a small, medium, high rating scale for sin and evil. All it takes to block you from heaven forever is one sin of any kind. Living a "good life" will never be good enough. Apostle Paul said:

"Oh, what a miserable person I am! Who will free me from this life that is dominated by sin and death? Thank God! The answer is in Jesus Christ our Lord." Romans 7:24-25.

So, you cannot redeem yourself. You were disqualified after one sin. This may seem unfair to you, but you are not God, who cannot tolerate sin, at any level. Therefore, you must submit to the sacrifice God planned for you when He sent His Son. Jesus is the only sinless man qualified to accomplish the feat of unconditional forgiveness for you. Jesus Christ is the point of Christianity.

"Christ is all that matters and he lives in all of us." Colossians 3:11.

By faith, you believe that Jesus Christ alone can satisfy God's standard for saving your soul. Your faith in Jesus is not based upon emotions or feelings, but upon your will. Asking Jesus Christ to take your soul is a deliberate, *willful* act.

Jesus explained this to a religious leader named Nicodemus who wanted to be saved:

"There was a man named Nicodemus, a Jewish religious leader who was a Pharisee. After dark one evening, he came to speak with Jesus. Rabbi, he said, 'we all know that God has sent you to teach us. Your miraculous signs are evidence that God is with you.' Jesus replied, 'I tell you the truth, unless you are born again (accept Jesus sacrifice), you cannot see the Kingdom of God.'" John 3:1-3.

Jesus was not talking about a second physical birth, that would be absurd. He was referring to a "spiritual rebirth" where God erases **all** your sins in order to make you acceptable to Him and destined for heaven.

The central theme and essential belief of Christianity is Jesus. The most important points are that Jesus is God's only son, He came to earth as a man, taught Christianity to the disciples and thousands of others, performed many miracles, died on the cross for our sins, was buried, on the third day rose from the dead, ascended to heaven to live with His Father and will return to take all believers to heaven with Him.

This was all prophesized in the Old Testament portion of the Bible, centuries **before** the events occurred. A few of the hundreds of prophesizes include:

Virgin mother: **"The Lord himself will give you the sign. Look! The virgin will conceive a child! She will give birth to a son and will call him Immanuel ('God is with us')."** Isaiah 7:14.

His birth: **"But you, O Bethlehem Ephrathah, are only a small village among all the people of Judah. Yet a ruler of Israel, whose origins are in the distant past, will come from you on my behalf."** Micah 5:2.

Jesus entering Jerusalem: **"Rejoice, O people of Zion! Shout in triumph, O people of Jerusalem! Look, your king is coming to you. He is righteous and victorious, yet he is humble, riding on a donkey – riding on a donkey's colt."** Zechariah 9:9.

His crucifixion: **"My enemies surround me like a pack of dogs; an evil gang closes in on me. They have pierced my hands and feet. I can count all my bones. My enemies stare at me and gloat. They divide my garments among themselves and throw dice for my clothing."** Psalm 22:16-18.

His resurrection: **"For you will not leave my soul among the dead or allow your holy one to rot in the grave."** Psalm 16:10.

I know, this is the most radical, wildest biography you have ever encountered. The entire Bible is infinitely more creative, prescient and all-encompassing than any other contemporary book, movie, game or alternative reality, fiction or nonfiction, you have ever experienced. When you believe in a God so big and powerful that you will never fully understand His power, reasons, ways and plans, this is what you get. Who would want a god that we simple humans could fully understand or figure out?

There is no middle ground. Is Jesus really who He and the Bible say He is? If your answer is yes, then He changes everything. If your answer is no, then the Christian faith is useless to you and you are on your own.

God sent His son Jesus to earth to save all of us; dividing history into BC (Before Christ) and AD (anno domini, "in the year of the Lord", the year of Jesus birth). Christmas celebrates Jesus birth and Easter His death, resurrection and ascent to heaven. Why have the Christian holidays, BC/AD, the church, the Bible and faith persisted for centuries? Because it is all true and deserves to be celebrated. It is an eternal message of forgiveness, love, peace and hope that nothing else offers.

In John 14, Jesus describes the way to achieve eternal life, that He and His Father are one in the same and that if you are aligned with the will of God, your prayers will be answered. For me, this is one of the most amazing verses in the Bible.

"Don't let your hearts be troubled. Trust in God and trust also in me. There is more than enough room in my Father's home (heaven). If this were not so, would I have told you that I am going to prepare a place for you? When everything is ready, I will come and get you, so that you will always be with me where I am. And you know the way to where I am going."

"No, we don't know, Lord," Thomas said. "We have no idea where you are going so how can we know the way?"

"Jesus told him, 'I am the way, the truth and the life. No one can come to the Father except through me. If you had really known me, you would know who my Father is. From now on, you do know him and have seen him!'"

"Philip said, 'Lord, show us the Father and we will be satisfied.'"

"Jesus replied, 'Have I been with you all this time, Philip, and yet you still don't know who I am? Anyone who has seen me has seen the Father! So why are you asking me to show him to you? Don't you believe that I am in the Father and the Father is in me? The words I speak are not my own, but my Father who lives in me does his work through me. Just believe that I am in the Father and the Father is in me. Or at least believe because of the work you have seen me do.'"

"I tell you the truth, anyone who believes in me will do the same works I have done and even greater works, because I am going to be with the Father. You can ask for anything in my name and I will do it, so that the Son can bring glory to the Father. Yes, ask me for anything in my name and I will do it!"** John 14:1-14.

There is no question that Jesus existed and walked the earth. Even most non-Christians agree. However, Jesus was not just a good guy or a prophet; He never left those options open to us. He claimed to be God. Read some of Jesus statements,

"The Father and I are one." John 10:30.

"I am the resurrection and the life. Anyone who believes in me will live, even after dying. Everyone who lives in me and believes in me will never die." John 11:25.

"That is why I said, that you will die in your sins; for unless you believe that I AM who I claim to be, you will die in your sins." John 8:24.

The Crucifixion

The death of Jesus was not the fault of either the Romans or the Jews. No one "killed" Jesus. He *gave* His life; there is a significant difference here. Jesus Christ was not victimized. He was intentional in dying for us. He said:

"No one can take my life from me. I sacrifice it voluntarily. For I have the authority to lay it down when I want to and also to take it up again. For this is what my Father has commanded." John 10:18.

"Christ suffered for our sins once for all time. He never sinned, but he died for sinners to bring you safely home to God. He suffered physical death, but he was raised to life in the Spirit." 1 Peter 3:18.

This is the greatest act of love in history.

"For this is how God loved the world: He gave his one and only Son, so that everyone who believes in him will not perish, but have eternal life. God sent his Son into the world not to judge the world, but to save the world through him." John 3:16-17.

The suffering and torture Jesus went through is well-documented; three phony trials, whipped, crowned with large thorns, forced to carry a large wooden cross to His execution site at Golgotha and was nailed to the cross. There He hung for three hours, thirsty, in excruciating pain waiting to die for you and me.

Jesus sacrifice makes you and I sin free and pure in God's eyes.

"But he was pierced for our rebellion, crushed for our sins. He was beaten so we could be whole. He was whipped so we could be healed. All of us, like sheep, have strayed away. We have left God's paths to follow our own. Yet the Lord laid on him the sins of us all." Isaiah 53:5-6.

The above scripture, written by the prophet Isaiah, is amazing not only because of the selfless sacrifice, but this was a prediction written approximately 700 years before Jesus crucifixion.

"When we were utterly helpless, Christ came at just the right time and died for us sinners. Now, most people would not be willing to die for an upright person, though someone might perhaps be willing to die for a person who is especially good. But God showed his great love for us by sending Christ to die for us while we were still sinners. And since we have been made right in God's sight by the blood (sacrifice) of Christ, he will certainly save us from God's condemnation. For since our friendship with God was restored by the death of his Son while we were still his enemies, we will certainly be saved through the life of his Son. So now we can rejoice in our wonderful new relationship with God because our Lord Jesus Christ has made us friends of God." Romans 5:6-11.

My interpretation of the verse above, is that in spite of all my corruption, selfish choices, immoral behaviors, dishonesty, how I treat others and ignored the teachings of the Bible, He died for me anyway! Jesus purpose was and is to transform and save us, not condemn us.

This is how much God loves you, wants to reunite with you now in Spirit and after death in heaven forever. It doesn't matter how good, bad or lost you have been or currently are, He came to love and save you. You are His first priority!

"For the Son of Man came to seek and save those who are lost." Luke 19:10

The Resurrection

Jesus resurrection was the greatest event in human history.

First Jesus died for our sins, then He conquered death to give us eternal life. Believing Jesus rose from the dead is critical to the Christian faith and eternal life. It means that when we accept Jesus into our hearts we have the ability to live forever with God. The Apostle Paul describes what Jesus did:

"Christ died for our sins, just as the Scriptures said. He was buried, and he was raised from the dead on the third day, just as the Scriptures said. He was seen by Peter and then by the Twelve. After that, he was seen by more than 500 of his followers at one time, most of whom are alive, though some have died. Then he was seen by James and later by all the apostles." 1 Corinthians 15:3-7.

Just like Jesus, after death we are resurrected to live forever with God. God wants us to have a prosperous, happy and purposeful life. But, His real goal, His end game is for us to love Him and live forever with Him.

"But God is so rich in mercy and he loved us so much, that even though we were dead because of our sins, he gave us life when he raised Christ from the dead. For he raised us from the dead along with Christ and seated us with him in the heavenly realms because we are united with Christ Jesus." Ephesians 2:4-6.

The Ascension

Jesus spent 40 days with the apostles, disciples and numerous others after His resurrection, before He ascended to heaven.

"Then Jesus led them (the disciples) to Bethany, and lifted his hands to heaven, he blessed them. While he was blessing them, he left them and was taken up to heaven. So, they, worshiped him and then returned to Jerusalem filled with great joy. And they spent all of their time in the temple praising God." Luke 24:50.

Additionally, Jesus promises to return to earth one day to first take all believers to heaven with Him (the rapture) and later to judge and rule over the earth (second coming). We have no idea when He will return so we must always be ready for His sudden return.

"As they strained to see him rising into heaven, two white-robed men (angels) suddenly stood among them. 'Men of Galilee,' they said, 'why are you standing here staring into heaven? Jesus has been taken from you into heaven, but someday he will return from heaven in the same way you saw him go!'" Acts 1:10-11.

"For you know quite well that the day of the Lord's return will come unexpectedly, like a thief in the night. When people are saying 'Everything is peaceful and secure,' then disaster will fall on them as suddenly as a pregnant woman's labor pains begin. And there will be no escape." 1 Thessalonians 5:2-3.

As a believer in Jesus and a child of God, Christians believe that upon His return, Jesus will take you with Him to heaven for eternity.

"And I am convinced that nothing can ever separate us from God's love. Neither death nor life, neither angels nor demons, neither our fears for today nor our worries about tomorrow – not even the powers of hell can separate us from God's love. No power in the sky above or in the earth below – indeed, nothing in all creation will ever be able to separate us from the love of God that is revealed in Christ Jesus our Lord." Romans 8:38-39.

In the following verse Jesus says He is returning soon to take believers to heaven.

"Look, I am coming soon, bringing my reward with me to repay all people according to their deeds. I am the Alpha and the Omega, the First and the Last, the Beginning and the End." Revelations 22:12-13.

Holy Spirit

Jesus promised not to leave us alone between the time of His ascension and when He returns. Jesus referred to the Holy Spirit as "Advocate" and "Spirit of truth". The Advocate resides in every believer, to teach, guide, encourage and strengthen us to live according to the Bible, tell others about Jesus and our personal salvation story.

"But when the Father sends the Advocate as my representative – that is, the Holy Spirit – he will teach you everything and will remind you of everything I have told you. I am leaving you with a gift – peace of mind and heart. And the peace I give is a gift the world cannot give. So don't be troubled or afraid. Remember what I told you: I am going away, but I will come back to you again. If you really loved me, you would be happy that I am going to the Father, who is greater than I am. I have told you these things before they happen so that when they do happen, you will believe." John 14:26-29.

The Holy Spirit is the presence of God in each person who believes. Without the Holy Spirit in you, it is impossible to be saved, possess the power to change spiritually and have a loving relationship with God.

"Don't you realize that all of you together are the temple (our body and mind) of God and that the Spirit of God lives in you? God will destroy anyone who destroys this temple. For God's temple is holy and you are that temple?" 1 Corinthians 3:16-17.

"The Spirit of God, who raised Jesus from the dead, lives in you. And just as God raised Christ Jesus from the dead, he will give life to your mortal bodies by this same Spirit living with in you." Romans 8:11.

You can only receive the Holy Spirit by accepting Jesus as your savior. Others can tell you about God and Jesus and you can read the Bible, but only through your unconditional acceptance of Jesus as your savior, will the Holy Spirit enter your heart and soul. It is not an emotional experience or feeling, it is the awareness of God in you. Yet another inconceivable part of God's glorious plan.

📖 **"If you love me, obey my commandments. And, I will ask the Father, and he will give you another Advocate who will never leave you. He is the Holy Spirit who leads into all truth. The world cannot receive him, because it isn't looking for him and doesn't recognize him. But, you know him, because he lives with you now and later will be in you."** John 14:15-17.

Remember that when you encounter problems and failures on earth, whether illness, divorce, poor choices, a family loss, a bad day at the office, an argument with your spouse, irritable kids, a financial collapse…none of those things change the irrefutable truth. You will still spend eternity with Christ FOREVER! This is a perspective that helps keep life and everything else in its proper place and priority.

The Trinity

The term trinity is not used anywhere in the Bible, but it is described in several places. Jesus told His disciples,

📖 **"I have been given all authority in heaven and on earth. Therefore, go and make disciples of all the nations, baptizing them in the name of the *Father and the Son and the Holy Spirit.*"** Matthew 28:18-19.

The Bible teaches that God is three persons and yet one essence. The Trinity is composed of: 1. God - the father, He has existed forever and created everything; 2. Jesus - God's only son, who died for our sins and offers salvation to everyone; 3. Holy Spirit - The Advocate, is the presence of God within each of us, helping us live as God wants.

Our goal is to look for and recognize the Holy Spirit's presence in each of our lives and use the Holy Spirit's guidance and power to make better choices for living righteous lives. God is not in a church, He resides in each one of us through the Holy Spirit.

"Now all of us can come to the Father through the same Holy Spirit because of what Christ has done for us." Ephesians 2:18.

The Trinity is unfathomable to me. However, I am in awe of God, so I choose to believe and accept the Trinity based on faith.

I have experienced the supernatural small voice giving me divine direction, which leads me to better life outcomes. I cannot explain these encounters, but they have occurred and I know it is the Holy Spirit. I believe in a God that is all powerful, omniscient and the creator of the universe and humans. I want and expect nothing less from my awesome God.

How to Live Forever

We have studied God, laid out Adam and Eve's creation and poor choices, God sending His Son to cancel Adam's and our sins, examined the credentials of Jesus Christ, provided an overview of His crucifixion, resurrection, ascension, promise to return and described the Holy Spirit and the Trinity.

There's only one thing left to explain.

How you can personally make the decision to give your life to Jesus Christ, be saved and live forever in heaven with God?

It's your decision time and it is not rigorous or complicated.

Jesus is patiently waiting for you to open the door and invite Him into your life.

"God saved you by his grace when you believed. And you can't take credit for this; it is a gift from God. Salvation is not a reward for the good things we have done, so none of us can boast about it. For we are God's master piece. He has created us anew in Christ Jesus, so we can do the good things he planned for us long ago." Ephesians 2:8-10.

Jesus already did all the work for your salvation. There is nothing you can add to that sacrifice. All you can do is accept, ignore or reject it. Paul told the people of Corinth:

"As God's partners, we beg you not to accept this marvelous gift of God's kindness and then ignore it. For God says, 'At just the right time, I heard you. On the day of salvation, I helped you.' Indeed the "right time" is now. Today is the day of salvation." 2 Corinthians 6:1-2.

His personal invitation to you:

"I correct and discipline everyone I love. So be diligent and turn from your indifference. Look! I stand at the door and knock. If you hear my voice and open the door, I will come in and we will share a meal together as friends." Revelation 3:19-20.

His promise to you:

"If you openly declare that Jesus is Lord and believe in your heart that God raised him from the dead, you will be saved. For it is by believing in your heart that you are made right with God, and it is by openly declaring your faith that you are saved." Romans 10:9-10.

Now all you have to do is intentionally and sincerely accept His offer of eternal life by honestly praying in faith:

Lord Jesus, I need You. Thank You for dying on the cross for my sins. I open the door of my life and receive You as my Savior and Lord. Thank You for forgiving my sins and giving me the gift of eternal life. Take control of my life. Make me the person You want me to be. Amen.

That's it, you are saved! You just made the most important decision of your life. This was an intentional act of your **will** not your feelings. In time, you will have plenty of wonderful emotions and experiences through your relationship with God. I didn't feel anything when I first accepted Jesus as my savior. But, over time, increasing enlightenment, peace and miracles have come to me. Jesus said:

"I tell you the truth, those who listen to my message and believe in God who sent me have eternal life. They will never be condemned for their sins, but they have already passed from death into life." John 5:24.

Of course, God knows the condition and motives of your heart. You cannot fool God. You must genuinely believe the words in Romans 10 and the prayer you said. If you say the words without really believing or have deception in your heart you are not saved. God demands truth, steadfast faith and to be first in every area of your life. Easy to say, difficult to do. Nevertheless, your go-forward lifestyle is not complicated, in fact it can be summed up by the following verse:

"For the whole law (how to live) can be summed up in this one command: 'Love your neighbor as yourself.'" Galatians 5:14.

The ways of the Bible are frequently uncomfortable and definitely make you different from others and society, but this kind of different is way better. A "biblical lifestyle" doesn't assure "smooth sailing", but it is less painful and more rewarding than anything the world offers. If you believe the Bible and that God is the creator of the universe, then it is not a huge stretch to believe He knows, better than you do, how to successfully manage your life. He gives you the Holy Spirit to provide the wisdom and strength to live your new life.

"And I will put my spirit I you so that you will follow my decrees and be careful to obey my regulations." Ezekiel 36:27.

He will never leave you. You will never be alone again.

"This is my command - be strong and courageous! Do not be afraid or discouraged. For the LORD your God is with you wherever you go." Joshua 1:9.

Now, make sure you tell at least 2-3 Christians and a pastor about what you just did so they can congratulate and support you. If you take a log out of the fire within a short time it will burn out. That needn't happen with you. Your salvation is too important and must grow for the rest of your life. Call them now. Meet with them as soon as possible to establish yourself in your new life.

"He died for everyone so that those who receive his new life will no longer live for themselves. Instead, they will live for Christ, who died and was raised for them. So we have stopped evaluating

others from a human point of view. At one time we thought of Christ merely from a human point of view. How differently we know him now! This means that anyone who belongs to Christ, has become a new person. The old life is gone; a new life has begun! And all of this is a gift from God, who brought us back to himself through Christ. And God has given us this task of reconciling people to him. For God was in Christ, reconciling the world to himself, no longer counting people's sins against them. And he gave us this wonderful message of reconciliation." 2 Corinthians 5:15-19.

Your salvation decision and faith may start small, but will continue to grow in strength and impact as you read the Bible, mature in understanding and diligently practice your new faith. When you accept Jesus as your savior you are not just fixed or rehabilitated, you are completely recreated from the inside – you are a new person. You are now truly a child of God. New ways of thinking and behaving are coming to you. Your path is cleared for a continually expanding, exhilarating earthly life and eternity. Yes, it is an endless mystery and takes faith – but, there is no alternative.

"The Kingdom of Heaven is like a mustard seed planted in a field (your mind). It is the smallest of all seeds, but it becomes the largest of garden plants; it grows into a tree, and birds come and make nests in its branches." Matthew 13:31-32.

Now continue to grow your faith and relationship with God. Get a Bible, read it every day. Join a church and small group, interact with fellow believers so you support each other and continue to grow spiritually. Our calling or vocation is to become more and more like Jesus. Always, loving God, loving others and telling others about Jesus and the Bible.

"So now I am giving you a new commandment: Love each other. Just as I have loved you, you should love each other. Your love for one another will prove to the world that you are my disciples." John 13:34-35.

You could think what you just read is too simple, weird, unbelievable or too difficult for you to do. Don't. This is what is possible with a loving, wonderful, all-powerful God! Do you want joy, meaning, peace, contentment, miracles, hope and love; do you want to live forever – you need God.

"So now we can rejoice in our wonderful new relationship with God because our Lord Jesus Christ has made us friends of God." Romans 5:11.

It is your choice. Make your decision today, don't put it off. God is real, Jesus is your savior and everything the Bible says is true.

Take Away: If you are still reading, congratulations you know the basics of Christianity and how to live forever! The decision to live a biblical lifestyle is a choice to have a grander, more meaningful earthly life and eternity. Every other lifestyle choice is deciding to have a *lesser* life – now and forever.

"Because of our faith, Christ has brought us into this place of undeserved privilege where we now stand, and we confidently and joyfully look forward to sharing God's glory." Romans 5:2.

Is Jesus who He claims to be; whom the Bible says He is? If you say **yes**, then you will have eternal life with God. The Bible is the only permanent foundation for building your life on, all other earthly lifestyles never satisfy long-term and will not take to heaven. Read Romans 5 - it simply and succinctly lays out what faith in Jesus accomplishes.

If you answer **no** to faith in Jesus, then you are on your own.

Why I believe the Bible

You deserve to know why I believe the Bible. My desire for telling you is to prompt you to passionately find your own reasons to read the Bible and use it as "**Your Life User Manual**".

"Therefore, we never stop thanking God that when you received his (God) message from us, you didn't think of our words as mere human ideas. You accepted what we said as the very word of God – which, of course it is. And this word (Bible) continues to work in you who believe." 1 Thessalonians 2:13.

Each of us discover the Bible and God differently; some choose to ignore or deny it completely. It is a very personal and critical decision. Your approach to learning about God will be unique and your reasons for believing may be different from mine. Never-the-less, here are a few of the reasons for my faith in God and trust in the Bible.

The World and Universe Around Us

Look around you, from the glorious universe, to our beautiful earth and all the extraordinary detail and complexity in animals, vegetables, minerals and mankind – to me, there is no question that a Master Designer created all this. The earth is the strangest planet in the entire lifeless universe. There is nothing else like it in the cosmos. The atmosphere works to protect us from the sun, asteroids and seamlessly supports human life. Our small blue sphere, in the middle of nothingness, just happens to be perfectly matched to support our breath, nutrition, temperature and every other human necessity. Is our earth all random, luck or freak of nature?

There was a total solar eclipse on August 21, 2017. The reasons for an eclipse of this scale is mind boggling in distance, timing, orbit, scope, speed, gravity and the resulting supernatural effect. It turns out the sun is exactly 400 times larger than the moon and the sun is 400 times further from earth than the moon, exactly the right distance for the larger sun to be perfectly eclipsed by the much smaller moon. Only the sun's corona is visible at total eclipse. Combine the exactness of all those dynamic factors, with the moon orbiting the earth (2,288 MPH), the earth's elliptical orbit around the sun (67,000 MPH), the earth's rotation (1,000 MPH at the equator), the tilt of the moon and the earth, the gravitational forces involved and the solar eclipse is beyond **astonishing!** Coincidence? Not likely.

Our bodies are marvels of enormous complexity, renewal and resilience. Every part of our body, mind and soul is amazing! Think about how your skin, eyes, ears, heart, stomach, intestine, organs and brain all work independently, yet in total *harmony*. Our minds store visions, pictures, movies, facts, smells, sounds, feelings and integrates it all into something logical and, occasionally, an idea that transforms us and the world.

There are endless variations of us, we are each unique and special. No two are alike. We are astounding creations – I cannot possibly imagine that we are accidents, happenstance or an arbitrary, lucky quirk of nature. Someone or something created us with a plan, purpose and love.

"They (all of us) know the truth about God because he has made it obvious to them. Forever, since the world was created, people have seen the earth and sky. Through everything God made, they can clearly see his invisible qualities, his eternal power and divine nature. So, they have no excuse for not knowing God." Romans 1:19-20.

Welcome to God's Creation. His fingerprints are all over the universe, earth and each of us.

Archeology and Science

Archeology and Science continue to document and verify the stories, people and events in the Bible. Little by little, the places and people in biblical times are being proven accurate through uncovering historical documents and ancient remnants. Scientists persistently discover scientific proof of what the Bible describes and predicts. The Dead Sea Scrolls, discovered in 1947, confirm most of the Bible's Old Testament. Likewise, over 5,000 copies of the New Testament, written by meticulous monks, have been discovered. I believe scientists, historians and archeologists will continue to confirm the Bible's authenticity.

Even for a precise, logical man like myself, the factual evidence is mounting that God is real and the Bible is not only accurate but filled with timeless wisdom. You can find as much evidence for and against the accuracy of the Bible as you like using the internet. Try it and make your own factual decision.

However, I believe God will continue to baffle conclusive human proof, because then faith would not be required. You don't "prove" God by facts. Irrefutable proof will only arrive after you die and when Jesus returns to earth, as the Bible predicts. Then we will experience, face to face, the existence and glory of God. Of course, then it will be too late for you to change your views. **Your choices, values and beliefs during your lifetime** will take you to your chosen destiny, for all of eternity.

Old Testament Prophecies

Jesus said:

"Don't misunderstand why I have come. I did not come to abolish the law of Moses or the writings of the prophets. No, I came to accomplish (fulfill or finish) their purpose." Matthew 5:17.

Factually, there are over 300 prophecies in the Old Testament. I found many and mentioned a few; you can and should do the same. Centuries before Jesus came to earth as a man, Old Testament prophecies clearly detailed His life and links to Jesus as the Messiah. From His heritage in the tribe of Judah and the House of David, to details of His birth, life, ignominious death and resurrection.

Jesus was crucified at Passover time, arose from the dead three days later and He ascended to heaven 40 days after His resurrection. The Holy Spirit came 10 days after His Ascension, called Pentecost. Remarkably, this was predicted approximately 700 years earlier in **Joel 2:28 and Isaiah 53.** The story is also described in the New Testament books of **Acts 2** and by John the Baptist in **Luke 3:16.**

It is impossible that a mere man could have manipulated his life to align with all the Old Testament predictions.

The Best Seller

So why does the Bible continue to be the worldwide best-selling, most translated book of all time? I believe it is because it is truth and that God wants it to endure so no one has an excuse for not knowing His plan for them. The Bible has been under attack, disputed, dissected, debated, even hated for centuries, yet continues to hold up to relentless scrutiny, as well as, the test of time. The Bible was written somewhere between approximately 2,000 and 3,500 years ago. I believe the Bible continues to influence our culture today, because it is the greatest source of truth ever written. It is the most important and influential book I have read and beneficially transformed my life more than any other source. Regrettably, I suspect that, in spite of its worldwide availability and sales figures, it is seldom read and often misunderstood.

The Apostles and Other Eyewitnesses

Of the original 12 disciples who followed Jesus ten of them died excruciating deaths as martyrs. John died of natural causes and Judas killed himself. These brave men were tortured and ultimately killed by crucifixion, boiling oil, fire and wild animals.

The question screams; "Why would men die for someone or something if it wasn't true?" They gave their life for the truth; that Jesus Christ is the Son of God. No fool would allow himself to be killed for something he didn't fervently believe.

All any one of these men had to do to avoid being killed was to denounce Jesus Christ. None did, a powerful statement to the reality of God and Jesus. If they thought Jesus was fake they would have denied Him, lived normal lives and died of old age. Their motivation was truth and compassion for others. These individuals were able to make the right choice where reality, faith and biblical authenticity converge.

Additionally, Jesus predicted His own death and resurrection in the New Testament; **Read Mark 8:31, Mark 9:31 and Mark 10:33-34.** And following His resurrection, appeared to several individuals; **Read Luke 24:13-34, Mark 16:9-14, Luke 24:13-31.**

My Own Experience

Sit in a church service, Bible study group or Christian camp and observe the miraculous stories of men and women, of all ages and backgrounds passionately describing how Jesus changed their lives. These are not crazy people; they are human beings, just like you and me, who are honestly recounting what God has done in their lives. They sincerely believe if God can help them then they must help others by telling their story. This is powerful proof in the human experience. I have found that all I am responsible for is telling my story and it is God who saves people. Based on my own experiences and encounters He is really good, even miraculous at saving people.

"Gently instruct those who oppose the truth. Perhaps God will change those people's hearts, and they will learn the truth." 2 Timothy 2:25.

Like others who have been amazed at God's reality, I have seen hundreds of changes in my own life. I cannot explain away, nor find another way to rationally explain the transformation I have and continue to experience. The compassionate work of God, through the Bible, redirected my life, healed my heart and gradually taught me how to be a better man.

I love the Bible's intermingling of encouragement, inspiration, practical advice, fascinating stories, humor, faith, love and connection to the supernatural. I would have completely missed all of this truth if a few brave individuals had not told me to read the Bible.

God is as grand and over-the-top as anything or anyone I have ever experienced. I am sure we will never fully comprehend or understand Him. Thus, you must have faith to wholly accept and ultimately believe in God. For instance, I cannot see compassion, joy, mercy, anger, hate, emotion or love; yet I know they are real. Similarly, I have not seen God, but I know He is real. That is what faith is, believing what you cannot see, fully explain or conclusively prove, but know actually exists.

"Seek the kingdom of God above all else and live righteously and he will give you everything you need." Matthew 6:33.

Powerful Authors

When I was originally studying and testing the Bible, I read ***"A Case for Christ," "The Case for Faith" and "God's Outrageous Claims,"*** all written by Lee Strobel. As a professional investigative reporter, he set out to disprove everything about Jesus and the Bible, but ended up a believer. His detailed and thought-provoking descriptions of how he dissected, questioned and tested the Bible are methodical as only a seasoned investigative reporter could accomplish.

I also liked, **"The Reason for God - Belief in an Age of Skepticism,"** by Tim Keller. It is a powerful read for skeptics.

"The Road Less Travelled," by M. Scott Peck, M.D., has influenced my life significantly for decades. Not really a religious book, it is an interesting and meaningful mix of psychology, human nature, reality and God. He emphasizes self-responsibility, freedom of choice and "reality at all cost" to achieve a life well lived.

The brilliant intellectual, C.S. Lewis, who came to Christ later in his life summarized the various identities of Jesus Christ into an inescapable conclusion.

"A man who was merely a man and said the sort of things Jesus said would not be a great moral teacher. He would either be a lunatic — on the level with the man who says he is a poached egg — or else he would be the Devil of Hell. You must make your choice. Either this man was, and is, the Son of God, or else a madman or something worse. You can shut him up for a fool, you can spit at him and kill him as a demon or you can fall at his feet and call him Lord and God, but let us not come with any patronizing nonsense about his being a great human teacher. He has not left that open to us." C.S. Lewis.

Many educated biblical researchers have declared that "Jesus is either a liar, legend, lunatic or Lord." Jesus, based on His comments in the Bible, left no room for any other options. What description do *you* assign to Jesus?

This Book

The book you are reading is not only the work of Evan Wride; it is the culmination and inspiration of the living God and direction from the Bible. I take credit for operating the keyboard, researching the Bible and talking with many believers and non-believers. However, the stimulus, drive, core and purpose of this book are from God. He patiently and persistently transformed me until I was ready, a more mature Christian. I know I could not have written this book by myself. If you knew me, you would fully comprehend the truth of that statement!

"When the Spirit (Holy Spirit) of truth comes, he will guide you into all truth. He will not speak on his own but will tell you what he has heard. He will tell you about the future. He will bring me (Jesus) glory by telling you whatever he receives from me. All that belongs to the Father is mine; this is why I said, 'The Spirit will tell you whatever he receives from me.'" John 16:13-15.

I don't expect you to take my word for it. My encouragement and hope are that you will read the Bible every day, live your life according to its teachings for a year and see what happens to your life – then decide for yourself. The Bible tells us to test what we hear and believe.

"Dear friends, do not believe everyone who claims to speak by the Spirit (to speak for God). You must test them to see if the spirit they have comes from God. For there are many false prophets in the world." 1 John 4:1.

So, keep an open mind and heart which will allow you the opportunity to discover your new and greatly improved future according to the Bible. Let the factual evidence speak for itself. Don't take anyone else's word for it. Do your research and discover your own informed decision.

"I am counting on the Lord; yes, I am counting on him. I have put my hope in his word." Psalms 130:5.

Take Away: I have diligently searched, worked at, practiced and tested many life options to evaluate and clarify what I believe. Now it is your turn.

Everyone is a believer; we all believe and put our faith in something or someone. Who and what do you use as your authority for managing your life? Many rely on themselves, others, society or government. What are your conclusions about God, Jesus and eternity?

The only hurdle between you and God is your pride. Your partner, your Sherpa is patiently waiting, inviting, even enticing you to commit to Him; wanting you to love Him as much as He already loves you. I have no doubt He will take you on the wild, miraculous, and meaningful "life-ride" that He has planned for you.

Stop wasting your precious life, decide to turn your life over to God and live like only a God inspired person can.

Next Steps

There will always be more to understand about the Bible, God, spirituality, love, life and many other subjects. God has a specific plan for each of us and it is all spelled out in the Bible.

"Seek not to understand that you may believe, but believe that you may understand." Saint Augustine.

This book describes what I believe. But, why should you believe me? You don't know me. You only know what I expressed in the book. In fact, you shouldn't believe anyone without doing your own research and verifying. Anyone claiming to know what is best for you, that does not align with the guidelines and teachings of the Bible, must be questioned. Your one unique life and eternity are too important.

So, stop wandering, pretending and wasting your life-time. If you must, ignore religion and view the Bible strictly from an intellectual perspective. I have tried "out thinking" God, many times, and it always turned out badly for me. The world according to me leads to unfulfillment and pain. The world according to God leads to forgiveness, meaning, joy and love. I finally stopped wrestling with God and got onboard with His eternal plan.

I had to write this book to tell others what I have learned about my purpose and how I manage my wonderful life according to the Bible. I am not always confident nor good at telling others about my faith. But, I have found that if I candidly explain a few specifics of how the Bible has improved my life, it is much easier. The following verse has motivated me to learn how to confidently tell others about God, Jesus and the Bible. Jesus said:

"If anyone is ashamed of me and my message, the Son of Man will be ashamed of that person when he returns in his glory and in the glory of the Father and the holy angels." Luke 9:26.

I highlighted hundreds of examples and related verses for how to not only intellectually read the Bible, but use it as a life guide to ardently follow in every area of your life. Just as it is impossible to be "a little pregnant," it is equally ridiculous to occasionally depend on the Bible, only fall back to it when in crisis or only use it in a few areas of your life. I strongly urge you to read the Bible every day and directly apply it to your entire life so it becomes a habit.

"But don't just listen to God's word. You must do what it says. Otherwise, you are only fooling yourselves. ... But if you look carefully into the perfect law that sets you free, and if you do what it says and don't forget what you heard, then God will bless you for doing it." James 1:22 & 25.

I want to leave you with a few specific **next steps** to motivate and encourage you to continue your biblical journey by reading more of the Bible. These are relatively easy action steps to help jump start and continue your journey.

Next Step: Go buy your own, easy to understand Bible. There are numerous translations to select from, ranging from an early King James version that uses older language to a translation called the "Message", which is written in very contemporary terms. It should be written in a way that you easily relate to so you can immediately apply the teachings in your life. Your Bible should provide commentary and interpretations for key stories, chapters and verses to help clarify its meaning and indexes to related passages and topics.

It is only as you personally "get into" the Bible that you will discover its incredible advice and wisdom. I use the New Living Translation (NLT), Life Application Study Bible, where most of the Bible quotes came from in this book. It is written in a contemporary way and provides lots of commentary and references to help me interpret and apply the Bible's relevant guidance directly in my everyday life. Thank you, Tyndale House Publishers for the NLT Bible and the excellent notes, index, dictionary and concordance.

"All Scripture is inspired by God and is useful to teach us what is true and to make us realize what is wrong in our lives. It corrects us when we are wrong and teaches us to do what is right. God uses it to prepare and equip his people to do every good work." 2 Timothy 3:16-17.

Additionally, if you do not already attend church regularly, you must find one that you relate to, feel comfortable attending and inspires you to learn more about God. Search for a Bible based church, a pastor who speaks in a manner you can understand and offers groups that meet during the week. You may have to "church shop" before you find the one that you feel comfortable with and can learn from.

Excellent Christian churches reach out to everyone, don't judge and are there to help everyone. If unusual, imperfect, hurting people and sinners are not overtly welcomed at a church, look for a new church. Genuine, God filled, Bible driven churches are the most inclusive organizations because they intentionally and diligently help everyone who attends, saved or not, as well as, the community at large, by unselfishly serving where needed.

Next Step: Keep reading the Bible, start by reading:

Proverbs. No other book is quite like it. Proverbs is filled with wise and thought-provoking verses. Don't read it straight through, read a few verses or a chapter a day and let it sink in. It is literally a text book filled with prudent, moral and "how to" wisdom for living a smart, spiritual and wonderful life. Each of the "one-liners" has the potential to literally change your perspective and profoundly alter the trajectory of your life.

"These are the proverbs of Solomon, David's son, king of Israel. Their purpose is to teach people wisdom and discipline, to help them understand the insights of the wise. Their purpose is to teach people to live disciplined and successful lives, to help them do what is right, just, and fair. These proverbs will give insight to the simple, knowledge and discernment to the young. Let the wise listen to these proverbs and become even wiser. Let those with understanding receive guidance by exploring the meaning in these proverbs and parables, the words of the wise and their riddles." Proverbs 1:1-6.

Ecclesiastes was written by King Solomon as he neared the end of his glorious life. This was a man who had intelligence, power and wealth, but asked God for only one thing - wisdom! His writings represent his learning and reflections, evaluating his life. His hope was to teach others what he had learned so they would not have to make the same mistakes he did in their search for a meaningful life. While some of his conclusions are cynical and strange, he sounds just like what many of us experience in our search for a purposeful, love filled life. In spite of his enormous wealth and power, he was an ordinary man struggling to discover what really mattered in his life.

📖 **"That's the whole story. Here now is my final conclusion: Fear God and obey his commands, for this is everyone's duty. God will judge us for everything we do, including every secret thing, whether good or bad."** Ecclesiastes 12:13-14.

James was Jesus half-brother. In the book of **James,** he takes on the topic of living according to the world's ways or the Bible's. His practical wisdom is straight forward, easy to understand and apply in today's modern, technological advanced, yet confusing world.

"What good is it, dear brothers and sisters, if you say you have faith but don't show it by your actions? How can you show me your faith if you don't have good deeds? I will show you my faith by my good deeds." James 2:14 & 18.

I love these relevant books of the Bible. After you read them my prayer is that they will lead you deeper into the Bible, to God, a meaningful life and eternity.

There is a distinct difference between those who *claim* to be Christians and those who truly live by the truths of the Bible. The former is a human attempt to justify their worldly behaviors with church attendance, a donation and a few rituals; they are fake Christians. It is hypocritical Christians who give God and the church a bad reputation. Jesus has strong words for hypocritical religious teachers and nominal Christians. Read all of Matthew 23.

"What sorrow awaits you teachers of religious law and you Pharisees (social movement, political party). Hypocrites!" Matthew 23:13.

My guess is that only about a third of those who regularly attend church actively use the Bible to *directly* manage their lives. I was in the 70% group for many years. I guess I thought the Bible was entertaining and, at times inspiring, but wasn't relevant to my daily living. If you aren't determined to behave, reason and make life choices according to the Bible all the time, then you are just like everyone else.

Your decision to commit your life to single-mindedly living out the instructions of the Bible, from the moment you wake up until your final thought at night, will be profoundly life changing. Most think about the Bible only on Sunday morning and pay only lip service to a biblical lifestyle the rest of the week.

The Bible is your Blueprint for a meaningful life and God is the architect.

Let there be no mistake; God wants you to not just call on Him in times of need or desperation; but to depend on Him in every area of your life, every day. We are His creation, His children, His joy and His eternal love. Nothing is more important to Him. This is the God I know.

Take Away: We all believe in someone or something to manage our lives. Find your own rational for what you believe in. What are you betting your life on?

I am betting my life on the Bible and the forgiveness, grace, hope and love of Jesus. Everyone would like to know the Jesus I know. I believe that how you assess, perceive and know God is the most important life judgement you make.

Free will and choice are powerful. Your choices take you through life, determine your earthly outcomes and your destiny beyond death. Remember, all your wisdom, power, strength and success come from God, not your worldly strength, knowledge, accomplishments or acquisitions. So, organize and orient your entire life around the teachings of the Bible; it is a love letter from God to you. Use the Bible as **"Your Life User Manual"**, you will never regret it and you will find a new, better way to live, thrive and know God.

Epilogue

"The book to read is not the one which thinks for you, but the one which makes you think. No book in the world equals the Bible for that." Harper Lee, author.

God wrote the Bible specifically to communicate directly with us and transform our lives. More than intellectual faith, God wants a relationship with each of us and for us to *experience* the transformational power of the Bible. The purpose for the Bible is to tell us about Jesus and the life restoration He offers. The Bible will guide you to a wonderful life on earth and into eternity. God knows there is no better proof that Jesus and the Bible results in a new, better way to live than for us to live fulfilling and successful lives.

The reason I wrote this book was to help me unravel, think through and thoroughly understand the Bible. Writing this book has been one of the great blessings of my life. I am a simple guy, thus I needed to fine practical, relevant and meaningful rules to guide me in today's modern world. I believe anyone can benefit by taking the Bible a lot more seriously. I've worked painstakingly and humbly, to capture the true essence of the Bible, while keeping it contemporary and real-world.

I am uniquely knowledgeable in what the Bible has done in *my* life. I am the only one with first-hand experience at my own special life. Telling others about my experience with the Bible and Jesus is the Great Commission. Some may disagree with my point of view and beliefs, but they cannot dispute my own life experiences.

"For I can do everything through Christ, who gives me strength." Philippians 4:13.

The God inspired Bible is the greatest message, the Holy Spirit is the perfect messenger and Jesus is the perfect example. I purposely filled the book with hundreds of Bible verses to make it easy for you to access a few of the Bible's truths and see how they directly relate to your everyday life.

"I have a fundamental belief in the Bible as the Word of God, written by those who were inspired. I study the Bible daily." Isaac Newton, mathematician, author and physicist.

I want to leave you with a couple of thoughts and present them as sensitively as possible. If you say you don't or can't believe in God, maybe you don't really know the God of the Holy Bible; at least the one that I have come to know. Likewise, just because you don't believe, doesn't mean that God and Jesus are not real, that eternity doesn't follow death, nor that the Bible is not true. I strongly urge you to dig deep, evaluate all your beliefs and think long and hard before reaching a conclusion. Based on what I know, this is a vital, if not the most important choice of your life. Jesus asked this question of the religious leader of His time.

"What do you think about the Messiah? Whose son is he?" Matthew 22:42.

If you don't believe that Jesus is who the Bible says He is, all the other religious questions are irrelevant.

After Thoughts

"Thoughts disentangle themselves when they pass through your fingertips." Dawson Trotman, Evangelist and founder of the Navigators.

Here are a few personal thoughts and perspectives on how I think of this book.

Notwithstanding what I intellectually think, I don't really know why or how I was compelled to write this book, but God does. I am not an author or writer, but God is. I have no formal theology, religious or spiritual training, but God does. It took me five long years of hard, solitary, exasperating work to search the Bible for proof of what I was theorizing. I often became frustrated and impatient, but God is infinitely patient, had a plan and didn't give up on me.

You have to understand this book is surprising and amazing to me; its existence is nothing short of a miracle! I am an ordinary man, the product of divorced parents and about as 'average' as you can get. I came of age in the turbulent 60's, made countless bad choices, yet through the grace of God, I survived and thrived. I am astonished this book actually exists. I view it as a contemporary, real-life, genuine miracle from God, just like the miracles I read about in the Bible!

"Has the Lord redeemed you? Then speak out! Tell others he has redeemed you from your enemies." Psalm 107:2.

Remember **this book is *not* the Bible**. There isn't and never will be a replacement for the Bible. This book barely scratches the surface of the Good Book's endless wisdom. This is simply my description of how I used a few morsels of the Bible's supernatural wisdom, direction and power to improve my life and open the door to eternity.

The Bible is the greatest story ever told! It is complex, deep, far reaching, intriguing, wild and, most importantly, life transforming.

There is much more to write, but it's time to stop. It would be a never-ending obsession to comprehend and express all the Bible has to say. I will never be done, biblical insights are confoundingly limitless. So, I will stop writing, knowing I have not captured everything I wanted to say. Tomorrow I will think of something new I would like to have written. If I don't stop now, I can't move on to the next challenge or epiphany God has for me.

This may be the book's conclusion, but there really is no conclusion to life. We all live forever via our souls and we are the stewards and developers of our own souls while on earth. Choice by choice you decide the ultimate destination of your soul. The only question is: Will you spend eternity with God or someplace else?

I sincerely hope you enjoyed and, maybe, learned a little from this book. But, infinitely more importantly, I hope and pray that you are inspired to read the Bible and live according to its direction, promises and protection for your life. Now start your own never-ending journey to have an earthly and eternal relationship with God. While your earthly life is critical, eternity is the only destination that is far better than the actual journey. The choice before you: Who will be in-charge of your life?

You or God?

"If God is for us, who can ever be against us?" Romans 8:31.

Acknowledgments

I owe a significant thank you and much more to those who patiently encouraged and helped me through the many challenges, unknowns and struggles to write this book. I always thought "how hard can it be" to write a book? It was much harder than this humble man ever thought. I now respect anyone who can succinctly and clearly express themselves through only words.

First, God wrote this book, not me. It is that simple - there is no way I could have single-handedly written this book. Somehow and for some reason, He wrote this book in spite of and through me. I believe it is proof that with God, anything is possible and that He uses the weakest humans to do His work. All the glory to God.

My wife is my soul mate - my everything! She contributed as much to this book as I did. We are life partners in everything. God has overwhelmingly blessed us individually and together. We learned that with God even two flawed, struggling, selfish, impatient humans can become Christians on a mission to live good lives and help others to find their own way to God.

I don't have words to accurately describe my only brother. For some reason, he has continued to like, support and even love me, in spite of me being me. He knows that I love him and his wife. No human walking the earth has known me longer. God bless him. By the way, any childhood memories in the book most likely came from him, since my memory is quite porous.

My children, are blessings for me, every day. I have and continue to do my best to be a good dad, but, as they know all too well, I am lacking in many ways. Thank you both for still talking to me and helping me to find my way. I hope I do the same for you.

My mother selflessly raised, cared for and loved me - always. She was my "body guard" during my vulnerable, early years. Even now, I recall her and learn something new or am reminded of her honest, practical wisdom and love. All of the good parts of who I am came from her.

I don't have tons of friends, but the ones I do have are priceless. These relationships help guide me, contributed to this book and are always there for me. Of special note are the three men who lovingly accepted me into a men's Bible study group and continue to show me, through their example and counsel, how to be a Christian man.

Patrick Hurley, editor, opened my eyes spiritually, creatively and literarily. His skills, encouragement, patience and guidance made this book possible and readable. Somehow, he found a way, to mentor and work with a Type A, random thinking, opinionated and inexperienced author.

I owe countless friends, mentors, teachers, work associates, neighbors and random individuals a great deal, each one contributed to the man I am today. Of special note is a childhood neighbor couple who took my brother and I to Sunday school for the first time.

Every pastor I encountered inspired me. They are the bravest of humans. I pray that God blesses, strengthens and inspires every one of these selfless individuals. The challenges they generously face every day to help others is not understood by most. A personal thank you to pastors Thom and Bevan for bring me back to God.

"If someone among you wanders away from the truth and is brought back, you can be sure that whoever brings the sinner back from wondering will save that person from death and bring about the forgiveness of many sins." James 5:19-20.

I have learned more than I can ever express in this book. Everyone who touched my life, positively or negatively, made me who I am. I learned from every life encounter at the moment it happened, as well as, now when I recall my journey to where I am today.

All blessings and love come from God. Find God and you will find life.

"For whoever finds me (wisdom) finds life and receives favor from the Lord." Proverbs 8:35.

www.ingramcontent.com/pod-product-compliance
Lightning Source LLC
Chambersburg PA
CBHW070140100426
42743CB00013B/2770